Times Past in the
COUNTRYSIDE

Reader's Digest

Times Past in the
COUNTRYSIDE

EVERYDAY LIFE
IN A BYGONE AGE

Valerie Porter

Times Past in the Countryside has been produced by
David & Charles in association with
The Reader's Digest Association Limited.

This edition © David & Charles Ltd, 2009
Text © Val Porter
Images © see page 256

David & Charles is an F+W Media, Inc. Company
4700 East Galbraith Road
Cincinnati, OH 45236

Some of the text and first-hand accounts contained in this
edition were first published as *Yesterday's Countryside*.

A catalogue record for this book is available from
the British Library.

ISBN: 978-0-276-44404-3

Printed in China by RR Donnelley
For David & Charles Ltd
Brunel House, Newton Abbot,
Devon, TQ12 4PU

For David & Charles:
Director of Editorial and Design: Alison Myer
Commissioning Editor: Neil Baber
Editorial Manager: Emily Pitcher
Art Editor: Prudence Rogers
Designer: Joanna Ley
Picture Research: Wyn Voysey
Project Editor: James Loader
Production: Beverley Richardson

Contents

Introduction

For many decades, there has been an enormous nostalgia for the 'traditional' British countryside – a dreamy place full of birdsong and meadow flowers, purple heather and misty hills, honest old gaffers exuding wit and wisdom, eccentric squires and lairds playing at and with life, cottages nestling in the landscape, cosy self-sufficient villages, children thriving in the fresh air … and all that. Of course, such a perception is largely in the imagination, but versions of it have served as an inspiration to many since Roman poets, condemned to city life, wrote lyrically of the countryside. Poets and other artists have continued the theme ever since.

Then there is the reality. For some born and bred in the country, the dream was to escape from it – but to where? All too often they were lured to the towns and cities, in search of work and better conditions, but never found their pots of gold there. Within two or three generations their descendants had reversed the dream and sought to return. The continuity had been broken, however; they found that they were strangers in the landscape and the dream, being a dream, remained elusive.

Some of us have been lucky enough to spend our childhoods in the country and discover our own reality, untainted by expectations. We have followed the natural urge to leave the nest and explore the wider world and, if we are truly lucky, we have come back, rejecting the undoubted attractions of urban life for the simpler but more deeply felt joys of a rural one. With our eyes wide open to reality, we have perceived the changes in the countryside – some of them deplorable, some of them to the greater good. This book seeks to highlight the ways in which living in the country, in all its aspects, has changed, as seen through the eyes of an older generation still living and through the written words of generations long gone. It also seeks to be optimistic about the future, where that is possible.

The biggest change, perhaps, is that country dwellers are very much in a minority now. The Domesday Book showed that the total population of England in the 11th century was two million people, of whom about 90,000 were cottars and bordars – peasants living in country cots in return for labour. Most people in Britain at the time lived in rural areas and this would be the case until the Industrial Revolution began to swell during the 18th century. By 1850, for the first time in Britain's history, as many people were living in towns as in the country, but their roots remained rural; most town dwellers still had close relatives in the countryside and liked to make day trips there for fresh air and the scenery. The pull remained strong: between the two world wars of the 20th century, there was a regular city exodus of tourists – country weekenders, caravaners, hikers, touring motorists and charabanc outings – but most of them only came for a break, not to live in the country.

By the outbreak of World War II, only one in five of the UK's population of more than 45 million people actually lived in rural areas, which was a dramatic depopulation in less than a century. During that war, more people returned to the countryside as evacuees from the cities and rediscovered the reality of it, which proved to be very different from the picturesque scenes that slid past their railway carriage windows. Suburbanites who came to live in the country as commuters tended to be civil servants, teachers and the like, and they were shocked to find themselves without electricity and with a bus only twice a week. The war also brought airmen, soldiers and others to a rash of aerodromes, camps and hospitals that littered the countryside, and some of them stayed on after a war that became a major turning point in the British way of life.

By 2001 the total UK population was nearly 59 million people (by July 2007 it had already risen by another two million). In England about 19 per cent of the population (9.5 million people) lived in rural areas – but that included 4.2 million living in small towns, which meant that only 4.7 million people (fewer than 10% of the entire population of England) lived in villages, hamlets and isolated dwellings. And of those who worked in rural areas, only 6% were employed in agriculture. Combining rural and urban workforces, only about 1% worked in agriculture, forestry and hunting. What a contrast to Victorian times!

The definition of rurality can be a problem when statistics come into play. With the rapid growth in the sizes of villages in many parts of Britain, their tendency to stretch out towards each other and the tendency of suburbs to spread far beyond their natural bounds, it can be difficult to decide where the countryside truly begins. Perhaps it is a matter of the heart. If you feel that you live in the countryside, then you do.

▲ FARM AND WOODLAND WORKERS, *born and bred in the countryside from generation to generation, formed the majority of the population in rural areas throughout the 19th century, but today they are a tiny minority. This skilled and self-sufficient worker in his makeshift camp, photographed around 1890, was typical of his time.*

1. The Country Village

The village was the heart of rural life. It was where those who lived in isolated homes spread about the countryside could come to meet and gossip, drink at the pub, get together for dances and festivals, go to church, buy essential goods and make use of a wide range of relevant trades, services and crafts. The villagers and those who lived in its hinterland were interdependent; each needed the other. The clustering of cottages, shops and social venues knitted a widespread community into a structured society dominated by the squire and the parson and cared for by vestry meetings, parish councils and village bobbies. But the rural community has changed in recent times, as influences have spread in from beyond the village; its social balance has altered and it has become less independent in managing its own affairs. Yet it survives, and the dream of many an urban dweller to live in a village persists.

In the countryside, every aspect of life is closely interwoven. But all the strands come together in the fabric of the village itself. For many centuries, the essence of the village was its self-sufficiency, a theme that threads its way throughout this book. For much of the 20th century that self-sufficiency was eroded and eventually apparently lost. But the urge for it still lurks beneath the surface and, when the need arises, the villagers rise to the challenge and once again stand on their own feet.

The community spirit that survives in villages today is different in detail from the old village's sense of kinship, in the days when most people were related to each other by blood or by marriage, and when perhaps many felt strangled by the apron strings of the village as one big family. It is different in that agriculture is no longer the dominant employment that determined everything from the nature of the trades and crafts in the village to the calendar of social events. It is different in its social structure, which is more multilayered and mingled than the rigid pyramid that existed right up to the two world wars, with the squire and parson at the top, then the professionals such as doctors and merchants and the yeoman farmers, then the village tradesmen and craftsmen, and finally a broad base of agricultural labourers and what were termed 'servants', whether working on the farms or in private houses.

▼ AN ARCHETYPAL ENGLISH VILLAGE, *Castle Combe, Wiltshire, (shown here in 1933) has set the scene for several films. Its market cross is evidence that the village was once a thriving medieval market town, its prosperity based on woollen cloth. There used to be several fulling mills powered by the local brook and many inhabitants of the lower part of the village worked as weavers and spinners in their Cotswold stone cottages.*

The traditional village, the picture-postcard village, had a street with a mix of small shops to meet basic needs, interspersed with cottages, and here and there a workshop – the blacksmith, the wheelwright, the cobbler and so on. There was a village green, maybe with its stocks still in place, and a large old tree under which people gathered. There was a church, of course, and near it a large parsonage. Distant from the church both physically and socially there might be a chapel or two.

Somewhere there would be the 'big house', either within the village, or set apart in its own parklands slashed by the long ribbon of its drive. There was at least one pub, a scruffy but friendly place that the regulars walked to, bringing their collies with them. There was a village school with just one large room, and a small playground outside. There was a handful of larger homes sprinkled here and there where you would expect to find a doctor, a retired army officer, maybe a banker and people of that ilk. The bigger cottages were home to tradesmen and craftsmen, and also their shop windows. The main village shop itself sold everything anyone could possibly need, but there would also be a butcher's and a baker's. Somewhere there was a village pump, with a horse trough close by, and somewhere there was a place where people hung about and chatted – maybe an old market cross or a square.

> '*There was definition to the village, a sense that it had grown slowly out of the soil until it fitted snugly in its landscape and then stopped, comfortable with its size and shape.*'

The street had people in it, wandering, gossiping, going about their business. Occasionally a horse and cart plodded by, or a donkey carrying panniers, or perhaps a small group of cows or sheep on their way to somewhere, leaving tokens of dung in their wake. Maybe a farm worker pedalled slowly past on his old bike, tinkling his bell to a friend and wearing string around his ankles to stop his trouser legs catching in the chain. A couple of dogs lying in the middle of the street would lift their heads lazily to watch the world go by, having a thoughtful scratch now and then or dozing in the sun. Children played on the green and in the street, bowling hoops or skipping with ropes or playing games to traditional rhymes.

There was definition to the village, a sense that it had grown slowly out of the soil until it fitted snugly in its landscape and then stopped, comfortable with its size and shape. Its buildings may have been of different ages but somehow they fitted together, they suited each other; there was an overall designer's touch that in reality was no more than

▲ MILK WAS USUALLY DELIVERED FRESH FROM THE FARM *in churns on a donkey-cart, or in milk-cans carried on a yoke across the milkman's shoulders. It would then be ladled into the customer's own containers. Some milkmen would even bring the cow with them to provide milk fresh from the udder. In the 1920s, during an agricultural depression, several farmers set up private milk rounds using old vans and these were the foundation of what became substantial dairies, some of which still deliver bottled milk to the doorstep in rural areas today.*

local tradition developing the vernacular over a few centuries. They were made of local materials and you could imagine that, one day, when the village finally died, its materials would simply crumble into the landscape and become part of it again.

Changes in the street

The reality of many villages today is traffic, for a start – cars on the move with muttering engines, cars parked along every available inch of kerb, lorries shaking the old buildings and rattling the manhole covers and bridges as they rumble through and almost scrape against the walls. People hug the pavement and are in a hurry, looking faintly angry until they see a familiar face and pause to say hello. If there is a village shop, it is self-service and sells mainly packaged goods, delivered to its back entrance by an enormous lorry. The smithy is now a garage, with cars choking its forecourt. The pub has been taken over by a brewery that likes background music, expensive food and no smoking. The cyclist wears Lycra shorts, wrap-around sun goggles and a streamlined helmet. The dogs have more sense than to be anywhere near the street and the same goes for the cattle and sheep. There are signs everywhere – road signs, shop signs, advertisements, public notices, estate agents' signs. There are streetlights and telephone wires, and white and yellow lines painted boldly on the road.

Some villages, that is. Some have managed to retain their charm, at least on the surface, and have only a few vehicles on their streets, but these are the ones that have probably lost their shops, their tradesmen and their crafts. They might, if they are lucky, see a bus once a week, twice a week, or even once or twice a day, if only to ferry the children to a school a few miles away because the village school closed long ago. Most of the cottages have been 'gentrified', and few of those who live in them were born in the village or work in the village. Television aerials or satellite dishes decorate the old

◀ **VILLAGE LIFE THRIVED ON GOSSIP** *and most families were closely linked. Everyone seemed to be related to everyone else – and they all knew about each other's romances, tragedies and problems. Gossip was essential to any village and often forms the basis of what is still known today about a village's history.*

rooftops. Through the windows comes the faint bluish flicker of television sets and computer screens.

And the village has lost its proper shape. It stretches way beyond its natural boundaries, with newer and newer buildings straggling along the outgoing lanes

▼ **MANY VILLAGES GREW AROUND RIVERS,** *which provided a source of water for the home, acted as the local launderette, watered horses and cattle, powered local mills and promised endless entertainment for children. Unfortunately the rivers also often carried away sewage, and so became a source of disease.*

▼ **THE HAND-OPERATED VILLAGE PUMP** *was a communal meeting point. It had originally been made from elm wood, or lead protected by a wooden case and frost-proofed with straw, but later pumps were of cast-iron. The pump shown here was still Cardington's only water supply in 1957.*

– bungalows, little blocks of flats, council houses, modern estates in their own little worlds, all eagerly marching down the road to join up with the next village, and the next, to form one day a town of a sort to give people the urban security they have in theory tried to escape but in practice still seek.

Estate villages and farms

Because of the old dominance by the estate or the 'big house', the relationship with the estate has always been of great importance to the village. Usually the livelihood of most villagers depended on employment by the estate, whether on the land, in the village trades, or in service at the big house.

In many cases, the nation's big landowners were philanthropical enough to benefit the villagers in a thousand ways in their everyday lives, by building a school or facilities such as reading rooms and parish cottages, ensuring work was to be had in all seasons, playing Lord and Lady Bountiful to the poor (and often the role was taken with great sincerity), finding doctors and nurses for the sick, building homes for agricultural workers and estate servants, and so on.

The major landowners often performed roles that today are played by the state. The village was a miniature kingdom and its

> *'The major landowners often performed roles that are today played by the state. The village was a miniature kingdom and its welfare was in the combined hands of the landowner and the Church'*

welfare was in the combined hands of the landowner and the Church – powers that sometimes worked together but sometimes were in opposition to each other, harbouring petty jealousies that inevitably impinged on the lives of all in the parish. Some landowners were not benevolent, or, rather, took no notice of their 'subjects'. A large estate thus has a lot more neighbours (and tenants and employees) than most of us; there are more people to be affected by the activities of the owner of that estate, which means that the responsibilities of that owner to the rest of the area are proportionately greater. Sometimes the obligations were forgotten and the squire lost his way, letting down the locals and blighting the whole neighbourhood.

Estate owners often built cottages or entire villages, many of them beautiful but giving away their planned origins in their uniformity of materials, period and

▲ THE 'BIG HOUSE' COULD OFFER A WIDE RANGE OF EMPLOYMENT, *either on its farms or directly serving the house and its gardens, stables and woodland. The domestic staff photographed here in 1900 were part of a larger group that included several gardeners, a coachman and an electrician for the private generator, and most of them were not local. Today the staff of the same house is reduced to one gardener/handyman and a housekeeeper.*

style. There are famous examples of model villages such as Great Tew in Oxfordshire, designed as part of an agricultural improvement scheme in 1808, and the Duke of Devonshire's village of Edensor on the Chatsworth estate in Derbyshire.

Many estate villages were built or improved with new money rather than old. In the 19th century especially, the old families of landed gentry with country pedigrees dating back many generations were being bought out by men who had made their money in commerce and industry and fancied the life of a country gentleman. They did not have an inborn sense of the rhythms of agriculture and village life but many of them had a vision and an urge to contribute to the rural environment in which they lived.

▼ ORIGINALLY A GEORGIAN FARMHOUSE, *this country dwelling in Sussex was lavishly extended in the late 19th and early 20th century to form a mansion four times larger, with huge reception rooms, and set in extensive landscaped grounds. The building work, which also included several new cottages in the local hamlet and on the estate farm, gave employment to many local trades for several years.*

All over the country there are small villages that do not attract much attention, but which the locals know owe their origins and sometimes their improvement to the local estate.

The squire

An important figure in social history, the influence of the squire in rural areas remained strong until at least World War I in many parts of the country. 'Squire' is an abbreviation of 'esquire' and was originally applied to landowners who were often but not necessarily always lords of the manor. The term can be used more generally to include those in rural areas whose power over a neighbourhood was usually based on being a substantial landowner.

The essence of the old-fashioned squire was that he was one of the gentry who came from an old and respected family and who preferred to live locally, and was involved with country society and village and farming matters, in contrast to the noble lords who preferred to live in the city and involve themselves in politics, court life, the arts and high society.

In 1850 squires were defined as 'lesser gentry' who owned between 1,000 and 3,000 acres of land and took an active interest in the farming of it. Their wealth was more in land than in other assets, and their land ownership gave them local power. There were about 2,000 squires in the country at the time and they were expected to have and maintain local roots. They were 'old money' – it was not until later in the Victorian period that 'new money' was accepted as being as valid as old.

A good squire, wielding that power justly and with a generosity of spirit, could command considerable loyalty and respect on his home territory, however much the urbane metropolitan aristocrats might sneer at his rusticity. Good squires were deeply concerned for the welfare of those who lived on the estate and in the village, and they had support in their role from their wives and families.

The women would take a particular interest in the village's poor, sick, elderly and children and could bring genuine comfort to those in distress, though some had a patronising air that could make your toes curl and some were downright arrogant or entirely cold in their manner. The family saw their concern for villagers as their duty, their responsibility, almost in payment for being better off than most and having what some judged to be privileges even when they were in reality burdens. The good squire would invite tenants, servants, employees and probably the rest of the village to celebrate joyful family occasions; he would share the

▲ THE PROXIMITY OF A MILITARY BASE TO A VILLAGE *sometimes gave the commanding officer the role of 'virtual squire'. Colonel Oscar Graham, Commander of Flowerdown (a base near Winchester) is seen here with Mr Arthur Deane at the opening of the nearby village of Littleton's cricket pitch in 1920. The first pavilion was a very large World War I military packing case, no doubt presented by the Colonel.*

game bag and ensure that every family had meat on the table at Christmas; he would put on 'teas' and fetes on the lawns of the big house; and find countless other ways of mingling with the village while maintaining his family's own way of life and privacy.

Of course, the village tended to know everything that went on in the squire's family, as those in service at the house were often from the village and were not averse to gossiping. In his own household and on the estate the squire might have a bailiff for the home farm and a steward to look after the estate, who would discuss with the squire whether a certain copse should be cut that winter, whether the oak bark had been paid for at a proper price, how the Alderney cow was doing or the poultry at the home farm, whether the pigsty roof needed a few new tiles or a cart needed new wheels, or whether

'The family saw their concern for villagers as their duty, their responsibility'

a tenant should be allowed to put up another shed. The steward would then give him the local gossip to keep him in touch – farmer Smith's sheep seemed to be dying, old Mrs Brown had taken to drinking, and poor simple Sally had given birth to a bastard.

There would also be a gamekeeper, a head gardener, a coachman, a groom, a butler of course, footmen, a governess for the children, a cook and a housekeeper, and most of these staff would have a team of lesser servants under their watchful eye and would chat with the squire or his wife now and then about whatever it was they were responsible for. Each had their own little kingdom, jealously guarded, with many a petty rivalry between them and often a degree of ganging up against, say, the snooty governess: her past was mysterious and she certainly wasn't a local – probably from some distant metropolis like London or, worse, a foreigner from France.

A squire might ride into market once a week, go to church every Sunday (always the best pew) and sit on the Petty Sessional bench weekly; he might ride to hounds in the hunting season, carry his gun about the estate to shoot rabbits or pheasants, do his

▲ **A GENUINE SQUIRE PREFERRED TO RIDE** *a good solid cob when going about his business, whether around the estate or into town. Squires who had bought themselves into the role rather than being born into it would be more pretentious in their choice of steed, and more likely to use wheels than saddle.*

▶ **JC HAWKSHAW WAS A BENEVOLENT SQUIRE** *for the family's 5,000-acre Hollycombe estate in Sussex. The son of the highly respected Victorian civil engineer Sir John Hawkshaw (and married into the famous Wedgwood pottery family), he travelled all over the world on the family firm's engineering projects but always found time to care for the welfare of his farm and cottage tenants at home.*

▲ **THE PARSON'S SOCIAL STATUS** *increased throughout the Victorian period. Freeman R Stratton's rectory, in a small hamlet, employed six domestic staff and he was influential enough to get what he wanted for his parish from local landowners and the government.*

paperwork in the study or library, read the newspapers, talk to a tenant with a problem or complaint, pop up to London now and then, go to the seaside with his family, and perhaps even take a trip across the Channel once in a while.

The parson

The parson could be as influential as the squire in village affairs and the two of them might work together or, perhaps more often, with a mild (or even bitter) sense of rivalry. The rivalry could be a useful balance in the village, ensuring that the views and ambitions of one person did not necessarily predominate. Sometimes, however, both roles were invested in the same man, naturally nicknamed the 'squarson'.

The Church was active not just in spiritual matters but also in the more practical problems of poverty, age and sickness in the village, as was the squire.

Many parsons took their pastoral duty of caring for the poor wholeheartedly and did their best to improve the grindingly hard life led by many in their rural flock, even into the 20th century. But now and then there would be a parson who seemed to be more interested in his own status than the care of his parish's poor, or whose arrogance and wilfulness upset the whole village. In the 19th century some of the livings were so meagre that the parson was forced to find little part-time jobs or other canny ways of increasing his income: some took up a trade in their spare time, or taught pupils, or sold the crops from their glebeland to make ends meet, or took on more than one benefice and spent their time rushing from one parish to another. Virtually every parish in the country has a fund of stories about its parsons and a rich stock of often eccentric characters to remember, with or without fondness.

▲ **REVEREND FH BARHAM WAS FACING A MAJOR CATASTROPHE** *when this photograph was taken in 1931: his church, the pub, the farms and the entire villages of Mardale Green and Measand were about to disappear under a new reservoir. Despite enormous public concern, Manchester Corporation went ahead with the development in 1935; the villagers were moved out, bodies in the churchyard were exhumed, the church was dismantled and its stones were ignominiously used for dam construction. Haweswater reservoir is now 200 feet deep and four miles long, and supplies water to urban areas in the northwest of England.*

The parson's influence, like that of the squire, began to wane in the 20th century, once local government in the form of civil parish councils, created in 1894, started to take on some of the Church's more secular roles and, more influentially, once the Welfare State was created immediately after World War II.

The village bobby

The village bobby did not exist until the mid 19th century. Some years after the 1856 County and Borough Police Act, counties were compelled to establish rural police forces to replace an older and more casual system of parish constables that, in one form or another, had existed since medieval times.

The old parish constable was one of four principal parish officers who were elected annually by the parish, the others being the churchwarden, the surveyor of highways and the overseer of the poor.

By the 19th century, the post of parish constable was no longer occupied by wealthier villagers and tradesmen wanting to serve their community, but was taken up largely by the unemployed, and often unemployable, in a job that nobody else either wanted or respected.

In some villages the old part-time parish constable was still around until the 1880s, but in most parishes he had been replaced during the 1870s by a respectable village policeman in a proper uniform whose job specification required him to be intelligent, able to read and write, of strong constitution and free of 'bodily complaints'. He had to be at least 5ft 7in tall and no older than 40. He had to have good references about his moral character and he had to be prepared to work hard, under strict discipline and for wages that were no better than those of an unskilled agricultural labourer. In some counties chastity was another part of the specification; in others his family was limited to two children.

He was discouraged from eating and drinking with the locals and from entering pubs except in the course of his duties. He worked a seven-day week and a 10-12-hour day, and was lucky to have one rest-day in every six weeks and an annual week of unpaid

▶ THE VILLAGE POLICEMAN'S UNIFORM, *as worn here by Police Sergeant George Kemish in 1910, was quite an advance on the early uniform, which included a dark blue swallow-tail coat and a glazed stovepipe top hat.*

▲ PARISH CLERKS WERE LAYMEN *paid by the parson to keep church records and accounts, summon worshippers to services by ringing the church bell, conduct and lead the hymn-singing and the efforts of the village's church band, read the epistles and lessons, and generally make sure that the congregation behaved properly. Henry Hilton, the Yateley parish clerk leading the donkey here, was socially inferior to the more smartly dressed churchwarden behind him: clerks were usually farm labourers, but highly respected in the village; whereas churchwardens (who monitored the fabric of the church, had considerable financial powers and made sure the parson carried out his duties satisfactorily) were often yeoman farmers.*

holiday. He worked mostly on foot, patrolling rural lanes and deterring crime by his very presence. In his spare time he ran the local fire brigade and ambulance, maintained the village lock-up, switched on any village street-lamps and, in due course, did speed checks on motor vehicles in his patch. It sounds like quite a hard and probably rather lonely life.

Vestry meetings and parish councils

An important part of village life was the vestry meeting, at which village worthies came together in the church's vestry (or more often adjourned to the nearest pub) to appoint each other to the various village caretaking posts that did not necessarily have anything to do with church matters. They appointed guardians and overseers of the poor, highway surveyors and way-wardens,

rates assessors and parish valuers, charity trustees, parish constables, parish doctors and medical officers, schoolmasters and others who were essential to the smooth running of the parish. They looked after almshouses, parish cottages and the parish workhouse; they distributed clothing, bread, flour, potatoes and other necessities to the parish's poor; they found things for paupers to do and dealt with vagrants; and they ensured that those who needed nursing were nursed (in some sets of vestry minutes there are references to the gloriously named London Truss Society for Relief of Ruptured Poor).

There was much more that the vestry meetings handled: they kept the parish roads in good condition, making sure that there were adequate materials, labour and draught animals to do so; they maintained pounds where stray animals were held until their owners paid a fine for their release; they sold lane-dropped manure; they dealt with footpaths and ponds, flooding and drains. Many of them set up parish fire brigades (the engines, of course, had to be pushed or

'*... there were very few aspects of village life in which the vestry did not become involved.*'

pulled by men or horses) and fire-fighting reservoirs; they maintained burial grounds and built schools; they kept an eye on the pubs and alehouses; they ensured that apprenticeships were available; they helped those who wanted to emigrate; they took adequate precautions to prevent the spread of smallpox or typhoid or plague in the village; they trod the bounds and cried the notices; they persuaded fathers to pay towards the wellbeing of their bastard offspring; they built reading rooms and created recreation grounds; they paid the parish constable's bills, provided him with parish handcuffs and a parish lock-up and offered rewards on the heads of criminals. In fact there were very few aspects of village life in which the vestry did not become involved.

This system continued vigorously until the early beginnings of centralisation occurred in the late 18th century, when parishes were advised to combine with others in the interests of 'efficiency'; for example, by jointly buying or hiring a workhouse to cover a wider area than just one village. New maps were being drawn up by assorted authorities, carving the countryside into regions or 'unions' of parishes under Poor Law amendments, often in the face of overridden but vehement opposition from parishes pointing out that they had no natural affinity with some of those parishes and would rather be placed with others instead.

Gradually these more centralised groups began to take away the vestry's powers to look after its own, and the whole business became increasingly less personal. People in trouble were judged by people who no longer knew them or their histories.

By the time parish councils were created in 1894, the vestry system had long since withered to a shadow of its former self and the new councils could do very little for their own poor and other disadvantaged villagers. It was all in the hands of other bodies in the towns. During the early 20th century, the villagers shrugged their shoulders and let 'them' get on with it.

▶ **FORMED TO ENCOURAGE WOMEN** *in the countryside to take a greater part in food production for the war effort, the timing of the WI creation was apposite: with Britain in the throes of World War I there was a need to boost home food production, as well as to fulfil an emotional void in the lives of women whose husbands and sons were away fighting.*

▲ **THE CREATION OF PARISH COUNCILS** *in 1894 provided women with a formal voice in village affairs. Candidacy was extended to women from the outset, and they even had the right to vote – much to the shock of male members. Few women actually succeeded in being voted on to parish councils until the 1920s and 1930s.*

' In these 'terribly British' groupings you would find examples of every clichéed character, which was part of the fun.'

Doing good

Between the World Wars a rash of initials came into the villages, full of worthy intent. Among the most influential groups were the Women's Institutes (WIs), based on a movement that had started in Canada in 1897. The first British WI was formed in the Welsh village with that famously long name, generally abbreviated to Llanfairpwll, in Anglesey. The aim of the institutes, which saw themselves as 'brightening the lives' of women in the villages, was 'to give countrywomen opportunities to improve conditions in their own homes and villages, and to increase their enjoyment of life'. The monthly meetings were divided into three parts: transaction of WI business; a talk or demonstration on a subject of general or local interest; and social activities after a cup of tea. Many institutes also organised drama or choral societies, art and handicraft classes or courses of lectures in subjects such as cookery and home making. Others became interested in further education; for example, in one village the mostly middle-aged wives of agricultural labourers chose medieval history as the subject they wanted to study. The village WI might walk the local footpaths, welcome foreign students studying community development, run a WI group in the local mental hospital or prison, sell members' produce in a weekly market in the nearest town – once a group of women got together, the scope was endless.

The essence of the WI was that it was for women in rural areas and embraced all levels of village society as equals, be they the rector's wife or the road sweeper's. These groups often became, as well, guardians of local history, listening to each other's memories and sometimes taking care to record them on paper, or even on tape, for future generations. Several WIs recorded on film, moving or static, and in paintings and needlework, creating visual records as well as verbal ones that local historians find invaluable. In these 'terribly British' groupings you would find examples of every clichéed character, which was part of the fun. There was always the rather fey, arty woman seeking to enlighten the masses. There was always a woman with a loud voice ruffling everybody's feathers, but there were enough of you to put her in her place.

Immediately after World War I, in 1919, the National Council of Social Service was formed (it would later be called the National Council for Voluntary Organisations) to strengthen the 'rich and varied pattern of voluntary societies' by bringing them together under one umbrella, where they could work in partnership with the new statutory services that were then being developed. Later in that year, the Council drew attention to the inactivity of parish councils and suggested setting up 'village social councils'.

In 1920 Sir Horace Plunkett appealed to the University of Oxford to take the lead in promoting a wider vision of 'better living as well as better farming and better business':

New ideas are stirring in the countryside. Men who have come back from service across the sea, women who have come back from work in munitions factories have learnt a new independence and a new vision ... The problem of making rural life as full of stimulus and as attractive as it ought to be can only be solved by educating village people themselves in the broad principles of cooperation in social and educational as well as in strictly agricultural matters.

That was a bit unfair: villagers had lived in a society of mutual cooperation for centuries (though it had slipped a bit in recent years), but he meant well. His appeal was heard by a Gloucestershire woman, Grace Hadow, vice-president of the National Federation of WIs, who in 1921 formed the first 'rural community council' (Oxfordshire), a group including leaders in adult education and spokespersons for various village clubs, to help the county's villages in social and educational work.

▲ THE NUMBER OF WI BRANCHES *in England and Wales had reached 7,000 by 1951, with a total membership of about 400,000; by the Golden Jubilee in 1965 (pictured above) there were 9,000 branches, all under the protective umbrella of their National Federation (inaptly based in London).*

In 1922 Professor WGS Adams, a pioneer of the National Council, said:

The tendency has been on the one hand to give the village what was considered good for it and, on the other, to turn to someone else for help on all occasions. The essence of the country problem is to find means to enable country men and women to help themselves, and to bring together all classes in cooperation for the common good.

It all rather smacks of condescension, but again, he meant well, and certainly the RCCs did pump new life into some of the villages. For example, there was immediate enthusiasm from voluntary groups of musicians and actors who went out to the villages to encourage an interest in the arts.

Then came the master-stroke. The RCCs realised that the best way of bringing all a village's interests together was to build a village hall, or improve an existing one. With the help of the National Council, they managed

▶ **ACCESS TO MEDICAL SERVICES WAS HARD** *for families who could only rely on public transport for getting about. By the 1920s local councils had become much more involved in community healthcare, and began to arrange for mobile clinics to come direct to the villages – especially dentists, as shown here.*

to persuade the Treasury to provide interest-free loans to do so. In those days it was loans; in the 1930s there were grants under the Physical Training and Recreation Act of 1937; today it is more likely to be grants from Lottery funds.

There are now RCCs in every county and they are an invaluable source of information and support for villages having problems with loss of services or in need of inspiration and cash. They have built up an enormous pool of expertise and knowledge; it is just a shame that they still base themselves in towns and that many of their staff are from urban, not rural, backgrounds who, albeit unwittingly, sometimes seem a little patronising towards their country cousins.

▼ **THE HARVEST FESTIVAL** *celebrated the end of the old agricultural year and the promise of the new planting season. This farmer, bringing harvest produce to decorate the church in 1934, was poised on a threshold between interwar rural depression and the boost to agriculture that World War II would induce.*

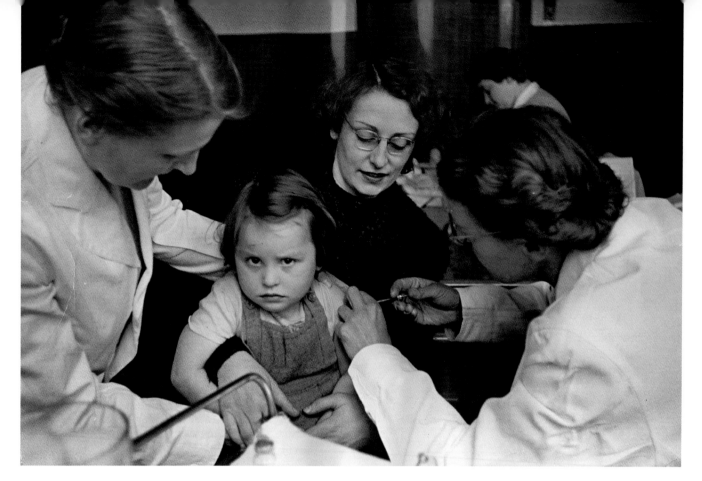

▲ POLIO WAS ONCE A COMMON DISEASE THAT COULD LEAD TO MUSCLE DEGENERATION *and partial paralysis. Huge improvements in hygiene have helped to control the disease, but prevention has largely been as a result of successful vaccination against the virus. The first national polio vaccination programme for British children was in 1956.*

▲ THE DISTRICT NURSE WAS THE RURAL ANGEL *on whom many families depended: they were more likely to know her than their GP. When few homes had telephones, the man of the house usually had to set out on his own bike to the nurse's cottage and hope that she was at home.*

The welfare state

In Victorian times, the sense of service to the village was strong among those at the pyramid's level of tradesmen, craftsmen, teachers and the like, many of whom played multiple 'official' roles in the village and its immediate neighbourhood. As well as paupers, their range of care embraced the sick, the elderly, the unemployed, orphans and bastards, widows, tramps and ne'er-do-wells. It was all part of the self-sufficiency of the old village.

For several centuries, the poor were essentially cared for by the Church and through acts of private charity, until the Elizabethan Poor Laws effectively transferred the responsibilities to the village itself. Wealthy individuals continued to feel better about their wealth by giving money, food, clothing, homes, education and other services to the deserving in their parish, but the essence of the Poor Laws was that most of the village contributed as well. And being a village, everybody knew who was in trouble and what was being done about it.

A very big change after World War II was the creation of the welfare state, which came with the shock election victory of the Labour Party in 1945. Its effects have been largely beneficial but there are disadvantages as well. The welfare state finally relieved the villagers of responsibility for their own, indeed even responsibility for themselves as individuals. Those in trouble were taken in hand by people who had no connection with the village at all, and sometimes they felt like numbers, just a case to be dealt with. In the old village, even in the workhouse, that would not have happened.

The welfare state also saw the final withdrawal of the squire from village life. Henceforth those in the big house and those with large land holdings became more self-centred and less willing to contribute to a village they perceived as being able to look after itself with the help of the state.

The new village

In the last decades of the 20th century the old 'class' barriers all but disappeared. There is still a degree of division by wealth in its extremes but there is a much bigger 'middle' class, a group of people who are neither major landowners nor in dire straits. In some places there is still a degree of division between original villagers and incomers but the lines are becoming blurred, perhaps largely because the incomers outnumber the families that have lived in the village for more than one generation.

With the blurring there is a loss of the great variety that once characterised the village. Too many people are similar now in their education, their outlook on life, the type of work they do, the clothes they wear, the entertainments they enjoy and the aspirations they hold dear. The spread of easy communications in the 19th and early 20th century injected a dose of life into villages that had been slowly dying, but ultimately good communications bred uniformity. And that might be a danger for the future.

It does seem that there are fewer 'characters' in the villages now, and far fewer of the eccentrics to whom 'conforming' was anathema. In their place, though, you will usually find that villages both old and new become motivated by a few individuals, who dare to stand out a little from the flock; they are the people who are always proactive, always doing something for the village and always asking others to help. Perhaps in villages where people habitually say 'No', these motivators eventually give up and become hermits, or leave for fresh pastures, and so the dying village perpetuates its own decay by suppressing initiative; but far more often people say 'Yes', and when they do a village can achieve whatever it wants.

▼ AFTER THE WAR, *in village halls up and down the country, people continued to look after their own by collecting money as carol singers and by other means to make sure that the older generation could have a good feast once a year, or as part of a monthly 'lunch club'. The charitable Darby and Joan clubs that were set up in many villages and towns provided (and still provide) regular social get-togethers for the over-sixties. These would often be under the auspices of the Women's Royal Voluntary Services, and would include outings and informal gatherings in the local hall. Larger clubs went further, providing help for the elderly and even setting up retirement homes.*

2. Cottage Life

The reality of living in a country cottage was a world away from the thatched rose-clad dream of the town dweller. Basic amenities came to rural areas much later than to the towns and the country housewife toiled endlessly to keep the home warm and the children clean and healthy, and to get food on to the family table. Everyday life in the typically crowded, damp, infested homes where the mass of agricultural workers were allowed to live as tenants at the whim of the landlord was a constant struggle. Every utility in domestic life was hard won and demanded physical labour, be it water for drinking and washing, fuel for cooking, or disposal of 'night soil' and rubbish. It would not be until after two world wars that services taken for granted today reached rural areas and cottagers could enjoy new homes – homes for heroes returning from the wars, bungalows, council houses with all their modern amenities, bringing such joy to the reluctant cottager's heart.

The country cottage: what an evocation of the lost idyll of a past that we never really knew; and what a deception, what a romantic hoodwink!

Between the wars, wistful would-be escapist townies yearned for a period cottage with character, facing south, with a view and a garden in the front, and with mains water and electricity as in the towns. The cottage should cost no more than £500 to purchase and preferably be 'isolated' but near enough to a city to soften the isolation. It would be a small(ish), cosy, pretty and intimate little home, with diamond-pane windows glinting irregularly in the sun and potted geraniums scarlet on the windowsills. Warmth would be suggested by woodsmoke curling gently from the chimney and the whole vision snuggled quietly and discreetly into its rural surroundings, frocked with flowers in a blowsy, abundant garden with a patch of healthy weed-free vegetables, ripe fruit for the picking, perhaps a few gentle dreamy-eyed cows in a buttercup meadow beyond the honeysuckle and wild-rose garden hedge, a few homely brown hens pottering in the dust of the lavender-hemmed garden path.

This pastel place was close to a friendly village where the settler was greeted by name in a shop whose owner had time to chat; there was a friendly little school where children learned in small classes and played safely in the fresh air. There was a church, a snug pub with a roaring fire, all just a stroll or gentle cycle ride away from the cottage down a lane whose hay-scented verges were sprinkled with wild flowers in yellow, white, blue and pink.

Was it ever like this? What was it really like to live in the country? And how is it different now? Was Dr Johnson right when

▼ THE OLD-FASHIONED HOMES *of South Uist in the Outer Hebrides (an example of which is photographed here as late as 1957) might be 'black houses' or they might be thatched three-roomed cottages. The oldest of the cottages had an open fire in the middle of the floor at the smoke-filled heart of the house (there were no chimneys), which formed the kitchen and working area, and sleeping-quarters roughly partitioned off at the ends – women at the 'up end' and men on the left-hand side of the front door. This system still existed in the early years of the 20th century.*

he said, 'No wise man will go to live in the country unless he has something to do which can be better done in the country'? Or, as FG Thomas put it in 1938 at the University College of the South-West in Exeter: 'Has the tradition and experience of urban life destroyed the capacity to live happily except in towns and cities?'

Begin with the distant view. Before the railways made feasible the transporting of bricks countrywide, there was a time when it was easy to recognise just where in the country you were by the style and substance of the local buildings. The substance relied heavily on what was locally available, and that was largely a matter of geology. The style relied on local tradition and suited the landscape. Today, as you journey across the country, you are likely to see endless boxes in similar styles and materials whether you are in Caithness or Cornwall, Carmarthen or Cambridge. The sense of place is dying.

Cottage crowding

In 1872 Richard Jefferies wrote to *The Times* about the Wiltshire agricultural labourers whom he knew so well and would write about frequently until his early death at the age of 38 in 1887. Having described a typical labourer in build, gait, clothing and eating habits, he turned to the cottages:

The cottages now are infinitely better than they were. There is scarcely room for further improvement in the cottages now erected upon estates. They have three bedrooms, and every appliance and comfort compatible with their necessarily small size. It is only the cottages erected by the labourers themselves on waste plots of ground which are open to objection. Those he builds himself are, indeed, as a rule, miserable huts, disgraceful to a Christian country. I have an instance before me at this moment where a man built a cottage with two rooms and no staircase or upper apartments, and in those two rooms eight persons lived and slept – himself and wife, grown-up daughters, and children. There was not a scrap of garden attached, not enough to grow half a dozen onions. The refuse and sewage was flung into the road, or filtered down a ditch into the brook which supplied that part of the village with water.

▲ THE LONG-HOUSE LINGERED FOR A LONGER TIME *in the crofting counties of north and west Scotland than elsewhere in the country. Crofters here rented their land from the local laird, but were encouraged to build their own home; having built it, the crofter could not actually sell his house as he did not own the land on which it was built.*

◄ COTTAGES AND FARMHOUSES *were made of local materials, especially stone, until the advent of affordable mass-produced bricks. This couple, Isaac and Ann Scarth, lived at Rock Head Cottage in Glaisdale, a North Yorkshire moorland parish about ten miles from Whitby. The local building materials were ironstone and slate: the barren hills around the fertile and picturesque Glaisdale Valley are rich in iron ore, and the local stone was also used for the dale's numerous drystone walls marking old field boundaries that once followed the snow-line.*

It is shocking to realise that those crowded children, had they reached a reasonable old age, would have been alive well within living memory and their own children are probably still alive today. And it is shocking to realise that among the latter generation there are those who can remember sleeping head to toe like sardines in a tin, several to the bed, in their country cottages, though they often claim to have had a far happier childhood than many. 'What you never had, you never missed,' is a common remark

The cottage within

The old cottages were always crowded – families were much larger than the present average of two or so children, even well within living memory, in contrast to the towns, in which the average in 1900 was much as it is today. In many a village, those who are now in their eighties often come from families of eight, ten or more, and each family would have been crammed into a cottage, or half a cottage.

In earlier times rural homes tended to be empty by day, when both parents might be working and the children would often be doing the same, if they were not at school. With limited artificial light, bed was the place to be once it was dark; there would be no sitting around in a living room at leisure, though the occupants might be bent over some cottage industry work to bring in a few extra pennies. The furnishings and decor of the cottage were minimal; they could not be afforded, there was little need for them anyway and they were rarely aspired to. Whatever was within the cottage was

▲ COTTAGES WERE OFTEN MADE COSY WITH CLUTTER. *Countless photographs of cottage interiors show men relaxing by a source of warmth while women, clad in aprons or pinafores, are busy doing housework, proving the old saying that a woman's work is never done.*

functional, essential to everyday life, and had little to do with comfort or aesthetics. Home was simply somewhere to escape from the cold and wet of outdoor work, somewhere to eat a hot meal and to sleep.

The key to rural domestic life was improvisation, creating for yourself what was needed from resources close to hand and preferably costing nothing. This was easier in the country than in the town. Perhaps the biggest contrast with the interior of the modern home is in uniformity: today goods are mass-produced, readily available all over the country and much the same whether you are in the Orkneys or the Isle of Wight, the Welsh hills or the Northumbrian coast. Wherever you live, you can recognise a cooker or a refrigerator immediately for what it is. There is no longer much need (or so much scope) to be ingenious in creating something out of nothing, recycling anything and everything to make for yourself whatever you require; or exploiting (say) the fact that natural running water or a hole dug deep in the soil can keep perishable goods cool – an option not usually open to town dwellers.

Heat and light

In Elizabethan times, Bishop Hall described a cottar's home:

Of one bay's breadth God wot a silly cote
Whose thatched spars are furred
*   with sluttish soote,*
A whole inch thick, shining like
*   blackmore's brows*
Through smoke that downe the headlesse
*   barrell blows.*
At his bed's head feaden his stalled
*   teame,*
His swine beneath his pullen o'er the
*   beame.*

The idea of keeping your horses and cattle close to your bed is comfortably warming, though perhaps you could do without the pigs rooting on the floor and the chickens sitting above your head on the beam. You can still find evidence of old wattle-and-daub cottages that are closely skirted by catslide outshots, which originally housed livestock on the other side of the wall from the family.

▲ **INGLENOOKS PROVIDED TOASTY PERCHES** *snuggling right into the nook, protected from draughts and so close to the flames that clothes could be singed. But sitting almost in the fire was necessary, as most of its heat went straight up the huge chimney.*

'*Whatever was within the cottage was functional, essential to everyday life, and had little to do with comfort or aesthetics*'

A major attraction for would-be cottage dwellers from the towns is an inglenook fire, burning sweetly scented logs from an old apple tree, the flames leaping cheerfully, throwing up little showers of sparks now and then with a comforting crackle, offering glowing red embers below for toasting bread and marshmallows or roasting chestnuts and potatoes. The reality tends to be more smoke than flame, and smoke that is determined to belch into the room rather than up the chimney. Modern cottagers prefer the efficiency of a wood-burning stove, if wood is the fuel of choice: the stoves don't smoke, they don't sulk and they throw the heat into the room instead of up that chimney.

The hearth may have been the heart of the home, and usually the only source of rural domestic warmth until the 20th century, but it was too often the cause of early death, either from lung disease exacerbated by the smoke or from the very real threat of the place catching fire. (Those with thatch on the roof would whitewash the thatch to make it less flammable.) The huge inglenook fireplaces, with their cosy built-in wooden seats, had big wide chimneys to match, virtually ensuring that they would billow smoke into the room. Cottagers did their best by draping little curtains from the inglenook beam, and by letting the fire ash build up as high as possible so that the fire itself was raised and its smoke more likely to find the chimney.

The fire was not simply for the pleasure of reading dream pictures into the flames, or keeping warm if you were close up to it. It was where kettles were boiled and family meals were cooked; it was often the main source of light in the evening; and it had a psychological, almost religious significance: many people insisted on keeping the fire burning continuously, summer and winter, night and day, because it was unlucky to let it die, as well as being a considerable labour to relight it and bring it up to a high enough temperature quickly. Even today, some of the older generation still keep their faithful Rayburn burning year round, and feel empty and lonely without its comforting background presence.

Cooking aids

Before the cooking could begin, there was the labour of finding something to burn. The luckier cottagers had commoners' rights to gather firewood, peat or turf for the hearth and in some regions they burned dried animal dung as fuel. Coal was already being used in some smaller country homes by the mid 17th century if it was mined locally; in the rest of the country coal did not become a common fuel until the railways made its transport cheap two centuries later.

Open fires, set in big wide fireplaces, were furnished with all manner of ironwork in the days when blacksmiths were thriving in every village and roving tinkers could mend your broken pots and pans. There was the essential heavy, cast-iron, fat-bellied cooking pot hung over the fire on its chain or ratcheted hanger, dangling from a wooden bar that was fixed some six or seven feet up the chimney, or the pot simply stood in the ashes on three stubby legs; whole cottage meals could be stewed in these hard-working cauldrons. A kettle might dangle from an 'idleback', a device that allowed you to tip the kettle for pouring the water without burning your fingers taking it off its hanger. There would be a gridiron, or a flat iron griddle or bakestone hanging over the fire for baking oatcakes.

▼ COOKING POTS WERE LARGE ENOUGH *to accommodate whole meals at a time and could be used out in the backyard (in summer, when the heat of the kitchen was unbearable) as well as indoors over an open fire or on a range. They were ideal for slow cooking: a woman could leave the meal stewing quietly to itself while she went out to work in the fields all day, the long leisurely process tenderizing old meat and suffusing it with taste.*

Farmhouses would have a meat-roasting spit resting on tall iron firedogs, turned by a wide range of devices – pulley-wheels, geared weighted winches driven by gravity, smoke jacks driven by the fire's hot air, clockwork-spring mechanical bottle jacks and the like; in poorer cottages they would simply rig up a system of twisted string.

In cottages, much of the food was boiled, or stewed. The iron pot might be kept simmering for days, more bits being chucked in to enrich the broth at intervals. Boil-in-the-bag was common well into the 20th century: you set your joint of bacon (the cottager's staple meat) to simmer in the pot; after a while you add potatoes tied in cotton bags and other garden vegetables in a separate cotton bag, and no doubt a suet pudding wrapped in a piece of old white sheet. The bacon would be eked out for several meals in different guises, and was inevitably a piece of your own pig, which had been living the good life at the end of the garden.

As many country people relied heavily on the pig for their protein and winter-warming fat, large chimneys often housed a bacon loft, or the sides of bacon were just hung in the chimney to smoke after being salt-cured. Home-made sausages often dangled in the smoke and were cut down for cooking as and when they were needed.

▲ **BAKING BREAD IN A VILLAGE BAKERY** *was similar in principle to baking at home for those who had cottage bread ovens built into the wall by the inglenook fireplace. The traditional cottage loaf was round, with a knob on top that many a farm boy liked to remove, before filling the loaf with something tasty like dripping, and replacing the 'lid' to carry with him into the fields for elevenses.*

> '... *people created an instant baking oven by turning the iron cooking pot upside down on the fire and surrounding it with hot ashes*'

▼ THE RANGE, *whether open or closed, succeeded the inglenook fireplace as the heart of the home in both cottages and farmhouses.*

Baking

Small loaves and cakes could be baked straight on the hot ashes, covered by an upside-down redware pot to act as a miniature oven, with more hot ashes heaped over the pot. In some cottages and farmhouses you might still find evidence of a bread oven, probably long since bricked off or converted into a cupboard. The oven, generally next to the main fireplace and sometimes built as a little extension, was usually a tunnel-like cavity, with a gently arching ceiling and an iron door. The method of baking was this: first, bavins or faggots must be gathered from the woods and commons – these were bushy twiggery, bound together in small bundles. The faggots were loaded into the oven and allowed to burn fiercely, with the door closed. When they had burned out, the oven was hot enough to start baking: the ashes were raked before the dough was slipped into the oven. You often found pieces of charcoal stuck to the bottom of your loaf.

Built-in bread ovens were something of a luxury as bricks were expensive. West Country cottagers might use portable earthenware ('cloam') ovens, the last of which were made in Truro in 1937. Elsewhere people created an instant baking oven by turning the iron cooking pot upside down on the fire and surrounding it with hot ashes, and these developed into lidded cast-iron baking pots or 'camp ovens', known in Yorkshire as yetlings.

Grates and ranges

With the growing affordability of coal, more efficient methods of cooking began to be developed. Although wood can be burnt on the hearth itself, or slung across firedogs, coal fires require grates, allowing the ashes to drop away from the coals. Grates became quite common in coal country in the 17th and 18th centuries, and in places like London, where wood was hard to come by but coal could be brought in by sea. The fireplace began to change: the old all-

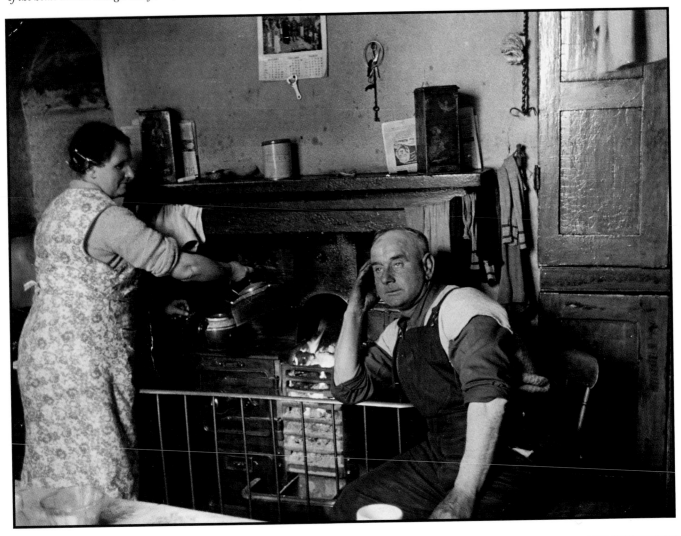

purpose inglenook became a much smaller area. Slow-burning grates on firebrick bases were being used all over the country in the final decades of the 19th century and the hearth became more suited to merely keeping you warm than being a place for cooking and bacon curing as well. Cooking over an open fire gave way to the challenges of the range, but rather later in country cottages, with their one main living room, than in town homes with their fancy parlours. Where wood was still plentiful, for example in southern Britain, cooking on the big old open fireplace persisted. Country people, well within living memory, often continued to cook on open fires but out of doors: typically a bonfire would be made up for cooking the vegetables, especially in summer when it was too hot to cook inside. The garden barbecue is nothing new.

Although you might have a hob grate for boiling a kettle, grates were more often found in kitchens. They were used for

cooking, and by the 18th century they were usually described as ranges, in comparison with 'stove grates' for heating living rooms.

The open range became an open coal fire with an iron baking oven on one side and a boiler on the other (if you were lucky) to replace the old portable copper, both with cooking hobs but also with the old beam for dangling your kettle over the open fire, where you could also roast the meat. It was not the most efficient method for either heating or cooking, and the next development was to contain the central fire under a cast-iron hotplate that kept the smoke and ashes away from the food and kept the heat where you wanted it. Traditionalists at heart, many country families claimed that the meat tasted wrong from such a range and they preferred to roast on the old open fire. Then during the 19th century manufacturers put iron doors across the front to make the closed range, which was particularly popular in the Midlands (where they were often called

▲ EVACUEE HOUSEWIVES FROM THE CITIES *were often shocked at the very basic kitchen arrangements they found in their temporary country homes during World War II. They would have expected electricity and mains gas for the cookers; instead they had to learn to cook on antiquated ranges and portable gas stoves.*

▲ **ANOTHER SHOCK** *for the evacuee housewife was the lack of mains water and plumbing in most rural homes. Before washing up, it was often a matter of drawing water from a well or the back-door pump, heating it in the copper or on the range and pouring it into an unplumbed sink. There would be no washing-up liquid. Afterwards, the plug was removed from the sink so that the dirty water splashed into a bucket underneath. The 'grey' water then had to be carried out to the garden for disposal.*

'kitcheners'), but many cottagers disliked not being able to see those warming flames, nor could they quite get the hang of dampers.

Manufacturers persisted, and created small, cheap ranges ideally suited to cottages. In 1929 the first Aga cookers, burning coke, came into Britain and proved ideal for farmhouse kitchens, though far too expensive for cottages. The latter eventually opted for the smaller, cheaper Rayburns that many still run today; they fitted perfectly into the smaller cottage fireplace and they were much easier to clean and more efficient at burning fuel than the old ranges. Anthracite was the ideal fuel, cleaner than coal and burning slowly enough to keep the fire in all night, but it was usually too expensive for cottagers. Nor did they benefit from the new fuels that town dwellers took for granted: piped gas still has not reached many country areas even now, and mains electricity did not come to the villages until at the earliest the 1920s and

more usually not until the 1950s or later. Even when electricity was attainable, many rural households distrusted it. Some chose oil stoves, which were often highly temperamental and filthy, with a tendency to set light to things and blow soot all over the kitchen. There were often problems with power cuts in rural areas, as branches and trees fell on overhead power lines.

Lighting

In the big houses, candles were the means of providing artificial light in the first part of the 18th century. Many cottagers could not afford candles until perhaps the 1830s, and some not even until the end of that century. Instead they relied on the flicker of firelight or they made their own candles from rushes gathered from the meadows in summer.

In the second half of the 19th century mass-produced paraffin-wax candles became widely available; these produced a steady, long-lasting and almost smokeless flame, and they were affordable. All sorts of candle holders and lanterns were invented, for reading and working by candlelight or for carrying around with you as you moved about the home, pottered up to bed, went along the garden path to the privy, took a journey by coach or ventured out into the weather to check your livestock.

By then, however, there was more competition in lighting. Oil lamps became increasingly sophisticated and again it was paraffin that led the way – it was cleaner and easier to use than the various fish, vegetable and other oils that were customary. Then came gas lighting (though rarely in rural areas) and, at last, clean and instant electricity, which relegated the use of candles to festive occasions and power cuts.

Water supplies

Household water is taken for granted now: a turn of the tap, and there it is, straight into the glass or kettle with no thought as to where it came from. Most households, even country ones, are now 'on the mains' for water supplies, though many rural ones still have private sewage disposal systems, just as they always did.

Town dwellers had piped water long before those in the country; and in many villages mains water was unknown even 50 years ago. In the early 1940s, 25 per cent of rural parishes had no piped water and 50 per cent had no sewage disposal systems. According to the 1951 census, 20 per cent of all private households in Britain still had no piped water supply, and it needs to be borne in mind that the majority of those would have been in rural areas, where about 20 per cent of the population of Britain still lived. For most unpiped households, every drop of water had to be drawn manually and often laboriously – caught from springs, dipped from streams and ponds, drawn from rainwater tanks and butts, hand-pumped or wound up from garden wells.

▼ **MAINS WATER SUPPLIES** *came to the towns much earlier than to the villages and hamlets. Most cottagers depended on garden wells or backdoor pumps but some entrepreneurs began bringing pump water to the house door on a donkey-drawn cart.*

'... in villages where cottages were grouped together on the big country estates the drawing of well water became a communal activity and a chance for a good old chat.'

vessel was heavy and wooden, narrower at the top to reduce spillage; sometimes two such 'stoups' might be carried with the aid of a wooden yoke across the shoulders; or a tub of water would be slung on a pole carried by two women; or perhaps a pitcherful of water might be carried on the head. Two gallons of water – which is what would be carried in a pail – is roughly what a toilet flushes today!

For some cottagers the well was conveniently just outside the door (in some farmhouses it was actually inside the kitchen, under a big flagstone) but for many the well would be across the yard or garden, or even farther away. In outlying rural areas each cottage usually had its own well, but in villages or where cottages were grouped together on the big country estates the drawing of well water became a communal activity and a chance for a good old chat.

Pumps and tanks

Some homes had pumps outside the back door, or within the scullery. But pumps had their own funny little ways and it was important to understand them. In particular, their pipes tended to freeze solid in winter.

Where groundwater levels were uncertain, people built underground water storage tanks which, in theory, retained enough water to last through the summer, though it was hardly fresh. Such tanks were rare for rural cottages until perhaps the 1920s or 1930s. Instead, smaller homes might rely on the water butt by the back door, collecting roof rainwater and all that went with it – moss, lichens, twigs, leaves, insects and algae, for example. In a good season you could store enough rainwater for all the household's everyday needs, perhaps even a bath once a week if the bathwater was shared by all the family. But not in summer.

▲ COTTAGERS NEEDED A WELL *if there was no natural spring or an easily accessible stream. The construction of the well was a skilled and dangerous craft. The well-sinker worked in a confined space and it was essential to support the sides of the new shaft as he descended, and also to ensure good ventilation – there were occasional tragedies from lack of oxygen during the work, and the men often carried candles to warn them of poisonous gases. For some wells the shaft might be only a few feet deep; others might need to be sunk to as much as 100 ft before reaching the underground water-table.*

Wells

There is an art to using a well. Novices who simply drop the wooden pail on its rope find to their surprise that it bobs about on top of the water. The knack is in persuading it to tilt so that the water can begin to spill over the brim. Well pails were traditionally of wood, built in the manner of a cask, with wooden staves bound by iron bands; it was not until late in the Victorian period that galvanised metal buckets began to be used.

Those same well novices have probably already knocked themselves out on the flying windlass handle when they let it go. Then there is the sheer hard work of winching the full pail up again and of carrying it indoors time and time again without getting yourself soaked by the slopping water. The usual

Water purity

Water purity was a major problem. Wells became fouled by dead rodents or by being too close to the privy; rainwater tanks, unless soundly sealed and lightproof, bred bacteria and insects; streams and ponds were also where livestock drank and paddled, cartwheels were dipped to swell them to fit their iron rims again, steam engines sucked up their water supply, sheep were washed before shearing, children swam, ducks and geese defecated, rats loitered – and those ponds were often the source of the water in the bowsers that were drawn by horse for delivery to your door. There is a theory that country people, living in constant association with polluted water, developed an immunity to it; and indeed this was highlighted during World War II when evacuees instantly succumbed to local water impurity in their temporary 'country-fresh' homes. Only the lucky homes had access to pure spring water.

Even when mains water did come to the countryside (in many places not until the 1950s), old habits died hard. Yes, it was a joy to turn the tap and watch the water splashing merrily into the sink, but could you trust the stuff enough to drink it? Oh no, not unless you boiled it first, especially if you knew that it had been stored in the local concrete water tower that was a landmark for miles around. Even after boiling, the taste depended on the local water source, and most of us still habitually run the cold-water tap for a while in the morning to get rid of funny overnight tastes and sediments.

▶ BUCKETS OR PAILS *for carrying water from the pump or well were originally made by the village cooper from wood bound with hazel withies or iron bands. Later the receptacles were made from iron or galvanised steel.*

Photo—J. S. HEWARD

▲ THE WELL HEAD PROTECTED THE WINDING MECHANISM *or windlass. For cottages, the mechanism was usually a simple wooden roller with a chain wrapped around it, from which a bucket was suspended: the bucket was lowered and raised by means of a plain iron winch handle to turn the roller. For farm wells the winding gear could be quite an elaborate system of fly wheels, cogs and brakes, and sometimes this was worked by a donkey walking inside a huge wooden wheel or by means of 'horse gear', a typical agricultural system whereby a horse plodded around in a circle to turn cast-iron gear wheels that operated water pumps or a winnowing machine or other machinery.*

'The waste water would be chucked into an open ditch just outside the back door'

Drains

Most of us now pull the bath plug or flush the toilet without a thought as to where it all goes, but some people in rural areas still rely on their own sewage-disposal systems in the garden – more advanced than of old, but reminders about being profligate with water.

Today those systems are likely to be septic tanks – a series of covered chambers acting like a miniature sewage works and from which, in theory, potable water eventually trickles into the local streams. Nobody ever inspects them to see that this is so, and often they pong with a sickly sweet smell, especially in summer. Septic tanks rely on beneficial bacteria, and modern habits tend to be antagonistic to those bacteria; detergents, bleach, chemicals used for cleaning toilets and baths, and various other substances that a household on mains drainage flushes away with gay abandon, leaving the problem to the water companies, must be used much more cautiously when you have a septic tank.

At least we now have pipework to remove soiled water from the house. In the 19th century most country homes had no such thing. The waste water would be chucked into an open ditch just outside the back door, creating a considerable health hazard to the residents and their neighbours. If you look in country churchyards you will often see evidence of the epidemics of typhoid fever and cholera that resulted.

Most Victorians realised that something must be done, in both the country and the town. During the 1870s there was an attempt to bring mains drainage to some rural areas but unfortunately it was so badly designed that it polluted local water supplies and put country people off the idea of public sewage systems for a very long time. In 1956, the National Federation of Women's Institutes published a survey of its member organisations: nearly every village at that time still put the improvement of sewage facilities at the top of its list of concerns, closely followed by water quality and

▶ SOME INGENIOUS PRIVIES *were flushed by rainwater gathered from the house roof into elevated tanks from which the water was fed by gravity through a pipe to a proper 'water closet' in the privy. A simpler system was to build a 'dry' privy to reduce odour: it had a solid base sloping backwards to drain liquid straight out into the garden through a little archway, with a baffle to prevent the escape of solids. An improvement was the earth closet: there was a hopper of ashes or dry earth (some can remember regularly drying garden earth by the inglenook fire so that there was a constant supply for the hopper) and you simply pulled a lever to cover solid matter with earth. Older privies sometimes emptied directly into the stream at the bottom of the garden.*

night-soil themselves: Dad would dig a pit
and empty the contents of the privy into it
when necessary. If you have a patch of nettles
at the end of your garden, that is probably
where the night-soil ended up.

The privy was usually a simple wooden
or corrugated-iron shed (or brick if you were
lucky), within which would be a scrubbed
plank to sit on, with a square hole or two cut
into it. Instead of the customary country
dock leaf, pieces of cut-up newspaper (the
Daily Mail for preference as its ink was less
likely to come off in use) might dangle from
a string or nail for your convenience. Beneath
the plank there might be no more than a
hole in the ground, with a simple soakaway
and a bucketful of dry earth or ashes that you
could sprinkle over the effluent to soak it up.
A new hole would periodically have to be
dug and a corrugated-iron privy would be
shifted to cover the new site.

In the more refined privy the effluent
would go straight into a galvanised lavatory
bucket; you still had to sprinkle ashes or
earth on top and Dad would empty the
bucket into his trenches and plant vegetables
on top. The next refinement saw chemicals
added to the bucket, which liquidised solids
but failed to disguise the stink.

Privies continued to be used by cottagers
until they had access to mains water and
plumbing, which, as already noted, might
have been only 50 years ago in many rural
areas, and as recently as the 1960s in some.
Wash-down indoor water-closets were
widely available in the late 19th century if
you had the plumbing, but cottagers
continued with their privies or used indoor
Elsans. Many have fond memories of the
privy as a place to which you could escape,
sitting in peace, listening to birdsong and
gazing at the flowers in your garden.

Privies were usually down the garden,
which meant creeping out in all weathers, at
night as well as by day, though a chamber pot
under the bed was useful at night except that
you had to empty it into the garden in the
morning. Imagine traipsing down the dark
garden path in the early hours in the rain,

availability (indoor WCs and running
water from taps were eagerly requested)
and electricity supplies. In a similar survey
in 1999, when more than 80 per cent of
the institutes still classified themselves as
rural, there was no mention of sewage,
water or electricity in the improvements
demanded.

Privies

In towns, in the latter part of the 19th
century, the local councils would remove
'night-soil' from people's privies on a fairly
regular basis and cart it away into the
countryside for dumping, or for selling to
farmers as manure. In the country there was
no such system. People dealt with their

▲ **A TIN BATH IN THE MAIN ROOM** *or kitchen was placed near the range when in use and hung on a nail on the wall for storage. It was common for evacuee boys to be scrubbed down by the farmer's wife in an outdoor tub when they were helping on the farms.*

with slugs and toads squelching underfoot, owls hooting, bats flying, bogeymen lurking … and being unable to see the spiders, beetles, snails and roosting hens that you knew lived in the privy. Many a child unfamiliar with the countryside would soil their bed rather than face such a challenge.

Bathing

When mains water first came to the countryside, most people opted to plumb a lean-to or outhouse. Gradually they found space for a bathroom (just a tiny one), because of course plumbing meant not only cold water on tap but hot as well, if you had an appropriate boiler. This was bliss indeed. No more firing up the copper to boil the bath water and then ladling hot water into a successively shared portable tin bath in front of the fire for the weekly dunking! No more emptying the bath by hand into the garden! No more showering under the cold water from the pump outside the back door!

The plumbing trend was led by the middle-class town dwellers who migrated to their 'romantic' country cottages and were shocked at the lack of facilities they had taken for granted in their urban homes.

For example, in an anonymous article written for *The Countryman*, a 'retired professional woman' described her hunt for a 'Victorian spinster's cottage' in the West Country. In the 1940s she eventually found one, in a considerable state of decay, with a pump outside at the back, 'a sink clinging forlornly to it, unconnected to any drainage'. Her first essentials were 'an indoor lift-and-force pump, to supply water tanks in the roof, and a water-closet'. The pump, installed by a local builder, produced only a thin trickle of pea-soup water, which, on analysis, proved to contain 'every kind of impurity', as did the water supply for the rest of the village.

Apart from that possible weekly bath, cold water was usually the order of the day

> ## 'No more showering under the cold water from the pump outside the back door!'

for personal hygiene – under the pump, or using plain enamel or prettily decorated Victorian jugs and washbowls.

Washday

The habit of using a washing machine almost daily would have amazed a generation born before World War II, and would have been unthinkable for earlier generations.

Most country people had few clothes and not much bedding; and what there was tended to be cumbersome to wash and likely to disintegrate if washed too often. Consider the time, labour and sheer drudgery of hand-washing when there was no soap except what you could make yourself from basic raw materials; no instant means of collecting the water, let alone heating it; no drains to take away the waste water; no means of drying the washing except by passing it through a hand-turned mangle and draping it on a hedge out in the fresh air or in front of a smoky fire. It is hardly surprising that the washing was at the most a weekly event.

On a washday the water needed to be drawn from the well or other source, and carried to be poured into the copper – a very large and very heavy container (sometimes of iron rather than actual copper) with a rounded base, set into a brick plinth in the scullery, if you were lucky enough to have such a place. The copper had its own tiny fireplace beneath, fuelled with bavins, and its own little chimney. Washday had to start early: it took time to get the fire going to heat such a large volume of water, and then the whole room (very often the living room) would fill with steam the day long.

There would be a row of earthenware redpans: one for white bedding, with a blue bag in the water to whiten the material; one to soak dirty working clothes in soapy water; one for coloured clothes and another for underwear. Then you had to scrub the dirtiest clothes, rubbing them against a corrugated washboard with a brush or your red-raw knuckles – or you could dump the clothes in a wooden barrel and bash them with a wooden dolly to loosen the dirt first.

◀ HOME LAUNDRY *traditionally took place outside the back door using cold water in a wooden tub; the clothes were pummelled with a wooden washing bat or 'dolly' to loosen the dirt. Well within living memory, wooden scrubbing or rubbing boards were used. Mass-produced galvanised tubs replaced the wooden version. Larger items were often draped over the garden hedge to dry.*

▲ KEEPING CLOTHES CLEAN WAS A DIFFICULT TASK, *and only the luckiest laundresses had a mangle to help dry the clothes. Wood ashes from the fire would be put into a sieve over a tub and water poured in, before being further filtered through muslin. The final alkaline liquid, or 'lye', would then be poured over loosely folded clothes to reduce soiling, or boiled with animal fat and salt to make a soap. Chicken dung and urine also sometimes found their way into the lye, and anything from hoof parings to ivy leaves and nettles were boiled as fabric conditioners.*

Each pan had to be filled with water from the copper, carefully transferred in a pitcher, and hand-emptied afterwards; usually the water was thrown into the garden. Then the clothes had to be wrung out (twisted by hand unless a hand-wound mangle could be afforded) and pegged with gypsy-made split wooden pegs on a clothesline made of wet-heavy hemp, or, by about 1900, a line of galvanised wire that sometimes leaked rust. Bed-linen was often flung over a hedge to dry. All this was fine in summer, but in winter the drying would be indoors, so that already cramped and damp quarters would be full of heavy clothes and bedding for days on end.

Then came the labour of ironing. Before electricity, heavy flatirons had to be heated by the fire or range (you spat on them to test the heat) and the 'ironing board' was usually the kitchen table covered with an old sheet.

In the 1920s, women's magazines were advertising washing machines, but these could only be afforded by those who could already afford someone else in the village to do their laundering for them. Washing machines also needed piped water and plumbed drainage.

Plumbing

Plumbing: what a boon it was, once it came, to people who were used to carrying every drop of water they needed and carrying away every drop of wastewater! The joy of turning a tap for instant water, even if the quality was less than perfect; the joy of pulling the plug or yanking the chain! Yes, you might still have to arrange for the emptying of your cesspit every month, or your septic tank once or twice a year, but with luck you would be linked to a communal village sewage works and, eventually, to the mains sewage system so that your waste was no longer your own problem, nor even that of your local community.

Rubbish

In the decades after World War II, we all became less green in our recycling of rubbish, though there is a trend back to the old ways now. In the country, the disposal of rubbish used to be entirely your own concern; there were no council collections from your bin, no communal dumps, no recycling centres. Whatever waste you produced, you had to find a place for it yourself. There was far less of it than now, largely because most people could not afford to be profligate. They used things until they were worn out, and then they turned them into something else.

There was very little unwanted packaging bought from shops until after World War I: you took your own containers with you for

▲ THE LABOUR OF HAND-WASHING LAUNDRY *was compounded by the challenge of drying it. Few cottagers had their own wringers or mangles, and they were faced with the vagaries of the weather for drying. Gypsies were well known for making and selling wooden clothes-pegs for hanging out the washing on lines made from hemp (which also marked the clothes). The station platform at Theobalds Grove, Hertfordshire offered the ideal solution in the 1930s. Passenger services had ceased on this rural loop line in 1909, and there was only the occasional freight train coming through.*

loose groceries, or bought goods packed in biodegradable materials; and anyway in the country you produced most of your own food. Waste paper was recycled as toilet paper, or used to stuff draughty gaps or to decorate the walls, or as a last resort would be composted or burned – cottagers seemed to be always be having bonfires for burning rubbish, and also for cooking up scraps for the chickens and the pig. Waste food that was not recycled through the pigs and chickens was put on the compost heap.

There was no plastic and there were no polythene bags, of course. Empty tins and jars, such as there were, might be buried at the bottom of the garden or in the hedge bank, or in nearby woods or wasteland. The more careful cottager saw empty jars and bottles as reusable in their obvious storage role or as decoration, perhaps in the garden to edge or form a path, or to make a bottle wall. Broken crockery was simply thrown into the garden soil for good drainage.

So the main methods of waste disposal were, first of all, recycling; then composting, burning or burial, depending on what the rubbish was. Whichever method was chosen, it was done essentially on your own premises, so that you were constantly aware of it. Today, like wastewater, rubbish is dumped miles away and is somebody else's problem.

Town councils were collecting rubbish from urban dustbins in the 1930s. Such a service came much later in rural areas, where the old habits of frugal recycling and using items until they really could no longer be patched and tinkered lingered on, and sometimes still do. Most of a country bin would be filled with ash from the coal fire or the range; it was not as useful as wood ash, which could be spread in the garden or used to make soap, though clinkers were handy for surfacing garden paths.

Homes for heroes

The tumbling insanitary cottages that various beneficent landowners replaced throughout the 19th century were the real cottages – places from which those who were born in them wished only to escape. The buildings were usually set on low-lying land that held the wet and the sewage, and in general the homes were cold, draughty, smoke-filled, crowded, damp, dark, extremely uncomfortable and unhealthy, and very demanding on the housewife in particular. The state of rural cottages was a matter of

▲ WHEN COTTAGERS MOVED INTO MODERN BUNGALOWS *and council houses, many of them experienced electricity and plumbing for the first time in their lives and were so fascinated by these new amenities that they took an almost childish delight in flicking switches on and off just because they could. They also found imaginative uses for the toilet: one elderly man spurned the indoor facilities (he thought them unhygienic) and used the cistern to store his homemade parsnip wine.*

concern to many at regular intervals and this continued during at least the first half of the 20th century. Some landlords couldn't care less, but here and there the big landowners would take responsibility for building new cottages for their workers, or try to encourage people to help themselves. Landowners in the 19th century built modern cottages – plain, perhaps, and maybe no more than one or two rooms on the ground floor and two above, but solid enough and new. Yet immediately after World War I parish councils all over the country were expressing concern about the lack of good 'workmen's cottages' – affordable homes for the villagers. That concern persisted throughout the 20th century, and was tackled in different ways.

After World War I, every effort was made to welcome home the heroes who had been through so much. The government wanted to house them and find them smallholdings and jobs to give them a fresh start in civilian life and at the same time help to revive rural areas. By the 1930s many villages found that their boundaries had been stretched, with countless bungalows being built along the lanes leading out of the village, and old cottages were being knocked down and replaced by new houses.

Some even lived in converted railway carriages, which were quite acceptable in the odd field here and there, and were an ingenious way of recycling whatever was available to make a home when homes were in short supply.

Bungalow heaven

In the late 1930s, when there were continuing attempts to improve conditions under the Rural Workers' Housing Act of 1926, a programme was broadcast on BBC radio about housing design – a subject that concerned many a good-hearted social worker. A village group of men and boys listened to the broadcaster praising the beauty of older houses and disparaging the rash of bungalows that were appearing on village outskirts. The villagers discussed the broadcast in a typically roundabout rural way, but the most telling comments came from one old man. 'What 'ee say about Tudor 'ouses and the like be all right, but I'll give all these 'ere cottages, thatch an 'all, for one of them there bungalows.' 'With water laid on,' said another. 'And a ceilin' you don't bust your 'ead on every time you stand upright,' commented a third. In the early 1950s, a grateful local wrote a short poem (published in *The Countryman* in 1952) to the rural district council that had built bungalows for old people:

Before our bungalows were built
We lived in one large room
No gas, no water, no proper stove
For two years was our doom.
But now all this has changed and we
Have light and heat and space,
With baths and stoves and other helps –
The world's a pleasant place.

Social housing

The first council houses were built in the 1890s, and thereafter in waves of enthusiasm, especially after each of the two world wars. The aim was to provide modern housing at affordable rents, and they were highly sought after by the many people in rural areas who still lived in damp, cold cottages with no conveniences. Right from the start, the

▲ OLDER VILLAGE HOUSING WAS OFTEN DEMOLISHED *to make way for new council houses. Because the new housing tended to be built as a single estate (often on the edge of a village) it could create a social divide, rather than integrate the new homes among the old. Elderly residents in old cottages were encouraged to apply for council houses but many were resistant: they did not wish to leave what might have been their home for several decades, however humble others thought it to be. In some cases it was a matter of pride not to accept what could been seen as 'charity'.*

▲ 'SOCIAL HOUSING' IS NOT A NEW CONCEPT; *in 1808/9 the new planned village of Footdee was created to rehouse the local fishing community of Aberdeen on an isolated spit of land at the mouth of the harbour. It was laid out in a grid of regimented squares of 28 thatched single-storey homes with granite walls. Fishing dominated and knitted the social as well as the working life of the village. In 1880 some of the homes were sold to their occupants and the new owners began changing their homes, adding variety to the overall design.*

cottagers led the stampede into what for them was pure luxury and found it hard to understand the counter-stampede of town dwellers into their discarded homes. The country cottagers knew the reality of life in the cramped buildings they had shrugged off, and they pitied the incomers.

There was a problem. Most of the council houses were built in styles that were often completely alien to the locality. What is more, they were usually built en bloc, as estates, plonked on the edge of the village, rather than as individual houses scattered within the village envelope and thus integrated with everybody else. Then, although originally conceived as homes for the villagers, they were sometimes rented to people with no direct connection with the village. The combination of these factors often set the council house estate apart, storing up trouble in later years when villagers began to blame 'them from the

'Most of the council houses were built in styles that were often completely alien to the locality'

estate' for petty crime and other problems. Writing in 1947 about housing the country worker, Michael Tilley (a young architect who was the son of a farmer) pointed out that the countryman's needs differed from those of the town dweller and he stressed that rural housing should not be treated the same as urban housing. He was particularly alarmed at the 'sporadic and fortuitous layout of housing estates, related neither to each other, nor to the village, nor to the industries which they have to serve. There has been no overall conception of the village as a social and economic unit in the life of the countryside.' One wonders how much the planners, local councils and government have learnt about village housing in the intervening half-century.

3. The Cottage Garden

The garden offered cottagers a substantial degree of self-sufficiency and that was its main purpose. There were many uses for the cottager's patch, large or small, but above all it supplied the home with vegetables, fruit, animal protein and medicinal herbs. Useful plants grew in garden hedges as well as in the veg patch and orchard. The pleasure of garden flowers was a much lower priority, almost a luxury. It was more important to find space for beehives, poultry and the inevitable cottage pig, or perhaps a goat or two. Many cottagers were skilled gardeners – they needed to be in order to survive.

Despite the flowery image of the romantic country cottage, in reality a cottage garden was essentially practical. It was a place in which to grow food; it was a self-sufficient medicine cupboard where you grew herbs and other home remedies; it was a dumping ground for rubbish, ashes and dirty water; it was the home of the pump or the well; it was where you built beehives, sheds, wood piles and compost heaps and recycled the contents of the privy. It was also a refuge from the openness of the working countryside; hence the garden was often firmly enclosed by walls, hedges or fences, and sometimes there would be protective mountain ash trees to ward off the witches. It should be remembered that cottage gardens had once been large – very large.

In the 16th century it was decreed that all new cottages must have at least four acres of land, to accommodate gardens and cottage livestock, both of which were essential to the cottager's self-sufficiency and without which his family would probably starve. Gradually this allocation shrank, especially with the enclosures that began later in that century and peaked between about 1760 and 1820, depriving cottagers of common-land grazing for their animals and reducing their gardens very often to small patches around the home that needed to be planted intensively if they were to feed the family at all.

In the late 19th century the Liberals, in their ideas for the formation of grass-roots parish councils, found an election winner among rural labourers when they said that parish councils should be allowed to hold and let to villagers a certain amount of land as allotments and that each allottee should be 'limited' to four acres (three pastoral and one arable). The Act by which parish councils were created became law in 1894 but very few councils could come by enough land to offer four-acre allotments.

Thus the severely reduced cottage garden gave preference to essentials such as vegetables, fruit trees and beehives. In practical terms, a typical cottager would cultivate about 20 perches for vegetables and put quarter of an acre down to fruit trees, and run a flock of perhaps 50 poultry and a pig, in order to be reasonably self-sufficient. The cottage pig, along with meat and eggs from the poultry, reduced the butcher's bill, and both types of livestock did well on

▼ EVERY AVAILABLE SPACE *in a cottage garden seemed to be filled with something edible (incomers often preferred flowers). If there wasn't enough space in the garden cottagers would have an allotment provided by the big estate or the parish council.*

household scraps with a little supplementary meal, while their manure was useful for feeding the vegetable patch.

In the 1940s and 1950s many villages had produce associations, which catered for growers of food crops in gardens and allotments, and also for smallholders who kept bees, rabbits and poultry. With the war still a fresh memory, home food growing remained popular and encouraged the self-sufficiency boom of the 1960s and 1970s.

Vegetables

The essential crop in any kitchen garden was the potato. Turnips, carrots, parsnips and beets were other standard cottage vegetables, all neatly buttoned in rows with nary a weed in between, along with all kinds of onions and greens. Broad beans were popular, along with peas, runner beans and haricot beans.

The vegetable patch might also grow food for a smallholder's animals, such as cow cabbage, chicory, swedes, buckwheat (its blossom for bees and its seed for pigs and hens) and hemp (seeds for greater egg production, and the fibre for huckabuck cloth and homemade rope).

Runner beans were sometimes grown, as much for their clambering scarlet flowers as for their pods. Borage was grown as a vegetable (for its boiled roots and young shoots), a herb and a bee-attracting flower; it had the added attraction of self-seeding profusely. Horse-radish was another multi-purpose plant, for those who had a damp piece of ground for it: the hot roots were grated for horse-radish sauce and also added to a grease to relieve rheumatism and sprains. Ordinary radish seedpods could be pickled, or the roots could be eaten raw for their hot flavour or to solve bladder problems, or applied as a cure for warts and corns. Onions could be rubbed on bald men's heads with honey to make the hair grow, or applied to chilblains to ease them. Lettuces were more than a salad plant: you could dry the juice and use it as a mild opiate.

▶ **COMPETITION BETWEEN GARDENERS** *could be fierce, and they took enormous pride in growing the best vegetables. The village horticultural societies that flourished in the early decades of the 20th century always included classes for non professional cottage gardeners in their annual shows. Here, the 'radio gardener' Fred Streeter (right) presents the prizes at a village show in Sussex.*

▲ **MOST FAMILY MEMBERS HELPED IN THE GARDEN**, *and during World War II evacuee children also lent a hand; for many of them it was their first contact with the soil. Some developed a lifelong passion for gardening, or even took up horticulture as a career after a spell at agricultural college.*

THE COTTAGE GARDEN   **53**

Herbs

▲ ROSEHIPS ARE HIGH IN VITAMIN C
*and during World War II children were
encouraged to gather wild hips from the
hedgerows so that they could be converted into
rosehip syrup in the interests of public health.
The Delrosa company at Wallsend continued to
make rosehip syrup long after the war, and
many can remember being fed a spoonful once a
week to ward off colds. In one of those war years
500 tons of rosehips were harvested, yielding
the equivalent (when they had been processed)
of the vitamin C content of 25 million oranges.*

Sweet herbs were grown as much for
medicinal as culinary purposes, and every
country 'goodwife' knew from her mother
and grandmother what plant to use for what
problem well into the Victorian period,
though folk remedies had been fighting a
losing battle with orthodox medicine since
the 18th century.

Town dwellers had forgotten their
herbalism, but countrywomen knew that
camomile could relieve all manner of
digestive problems, mint did its trick for
indigestion and bad breath, rosemary was the
ideal rinse for brunettes, lavender was a moth
deterrent and room sweetener (as pot pourri
or burned like joss sticks), sage cleaned your
teeth and made a good gargle with vinegar

and honey, marjoram battled with colds
– the uses for cultivated herbs were endless,
and that was before you took your pick of
the wild plants that filled the woodland,
hedgerows and field margins.

World War I inspired the government
to encourage the growing of medicinal
herbs again, largely because it was no
longer possible to import them. Quite a few
enterprising people began herb farms, and
came into their own again during World
War II. The most important cultivated herbs
included aconite, balm, belladonna, burdock,
caraway, colchicum, comfrey, dandelion
(roots were required in large quantities),
elecampane, foxglove, henbane, horehound,
hyssop, lily-of-the-valley (all parts were
of medicinal value – it was even said that

*'It was said that a distillation of lily-of-the-
valley flowers could restore speech to those with
"dumb palsie"'*

a distillation of the flowers could restore speech to those with 'the dumb palsie' – and you could also get a good return by picking the flowers and getting them into market early for the florists), marigold, marsh mallow and mullein.

During World War I, when women were encouraged to attend gardening schools, a Women's Herb Growing Association was formed with the aim of cultivating and marketing medicinal herbs on cooperative lines. The supply of these herbs had hitherto come mainly from Germany and Austria, and there was a very strong demand for drugs from medicinal herbs during the war. The association sought to encourage women gardeners to organise themselves as herb growers at a time when prices for the herbs were rocketing. They wanted to create a central drug farm where some of the herbs most urgently needed could be grown in large quantities, but also to encourage women to grow herbs in their own gardens, large or small, and to provide them with an established system of collecting and marketing the small amounts they would be able to harvest. The herbs particularly required were monkshood roots, camomile flowers, deadly nightshade leaves and roots, thorn-apple leaves and seeds, henbane leaves, foxglove leaves (you could gather up to two tons from an acre), fennel seeds, opium poppy heads and valerian roots. Also needed were balm, feverfew, dandelion, yarrow, barberry bark, common nightshade branches, broom branches, henbane, sweet flag rhizomes and red poppy petals.

Shrubs and hedges

Hedges were planted around cottage gardens to keep out marauding livestock and wildlife and to satisfy the age-old human need to define personal space: this is my patch! The hedge sent out that message loud and clear to neighbours, strangers and animals, and it would be a productive feature of the garden.

Elder was one of the most useful country plants: both berries and flowers could be made into wine, and the flowers could be fried in batter or made into lotions and ointments with a wide range of applications. The hollow stems were turned into whistles or peashooters, and the wood was used to make toys, pegs, skewers and angling rods. Elder grows easily and fast, and the quickest way of establishing squatters' rights was to plant an elder hedge around your 'property'.

Blackthorn was another invaluable plant, for hedging and also for its sloes. Hawthorn was planted as a hedge and its young leaves made a tasty snack or could be brewed as a tea, while may blossom was another basis for a country wine. Holly made for an excellent defensive hedge in the many areas where it seeded itself freely.

Fruit

The more far-sighted landlords ensured that every cottage garden had at least one fruit tree – always apples, but also pears, plums, damsons, greengages and cherries where space permitted. Many an old garden would have medlars and mulberry bushes (both could be turned into a laxative syrup), nut bushes and aromatic quinces. Wild crab apples were eagerly gathered for jelly making, and their verjuice was used on sprained limbs.

More common in cottage and farm gardens were bush and cane fruits such as black currants (valuable for their vitamin C content), red currants, white currants, gooseberries and raspberries. Gooseberry growing often became highly competitive in some villages.

▲ **FRUIT GROWING COULD BE AS COMPETITIVE AS VEGETABLE GROWING** *in the cottage garden, and some districts specialised in enormous 'prize gooseberries' (one berry alone could weigh 1 oz). Entire shows would sometimes be devoted just to gooseberries, such was their popularity.*

▲ THE HORTICULTURAL SOCIETY'S SHOW CLASSES *included many categories for those wealthy enough to employ gardeners. The gardener sometimes paid the entrance fee himself, but was often neither credited by name nor given the prize: it went to the owner of the garden, who might not have lifted so much as a finger to grow and present the winning entry.*

Flowers

Only sometimes was the garden made more cheerful with cottage flowers, usually by the woman of the house and originally only with the flowering plants that had medicinal properties. After all, in the centuries before the widespread use of herbicides, the meadows and verges were full of wild flowers and there was no need to grow your own. But the love of flowers increased and when this was so the effects were striking.

Those who did develop a passion for flowers tended to cram them into every corner of the garden, in amongst the vegetables, along the garden path, clambering over the porch and the low-dipping roof. Indeed, the smaller the garden, the more densely would it be packed with flowers, crammed in wherever there happened to be a space, so that there was a gloriously random riot of mixed colour and form but an unplanned overall sense of harmony.

Gradually, then, the flowery cottage garden depicted by romantic artists became a reality. In the end it was often the cottagers who became the most adventurous flower growers, developing single-minded passions for pinks or dahlias or auriculas and creating new varieties by the score. And it was often the cottagers who swept the board at the local horticultural show with their prize flowers and vegetables. They rarely bought their stock; they drew on stock in the wild or swapped cuttings and seeds with their friends. Many a gardener can still remember who gave their grandparents which plant.

Tools and machinery

There was no place in a cottage garden for grass, except as pasture for livestock and grazing for geese. In the grounds of grander houses, however, grass set off fine buildings and plantings. The problem was one of maintenance. The original means of keeping grass short was the scythe, and this could be used by an expert to a degree that turned a potential meadow into something approaching a lawn, though there tended to be scalped patches here and there and the job took a very long time indeed.

◄ VILLAGE 'WISE WOMEN' *specialised in growing herbs and using them for medicinal purposes rather than for flavouring food. The wise women's remedies were often trusted more than those of doctors and pharmacists.*

Edwin Budding, a carpenter near Stroud in Gloucestershire, who worked as a freelance engineer for various mill owners, conceived the first grass-cutting machine, possibly inspired by rotary cutters he had seen being used to cut the nap off wool cloth. He patented the idea of a cylindrical grass cutter in 1830 and his partner John Ferrabee manufactured the first machine to this patent at his Phoenix Foundry near Brinscomb. The machine was seen not merely as an efficient way of cutting grass: 'Country gentlemen may find in using my machine themselves an amusing, useful and healthy exercise.'

By 1841 ponies were pulling lawn mowers instead: they could cut a lawn at the rate of an acre an hour. In the early years of the 20th century leather-booted ponies, donkeys and horses were still mowing parks and the lawns of country houses and continued to do so in some places right up to World War II.

By the late 19th century, there was also a wide range of hand-pushed mowers to choose from. In the 1890s steam-powered mowers were patented for the first time but petrol-driven mowers were already being designed and would become increasingly popular after World War I. In 1896 the first mains-powered mower was produced, though it was not until the early 1960s that battery-powered and electric mowers became widely accessible.

After World War I, it seemed that every suburban householder aspired to a patch of lawn and the great ritual of weekend mowing began, with countless less-than-fit men manfully pushing and sweating with their hand mowers. Gradually (as ever) the idea spread to country cottages as well.

Most cottagers were more interested in hefty orchard grass cutters like the Allen scythe or in petrol-powered cultivators than in lawn mowers; they were invaluable on smallholdings and in large gardens and allotments where food growing was a serious matter. In 1940, those intending to live in the country were advised to make use of mechanical power if they had more than 20 perches; for example, you could plant a hundredweight of potatoes in half an hour by machine, whereas the hours that it would take by hand were unthinkable.

In pre-mechanised days, employed gardeners had a very wide range of equipment, often made by the village or estate blacksmith. Each item was carefully

▲ COTTAGE GARDENERS KEPT THEIR TOOLS IN IMMACULATE CONDITION. *A properly cared for spade, always cleaned after use and with the blade kept sharp, did the work more efficiently than one allowed to become rusted and blunt. New handles could be fitted when the old ones wore out and many a proud gardener claimed his spade to be a century old whereas in reality the handle and the blade had been renewed alternately over the years so that no part of the original remained.*

'It was important for children to be brought up to value useful things, especially living things …'

chosen for the job in hand, and for the hand that held the tool. Each gardener had his favourite designs, many of them to a traditional local pattern, to cope with trenching, digging, forking, weeding, raking, turfing, trimming, pruning, cutting, scything, harvesting, planting, transplanting, dibbing, propagating. There were all sorts of different barrows, portable cloches, forcers, water carts, watering cans, rollers, sprayers, fumigators, syringes, containers and endless terracotta pots in the potting shed.

Cottagers made do with a trusty spade and fork, their metal parts and wooden handles polished with constant use. A rusting spade was a sign of a lazy gardener.

Backyard animals

Country people were practical by nature, and in general they kept animals because they were useful. Most of those who lived in the country would have enough space out back to keep livestock on a small scale, though they could hardly call themselves smallholders as the 'space' was probably just a patch of garden. But you could still be reasonably self-sufficient with only a patch.

Quite apart from the value of backyard animals to the family larder, William Cobbett had a deeper and more interesting concern. In his classic tract, *Cottage Economy* (published in 1823), he suggested that a labourer's child who had been brought

▲ ONLY THE WEALTHY COULD AFFORD POWERED MOWERS, *and after World War I wealthy country house owners began to discover the pleasures of doing their own mowing (many were shocked when the loss of so many men during that war led to such a shortage of gardeners that they had to turn their own hand to driving the motor car and other chores). A steam-powered ride-on mower was produced by Shanks as early as 1900 and a petrol-driven ride-on from Ransomes two years later. This photograph is of a 1926 model.*

up to take care of cottage livestock would make a far better stockman on the farm, especially if given responsibility for the care of small animals in his own childhood. It was important for children to be brought up to value useful things, especially living things. In childhood would be instilled 'the early habit of fondness for animals and of setting a value on them'. Cobbett understood the importance of a child seeing that his parents took great care of their animals and treated them with great kindness; he also stressed the importance of now and then letting the child have 'a little thing to call his own', thus instilling a love and understanding of animals that would last a lifetime. A person who is actually interested in animals will care for them better and, in commercial terms, get better returns from them.

The cottage pig

The idea of pannage is part of our history but it does still exist here and there. Pannage is the right to put your pigs into woodland to forage for acorns and beechmast, and the system persisted in the New Forest. It was recognised that acorns in excess could poison the Forest ponies and thus pannage for pigs was positively encouraged, in the interests of both species. The only problem today is the usual one of traffic. If there were no vehicles pigs could be as happy as in clover and swineherds would have a job for life.

Almost any cottager would have a pig or two at the end of the garden, pig meat being a staple part of the diet. The cottager's pig was a hardy beast and would usually be something spotty, though not classy enough to take the name of a breed. The pig was kept in a pen and fed largely on household scraps, perhaps supplemented with meal bought from the mill or the village shop. Ideally the pig was grazed on the verges and then run on the commons and in the woods to forage and fatten, because that was food for free.

The pig was generally killed in the winter, before Christmas if the weather was coldish. 'To kill a hog nicely,' said Cobbett, 'is so much of a profession, that it is better to pay a shilling for having it done, than to stab and hack and tear the carcass about.' Most people did call in the pig killer to do the deed, but they often did their own scalding or scorching (to remove the coarse hair), butchering, salting and smoking. As well as all of the generous produce from the carcass, there would be lots of manure for the garden.

▲ THE END-OF-THE-GARDEN STY *might house a sow whose litter could be raised to killing weight by the cottager, or he could sell off the piglets at weaning to other cottagers for raising in their own gardens. Most cottages would rear no more than one or two weaners.*

Flora Thompson graphically described the day the pig was killed by the travelling pork butcher or pig sticker, who happened to be a thatcher by day and so always had to kill after dark, by the light of lanterns and the burning straw of the bristle singeing. The killing was a 'noisy, bloody business' and the job was often bungled. If you want the details, read the first chapter of *Lark Rise* (written in the late 1930s) and blench.

Cottage cows and goats

Fewer cottagers had cows, as they needed more space. Villagers who had access to the verges and commons had more scope for keeping a cow or two. A cow was even more generous than a pig: she gave you milk, cream, butter and cheese and, with careful management, a calf every year as well. A cow could also be trained as a draught animal to plough a field or pull a cart and still give you all of this. Calves could be reared for meat, so the benefits of cows were numerous – and all that dung as well.

In many European countries, goats are the poor man's cow, but for some reason they never did fill that role in Britain. Yet goats were tough enough to take care of themselves and were easy to feed; they produced milk almost throughout the year and kids besides, for many years; they did not ramble from home and stood no nonsense from dogs; they could be 'clogged' or stumped out on the common, or kept in a shed or let loose to browse where they wished (coming in regularly of their own accord in the evenings, or when called). They are not the sort of animal that is recorded in agricultural returns and so it is hard to know how many there were in the country at different periods, but it was never as many as their virtues warranted. There would usually be a few goats around any village, but only a few, and the situation remains similar today.

Cottagers occasionally kept a ewe or two for milk, but the practice was not widespread. In medieval times almost all of England's milch animals had been sheep, not cows.

▲ GOATLINGS WERE OFTEN REARED *on the bottle, because a nanny goat's milk was destined for the house, not for her offspring. Most cottage goats were of no particular breed, though the youngster being bottle-fed here at a farm school in 1936 appears to be a British alpine.*

◀ AFTER BEING 'STUCK' *by the local pig killer, the cottage pig's still-warm corpse would be scalded with boiling water to remove its bristles. Many cottagers joined pig clubs to share the rearing of the pigs, which enabled them to buy pigfeed more cheaply in bulk, and they would share out the meat after slaughter.*

Hutch rabbits

Rabbits were instant meat in your backyard. They were easy to keep in hutches and were prodigious producers of young. Their food was for free, easily culled from the wild or grown in the veg patch.

Many households kept rabbits for meat during the world wars. They could be fed on household scraps mixed with bran, and with fresh weeds and grass cuttings. Some people literally cultivated dandelions for their rabbits, though in the country this was hardly necessary and you could grow kale, roots and clover to tickle their palates. Returns on rabbit pelts were still a useful source of income for smallholders in the 1930s and 1940s and there was also the production of silky angora rabbit fur as a small business.

Poultry

Backyard poultry included chickens, geese, ducks and turkeys. For most cottagers it was hens, for eggs and for the table. Anybody could keep a few hens, and they are what you usually see in Victorian paintings of cottages, scratching about in the lane or the farmyard.

Geese needed access to grazing on the commons and verges, given which they could provide you with a hundred eggs a year and live to a great age. To fatten them for the table you needed to provide corn and in some parts of the country cottagers specialised in the production of geese and ducks for the markets, or for selling to farmers for fattening on stubble for the table.

Ducks also produced plenty of eggs, though you had to take care as to where they had been laid or you'd end up with food

poisoning. They fattened well for the table on grass, greenstuffs and grain; apparently the Americans of Long Island fattened their ducks on a crab known as the horse-foot fish, and the meat gave away their diet in its smell and taste. In the garden and allotment, ducks did a marvellous job as slug-clearing machines as well as providing manure. Along with hens, ducks often feature in country cottage and farmyard paintings.

Turkeys, said Cobbett, 'are flying things', which might surprise some turkey farmers today – the ability has long since been bred out of them. Turkeys were native to America, where they were often shot as gamebirds in the wild, usually when they were peacefully roosting in tall trees. The biggest problem for the smallholder was the British climate: turkeys did not like the cold and young

▲ COTTAGERS AND SMALLHOLDERS OFTEN GRAZED THEIR COWS *on the lane verges and commons, either minded by children or tethered. Well within living memory, most villages in suitable regions were surrounded by countless small herds of milking cows to supply local needs – perhaps two or three or up to a dozen cows on each holding.*

▲ CHICKENS WERE CHEAP TO KEEP *and could be hugely productive fed on boiled-up kitchen scraps and allowed to forage for themselves, though most were confined to portable runs that were moved to fresh areas in the garden on a regular basis. Worms and insects (and even small rodents and amphibians when they can be caught) are as much part of a chicken's natural diet as grain.*

ones especially did not like wet weather and heavy dew. Turkeys also like 'room to prowl about', though if you raised the young under a broody hen she would teach them that rambling was not the thing to do. Nurture would beat nature. Turkeys were reared purely for meat and were therefore less useful to the cottager than other poultry.

In the late 18th century a few 'curious persons' kept guinea fowl. Like other poultry, they tended to be for family use, or as 'perquisites or pin money to the female part of the family'. This rather condescending description does highlight the point that many a farmer's wife kept poultry for a little income of her own.

Cottage bees

Many a cottager kept a few hives in the garden, usually in skeps made of rye straw as being warmer than boards. Straw was also cheap and therefore it was easily replaced every few months in the interests of hygiene. Apart from the hive, the cost of keeping bees was virtually nothing, either in expense

or in time and energy. Honey was not just a useful sweetener in place of sugar; it could also be turned into mead. And apparently bee venom could relieve rheumatism. And little old ladies could set up a sideline in 'teas' – home-churned butter on homemade bread with honey from their own hives.

Pets

Surrounded by abundant wildlife, even in the 19th century, country people tended to make pets of wild creatures. Favourites included slow worms, toads, tadpoles, beetles, songbirds, mice and baby anything-that-moved. Families would catch live birds and put them in cages by the door for the sake of their sweet singing; this was quite common among cottagers, who also kept captive corvids for their mimicry, much as people keep parrots today.

A country favourite, at least of boys, was the ferret, which is basically a domesticated polecat. Ferrets have been known in Britain since at least Norman times, if not Roman, and were widely used in the medieval

period for helping to catch rabbits for the pot. Ferrets in the pockets of boys and men would be frowned upon – not because of the distinctive odour of them but because their owners were more than likely to be poachers; ferrets work swiftly and quietly. Today quite a few men still keep ferrets for working the burrows, and, slightly to their disgust, there has been a growing trend towards the keeping of ferrets purely as pets.

Cats were kept largely for their ability to keep down the rats and mice that plagued country homes and particularly the farms, but they also became natural companions. Dogs, too, were kept more for the work they performed in the country, especially with livestock or as gundogs, but now they are more often pets and companions.

▲ **HIGGLERS VISITED COTTAGES AND FARMS** *to buy eggs and poultry for town markets. Some women made quite a lot more than pin money from their backyard poultry flocks.*

▶ **THE ANCIENT SKILLS OF BEEKEEPING** *were well understood by most country dwellers and tended to run in families, the tradition being handed down through the generations. At the end of the 18th century a lighthouse keeper at Dungeness put up some beehives on his tiny isolated patch of garden and harvested 12 pounds of honey a year.*

4. Country Supplies

Self-sufficiency from backyard produce could not provide most families with all their needs, but more food could be harvested, legally or otherwise, from the fields and woods beyond the garden. For the housewife, processing and storing food at home in the days before refrigeration was sheer hard work and required considerable ingenuity.

Cottagers turned to the village and the nearest market town (a focus for much more than merely buying and selling) for clothes, household items and other supplies and services, but also relied on itinerants, on foot, with donkeys or in carts, who delivered a wide range of goods and services direct to the cottage door. In their heyday, village shops supplied everyday needs and began their own home deliveries by bicycle and later by van. Country people began to be influenced by the spread of advertising, which changed the habits of a lifetime and presented a major challenge to village shops in trying to stock what its customers increasingly demanded.

Many of those living in country areas aimed to be as self-sufficient in food as possible, growing their own vegetables and fruit, raising backyard animals such as poultry (for eggs and meat), cottage pigs and perhaps a dairy goat or two or even a house cow for their butter and cheese; or they would barter with neighbours for homegrown crops or potter up the lane with a milk can dangling from their hands to the local dairy herd of ten or so hand-milked Shorthorns. They also supplemented homegrown produce by harvesting from the countryside around them, whether simply by picking wild berries or by catching rabbits and pigeons for the

'People would bring along their Sunday joints to the bakehouse on the way to church'

▲ PRESERVING VEGETABLES AND FRUIT *for the winter months took many forms. The methods generally consisted of drying, salting, pickling or converting into jams or wines, that would keep without the aid of refrigeration.*

pot and perhaps sometimes happening upon (or even poaching) other sources of meat, such as gamebirds and deer. Increasingly, though, food came from elsewhere, brought to the door by itinerants or bought from village shops (if they existed) and the weekly markets in the nearest town. These sources offered a great deal more than food.

Mealtimes

Getting meals on the table was a job in itself for most country women. Perhaps the nub of it all was that the country housewife needed much more space than the town dweller, because she needed to be more self-sufficient: she needed to grow and rear food, harvest or kill it, preserve or pluck and skin it as well as store and cook it. If the cottager was lucky enough to have a scullery in which to prepare vegetables, dish up, wash up and fire the copper, there tended to be friction because men would come into the house through the back door into the scullery, kick off their muddy boots, peel off their wet clothes and wash away the day's dirt just where and when the wife was preparing a meal. Oh, for a utility room, or just a downstairs washroom! (And that is one reason why so many cottages have downstairs bathrooms, preferably near the back door.)

The broadcaster CH Middleton, in his 1941 book *Village Memories*, devoted a whole chapter to 'Grub'. He looked back half a century to grandmothers who would scorn anything out of a tin or out of a foreign country, who made their own jam and cured their own bacon and distrusted any foodstuffs that had not been produced at home. Meat was all home-killed, with one weekly joint for a family at most; in between you ate your own bacon and ham, perhaps a rabbit from the fields and occasionally poultry from your own backyard, but rarely fish unless you lived near the coast.

Pig meat was the basis of the rural diet in the days when every cottager kept a pig or two at the end of the garden. The local pig killer would kill your pig and cut it into joints for half-a-crown. Pig killing meant a time of plenty for the family: you would roast the fresh spare rib as pork; you would make black puddings and sausages, basins of brawn from the head, faggots from unmentionable parts liberally flavoured with onion and herbs, and curly 'scraps' (little bits of skin) for breakfast. The chine of a large baconer would be rolled, cured and stuffed

with herbs. The great slab of solid white fat (the 'leaf' or 'flare') would be cut into small pieces and melted down for lard to be used for cooking or to be spread on bread as dripping with pepper and salt. The bacons and hams that were the bulk of the carcass would be salted and cured at home (sugar, salt and black treacle usually came into the recipe) and then hung in the back kitchen for a year. If you had a good big inglenook fireplace, you could hang the meat in the chimney and preserve it by smoking.

In the many homes that did not have a back kitchen or space for an airy walk-in larder, fresh and hung meat might be kept in a meat safe – a cupboard with perforated zinc sides or something similar that let plenty of air in and kept the flies and rodents out, preferably on an outside north-facing wall to keep it cool. Summer milk in some rural areas had to be delivered twice a day; it was unpasteurised and very likely to 'go off' rather quickly, which was only a benefit if you wanted it ripe enough to make butter or to turn it into cheese yourself.

When Middleton was a child in the late 19th century, bread was still largely baked at home in his village. Many cottagers even grew their own grain on their big allotments, harvesting and threshing it by hand and then taking it to the local mill for grinding into flour in exchange for the bran. Others made use of the village bakehouse – and not just for bread. People would bring along their Sunday joints to the bakehouse on the way to church; the joints, on trays complete with the housewife's own batter puddings and potatoes for roasting, would be popped into the baker's ovens and churchgoers would collect their sizzling hunks of meat after church to carry them home under a cloth.

In Middleton's Northamptonshire village the butcher would kill a bullock one week so that everybody had beef; the next it would be a couple of three-year-old sheep so that every family had hunks of mutton. His mother had a leg-of-mutton ritual: the meat would be hung in the back kitchen for a week and each day she would push a knife between bone and flesh to pour in

▶ WIDELY USED TO PICKLE VEGETABLES, *vinegar was also used to preserve meat (as shown here) and as a household remedy for curing hiccups and yeast infections, among other ailments. It was also a useful cleaning agent around the home.*

some homemade wine and vinegar. When the meat was adequately hung and pickled in this way she would roast it, fatty and full of flavour, on a jack in front of the fire. Bacon was equally fat and farmworkers ate bread and boiled fat bacon for their midday meal: fat is the perfect energy source to recharge a labourer's muscles and keep him warm.

Vegetables were stored and preserved in various ways. Root vegetables could remain in the ground until needed, or be stored in clamps – heaps of earth and straw to protect them from the frost. Haricot beans were dried; an excess of runner beans would be salted down in big earthenware pots; cabbage could be pickled. Fruit was eaten in season or preserved in jams and jellies; bottling in Kilner jars became all the rage for those who could be bothered with the sterilisation procedures, and for a while there was also home canning, until it became much cheaper and easier to buy ready-tinned food.

'The profession of warrener persisted into living memory and rabbit was a valuable source of lean and wholesome protein.'

Tinned meat was available as early as the 1820s, if you could afford it; but it was not until the beef farmers of Argentina started shipping tinned corned beef that the idea became popular. Then in the early 1880s they came up with refrigerated ships so that cheaply produced South American and Australasian beef and lamb carcasses could cross the oceans, denting the home-grown British fresh meat market in the process.

Refrigerators came late to the cottages, and freezers much later, though it was possible to buy ice from a travelling ice man in the 19th century or carve your own block from a frozen pond. If you put a block of ice in the cellar it would last for a while, and if

▼ BARNYARD FOWLS *often included ducks and turkeys as well as hens. As turkeys approached the age of 8–10 weeks their keepers would be on the alert for 'shooting the red' – a period during which the birds' colourful wattles would grow. It was important that the birds had been taught to roost before shooting the red, and that they received particular care during this fairly stressful time of their lives.*

you were really lucky you had an insulated ice chest. Home refrigerators came to Britain in the 1920s, though they did not become commonplace until after World War II, or even later in many country homes, as there was no electricity supply to power them.

Living off the land

Allotments and cottage gardens were only one source for the country larder and were supplemented by the natural harvest. As well as gleaning the wheatfields after the crop had been taken by the farmer, whole families would scour the local hedgerows and commons for blackberries, elderberries, wild strawberries, hazel and cob nuts, wild pears and crab apples, preserving what could not be eaten fresh, or turning all manner of fruits, flowers and roots into potent country wines. The habit of blackberrying is dying out now, especially since the laneside hedges became laden with traffic fumes.

They would also raid the meadows at dawn for mushrooms in the season, hoping for the occasional 'white-out' when after a few showers the whole pasture would be dotted with new white buttons that had burgeoned out of nowhere overnight, their gills still pink and their caps still earthy. In these occasional surplus years, the mushrooms would be dried for winter use as well as being eaten fresh. Most country people also knew enough about other fungi to harvest the edible and to teach their children which ones were poisonous and not to be touched.

Rabbiting

Rabbits are not native to Britain and were originally introduced as a source of food; they were kept carefully controlled in warrens and culled when needed. But Britain suited them admirably and they soon ran wild. The profession of warrener persisted into living memory and rabbit was a valuable source of lean and wholesome protein.

Two hundred years ago, especially in areas like Lincolnshire, land was deliberately 'planted' with rabbits: they were a crop, not a pest. Warrens were very carefully managed, fenced to keep the rabbits in and with properly made sod banks capped with furze faggots, and could be highly profitable. Skins were valuable: the rabbits would be netted and trapped for killing, then the skins would be carefully cleaned and dried over charcoal. Carcasses were much less valuable, mainly

▶ WILD RABBITS *were an excuse for sport. In areas where they were considered to be a pest, they might be ferreted, trapped or shot. Ferreting involved placing nets over the exit holes from rabbit burrows, then releasing a trained ferret into the burrow to scare the rabbits into the nets, which entangled them so that they could be dispatched with a sharp hand blow to the back of the neck.*

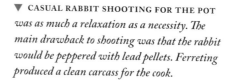

▼ CASUAL RABBIT SHOOTING FOR THE POT *was as much a relaxation as a necessity. The main drawback to shooting was that the rabbit would be peppered with lead pellets. Ferreting produced a clean carcass for the cook.*

'Rabbits had become a plague in Britain as well as down under, demolishing acre upon acre of crops'

▶ **RABBITS WERE A SOURCE OF PROTEIN** *that was cheap and readily available throughout the wars. One London schoolboy – who was evacuated to Sussex – quickly realised that his pelts had a market, and he soon set up a thriving little business supplying rabbit pelts and mole skins to London furriers.*

▼ **MYXOMATOSIS ARRIVED IN BRITAIN IN 1953,** *and by 1955 it had reduced the wild rabbit population by about 95%. Even those who regarded rabbits as a pest were shocked at the unpleasant symptoms of the disease, and it inspired poems by Philip Larkin and Spike Milligan.*

because a lot of farmers climbed on the rabbit bandwagon and flooded the market, and also because nearly all the rabbits were killed in the six weeks before Christmas as that was when the skins were in prime condition. A good warrener of the period could earn as much as £35 a year plus a cow, a house and fuel, and on top of that overtime for killing over a 16-week period at 18 shillings a week and other bonuses, bringing in an extra £18 a year. In Sussex in the early 19th century, although the rabbits that flourished on the wastes were described as nuisances, considerable quantities were sold to London markets.

Rabbits are prolific breeders and survivors. In 1788, for example, there were apparently only five rabbits in Australia's Port Jackson; within a century they had overrun the whole continent and between 1914 and 1924 Australia exported 157 million rabbits, quite apart from the number that were eaten or destroyed at home. Those exports finally killed off the British warreners in the 1940s, but many people continued to harvest wild rabbits for the pot, either by trapping, ferreting or shooting.

By the 1950s, rabbits had become a plague in Britain as well as down under, demolishing acre upon acre of crops, snatching grass intended for livestock and vandalizing tree plantations. Some people were quite happy to see them almost wiped out by the gruesome plague of myxomatosis in the 1950s. It was very ugly: rabbits with unseeing, bulging or closed encrusted eyes would hop miserably about the fields, or sit hunched and stark-furred on the verges, wholly oblivious to danger and taking a long time to die. It put a lot of people off eating wild rabbit.

Gamebirds

In many country areas, gamebirds have been on the increase in recent years. Pheasants are reared locally in their thousands, cosseted from eggs or chicks to young birds ready to fly. And then they are shot.

Until well into the 18th century, the British only shot birds for the pot and on the ground; their weapons and their skills were not good enough to shoot birds on the wing. With birds flying at speeds up to 50 mph, 'shooting flying' was a considerable challenge, but people learnt and their weapons improved. Then shooting became more of a sport than a pot filler.

Country people are ambivalent about gamebirds. In days gone by, game of all kinds was a source of considerable friction; it 'belonged' to the privileged few and was denied to the hungry many, and the penalties for poaching were severe. Today locals, being more often migrants from the towns than lifelong country dwellers, tend to tolerate rather than enjoy game shooting. Long gone are the days of touching your hat to the local squire and feeling that he had every right to do whatever he wished. Many do still become involved with the shoot, acting as beaters now and then as a good excuse to be out and about in the woods and fields in convivial company. But local people might question the scale of pheasant shooting, which has very little to do with feeding the family. As for poaching, it is now purely for

▼ VEGETABLE PATCHES WERE VULNERABLE *to predation by pigeons and other birds, with cabbages, broccoli and peas being particularly susceptible. Shooting was one way of protecting the vegetable patch.*

▲ ANOTHER WILD SOURCE OF PROTEIN, *pigeons were often a severe pest in crop fields. When human bird scarers (usually young boys) were no longer available the birds were controlled by shooting. As flock birds, they take fright easily and pigeon shooters tended to use hides. They would also lure the birds into the stubble with decoys.*

profit, carried out by ruthless gangs usually from the cities, not for the pot of a family whose stomachs are knotted with hunger. There is absolutely nothing romantic about the modern poacher.

Home shopping

When country roads were difficult to negotiate and most people had no means of transport other than Shanks's pony, much of such shopping as they did for food and for household goods came direct to their homes – on the backs of pedlars, or in panniers on hawkers' donkeys, or in carts. The carrier's cart would bring ordered goods from town shops and every now and then country people would go themselves to the local market town or to a fair (often travelling in the carrier's cart) to stock up on everything from food to clothes and household goods. Village shops, even for food, were fairly thin on the ground until the 19th century, though many a village would have an informal weekly market of its own on the green.

Itinerants

Those who brought their assorted goods to the country dweller were known by the general term of chapmen (and chapwomen – trading was by no means limited to men) or packmen. They tended to buy in bulk in the towns and cities and then sell for whatever they could get in the country. Those on foot, carrying their wares on their own backs, were pedlars, who 'peddled' their pedlary; those who could afford a donkey or pony to carry their panniers or pull a cart were hawkers. It was estimated that there were about 45,000 pedlars and hawkers in the country at the time of the 1871 census.

Pedlars walked the lanes carrying their goods in a sack or basket, or in a leather box that doubled up as a display cabinet when swung round to the front and opened. Inside would be useful bits and pieces such as needles, thread, ribbon and other haberdashery, matches, cheap toys, almanacs, song sheets and perhaps cheap jewellery.

Hawkers could carry bulkier items, such as ornaments, crockery, ironmongery, brushes, pots and pans. 'Cheapjacks' were not what the name implies: they tended to be hawkers with a better class of goods who bought tools, cutlery, cooking utensils,

▶ ITINERANT SERVICES *such as china-menders and knife- grinders tended to appear irregularly, setting up on the village green or a patch of wasteland, where their presence would soon be noticed. Some brought a wife or an assistant to knock on doors and drum up custom. Travelling knife-grinders were still seen in the heart of London as late as the 1960s, setting up their equipment in alleys and sending a shower of sparks from their grinding wheels.*

▼ CHAPMEN DEALT IN A RANGE OF GOODS, *including 'chapbooks' – printers' cheap paperback pocket-booklets, which might contain political or religious tracts, song sheets, stories, poems, almanacs and sometimes popular prints and were distributed in rural areas until newspapers became more accessible.*

leather items and so on from industrial areas and sold them across the country. Cheap Jacks and cheap Johns always claimed to be giving you a good bargain. Typical of the cheapjacks was a Sheffield cutler's agent who would turn up in villages in Oxfordshire in the spring and autumn during the 1880s and 1890s, driving a covered wagon drawn by two large black horses. He would remain for a month, setting up his van on the village green in the evening to display pocket knives, billhooks, garden spades and other tools. A lad would be paid a penny or two to shout the news of his arrival around the village.

Travelling widely, the various itinerants were an excellent source of information about the larger world, and usually good raconteurs who were quite happy to entertain locals with an evening of songs and stories. They often stayed a night or two at a farm and lent a hand with the farmwork.

Gypsies might come to the door selling their besoms, clothes pegs and split-willow baskets or offering to tell your fortune.

Near the coast you might be lucky enough to come across fishwives walking the lanes with baskets of crabs, winkles or fresh fish for sale. In the big fishing ports, such as Brixham in Devon (where in the early 19th century the fishing fleet was a hundred vessels strong), which sold mainly to London, Bath and Bristol, there was the custom of processing any summer glut of fish such as whiting, flounder, gurnet and 'thornback' by gently salting and then drying the fish in the sun. Known as 'buckhorn', this was much in demand by the Navy. If you didn't have a fishing boat, you gathered cockles and mussels at low tide and earned a great deal of money.

Trading was not just one way. The higgler came to the door of farmhouses and cottages to collect butter, eggs, poultry and other home produce; he'd pop the birds into wicker crates and pile the rest in the back of his cart to sell the goods in town on your behalf. The village butcher, delivering his meat to your door, might perform the same favour.

Services

The itinerants included those who gave a service, such as the travelling tailor who moved from house to house within a more limited area. Typically a farmer might buy

himself a length of cloth when he happened to be in town and would then wait for the tailor to stay at the farm for a few days to stitch the material into something useful, hunched over the kitchen table and being paid by the day to make new clothes and repair old ones. Some tailors did well enough to work from their home, visiting the big houses to measure up for a suit for the squire or 'uniforms' for keepers and hunt servants.

Chair-menders came with bolts of rushes on their backs and fixed the rush-bottomed chairs that were common in many farmhouses and cottages. Knife-grinders came with their heavy barrows: there would be a treadle-worked wheel to turn the grindstone for sharpening knives, razors and scissors. Wandering umbrella-menders had simpler equipment.

Tinkers usually had a donkey cart, raised high enough for there to be a hand-pumped set of bellows under the cart to make a

draught for a pan of glowing charcoal. The tinker would sit by his cart, pumping his bellows now and then and working with a grindstone, an anvil and a small vice. Despite often being skilled craftsmen, tinkers did not charge very much for mending pots and pans and took some of their returns in food instead of cash. They might set up camp locally, making a simple bender for shelter.

Another itinerant, though more often seen at fairs than in the villages, was the travelling quack selling unlikely potions claimed to cure every illness or discomfort that could possibly occur. He was less likely to persuade country folk, as most of them had their own traditional remedies based on herbs and probably knew a lot more about it than he did; they also preferred to consult the 'wise woman' they already knew rather than the visiting stranger. But some of these travelling 'doctors' were qualified pharmacists; they might have a shop in

▲ MARKET DAY *brought the country into town: farmers and growers came to sell their livestock and produce, while country families dressed in their best came to buy what they needed, enjoy the bustle and meet friends. The rural railway branchlines, carrier's vans and country buses were crowded with passengers on market day. Markets are once again popular, as people seek out local produce that has travelled less 'food miles' and support local businesses at same time.*

town, spending the winter behind the counter but the summer on the road, and some built up such a good reputation that they could live on their itinerant summer earnings, supplemented by a private mail-order business. Such men were still quite common in the lanes even in the 1920s, advertising their itinerary in the local press year after year and setting up their temporary consulting rooms in a spare room at the pub. The best of them had the integrity to advise their patients to see a qualified doctor where necessary; the real charlatans, however, took care not to return to an area for a very long time, whether they claimed to be doctors or mere tooth-pullers.

Market day

Almost every village was within walking distance of a market town, in the days when ten miles there and ten miles back in the same day was considered very reasonable. The weekly market day in town gave country people an opportunity to sell their goods and livestock – a very important source of income. They would spend as well, of course.

Market days were all bustle, with sheep and cattle being herded into their pens, auctioneers shouting, men prodding flesh, chickens squawking indignantly, women bartering at top pitch, others ensconced in the market hall with their panniers of vegetables and fruit and their bowls of cream and butter, the occasional loud argument between buyer and seller, and plenty of good gossiping in between. Later in the day there would be the bustle of homegoing: bewildered livestock being herded by their new owners for the long walk to the farm, dogs barking, carriers trying to find their passengers, horses and carts getting in each other's way, and many loath to leave the liveliness of the market.

Market was where you met friends you only saw on market day, and in some market towns today those of an older generation have not broken the habit of coming in from the countryside every Wednesday to meet those friends, have a pint at the pub and wander round markets that have now almost lost their point. Today's markets rarely have livestock in them; they have fruit and vegetables bought wholesale in city markets and recycled, rather than local produce; they have racks and racks of cheap mass-produced clothes and shoes and bits and pieces.

While you were in town you would buy goods that were not available in the village or from the itinerants. Very few Victorian villages had apothecaries, for example, and so you might visit the chemists and druggists to marvel at the coloured bottles in the window or to buy the shop's own remedies or patent medicines. You could buy a surprisingly wide range of goods there – household and cosmetic as well as medical.

Chemists often doubled as wine merchants, in that they sold 'tonic wines' anyway and it seemed only natural to sell alcoholic ones as well, which they did well into the 20th century. More often you bought your alcohol in the village, or made your own. 'Small beer' was the medieval answer to the problem of contaminated

▲ **LIVESTOCK MARKETS** *were held in market-town squares for the buying and selling of cattle, pigs, sheep, horses and poultry, well into the 20th century.*

'Market days were all bustle, with sheep and cattle being herded into their pens, auctioneers shouting and the occasional loud argument between buyer and seller'

drinking water: you boiled the water, flavouring it with common plants such as nettle or dandelion, and left it to ferment. Such brewing continued into the 18th century and here and there into the 19th; and the brewing of stronger ales and country wines certainly persisted in the villages. A home favourite was ginger beer, which began to be a popular refreshment sold on town streets in the 1820s and remained a cottage brew for at least a century thereafter.

Village shops

Mobility has always been a major factor in the economic health of the village shop, working sometimes in its favour and sometimes decidedly not. In the 18th century, when mobility was limited and roads were impassable even in the towns,

the customers of the village shop tended to be wealthy: goods might include silks and spices and the then luxuries of tea and coffee. The rest of the village relied on itinerant pedlars and hawkers, and occasional visits to fairs and markets, to supplement what they could not grow or make themselves or glean from common land. In the mid-19th century, with the railway network beginning to stretch across the countryside, the village shop gained access to goods that were mass-produced and therefore cheaper. In almost every village the number of shops increased dramatically between the 1830s and the 1870s, particularly the general stores that sold everything a villager might need. At the village store even the poorest could buy goods, albeit in small amounts and on tick.

Village shopkeepers were well versed in diversification; indeed, they had to be, in order to survive. Butchers might also sell vegetables, grocers might offer material and seeds, or in those blissfully unregulated times a cottager might simply open her front room to sell sweets, honey, backyard chickens, rabbits, stitchery, ginger beer, flowers, herbs and anything else she could muster to increase the income. Many shopkeepers ran their shops as a sideline (ideal for keeping up with the local gossip) and had other jobs to keep them going, especially in a Victorian age when most people spread their luck to harvest a series of incomes.

Each shop had its own special smell. In the days when many groceries were sold loose (well within living memory) the shop was fragrant with a strange mixture of shop-

▼ THE VILLAGE BUTCHER'S SLAUGHTERING METHODS *were crude in comparison with those of a modern abattoir, but the spiked end of a poleaxe would kill an animal instantly if the blow was powerful and the aim at its head accurate.*

blended tea, freshly ground coffee, hand-sliced bacon, flour, soap, candles, tobacco, dried fruit, vinegar, linseed oil, grain, paraffin, hessian, leather and cloth, sometimes combined with the unmistakable smell of the cats employed to keep down rodents.

Sweet shops were a childish heaven; the cheerful jangle of the shop's bell triggered by opening the door (to let the owner know it was time to emerge from nursing a cup of tea in the back room) still evokes for many the kaleidoscope of tall jars of loose toffees, gumdrops, striped bull's eyes, gobstoppers, fudge, pear drops, lollipops, pastilles and multicoloured boiled sweets. On the counter would be sticks of black liquorice to dip into triangular yellow paper packets of sherbet; there would be slabs of mintcake and butterscotch to be broken with a small hammer; there were red-tipped sugar cigarettes and, later, tubes of Refreshers and Polo mints and assorted chocolate bars. Those who remember sweet rationing after World War II (it finally ended in February 1953) valued every mouthful: Mars bars were carefully cut into seven chunks so that you savoured one piece a day for a week; lollipops were sucked for a while then put away for another licking later; loose sweets were bought by the quarter with saved-up pocket

money and were stored in a paper bag in your pocket along with rubber bands, pebbles, marbles and other bits and pieces.

While the ubiquity of packaged, tinned and frozen food has put an end to most of those lovely old grocery aromas, the butcher's shop still has its own smell of raw flesh, sawn bone and sawdust. The old butchers delighted in dressing their shop windows with fully feathered and furred game from the local shoot as well as plucked festive turkeys and geese, half sides of beef, lamb and pork (it was always abundantly clear where meat came from) and strings of homemade sausages. You would always expect to wait at least a quarter of an hour to be served, because the butcher was a chatty man and his customers loved him for it; he would also be taking time to select the right piece of meat, trimming and tying it to suit the customer as necessary. He reared his own animals in fields behind the shop, slaughtering, hanging and butchering them himself when he decided they were ready – not for them the stress of being herded into a lorry to travel to the bewildering noise and confusion of a distant abattoir. Today the butcher's fields are under a housing estate, and the old shop has been converted into a home. Perhaps the ghosts of the animals still

▲ **VILLAGE SHOPS COULD SPECIALISE** *as butcher or baker, but the best offered a great deal more. FW Chalk at Brockenhurst, a Hampshire village in the New Forest, described himself as a fishmonger and grocer, but the display outside the shop in 1910 reveals his wider range.*

▲ **SUCCESSFUL VILLAGE SHOPKEEPERS** *might progress to premises in the towns and cities.*

DONKEYS WERE WORKHORSES *for those who couldn't afford to buy and keep a horse. They were cheap to keep, lived a long time, plodded amiably, and were reliable and adaptable. One place in Surrey was known as Donkey Town for its large number of donkeys. Pack donkeys were gradually replaced by delivery bicycles and motorbikes.*

wander in the gardens, and if you listen hard enough you might catch up on the gossip of 50 years ago.

Deliveries

Accustomed to visits by itinerants and by the carrier's cart, rural households continued to rely quite heavily on deliveries even after many of them had private cars. The butcher from the village would visit outlying cottages and farms in his cart, using the tailgate as a chopping block and counter. Fish hawkers would bring their fresh herring and mackerel to homes near the coast, having spent the night close to the beach, sheltering under a boat or by a hedge, so that they could have the pick of the fresh catch as it was landed. Bell-ringing ice-cream vendors brought their loudly painted barrows and donkey carts to remote crossroads long before the days of piped-music ice-cream vans, and in winter they might sell hot baked potatoes and chips.

Most deliveries came by bicycle, with a large basket on the front, or by van, and the custom persisted into the 1970s. Up until the late 1950s the lanes were almost teeming with deliveries and quite a few of them were still by horse-drawn cart (gardeners rushed out to scoop steaming dung into their buckets). Boys on delivery bikes could earn five bob a week after school and Bernard Parke remembers carrying 'at least 28 pounds of sugar and a side of bacon from the grocery wholesalers down the High Street, only to find the back end of the bike rising into the air from the weight'. He recalls that customers were bound to use just one shop during World War II and up until the mid-1950s: they had to be registered with the shop because of the system of food and sweet rationing. Clothes were also rationed but only until just after the war. But then shopkeepers began to find that deliveries were no longer economical and the service waned, forcing people to take their own cars out more often. Those who relied on the declining bus service were seriously disadvantaged by the loss of delivery services.

The news still got through, of course. In the 1920s the Sunday newsagent brought the weekly journals to cottagers; most of the Sunday papers had their own agents who would collect the journals from the carrier and distribute them. Cottagers in particular looked forward to their weekly read of the often lurid papers, full of murders, battles and society gossip as well as politics and endless advice on every practical aspect of life. With improving distribution networks people began to take in daily papers as well, and in many rural areas they would have been delivered by a boy on his bike, ringing his bell to announce his approach.

Transactions

In Victorian times, life seemed simpler. Before advertising you bought what you knew from experience to be good and to be what you actually needed. Products were slow to change; a manufacturer's catalogue could remain current for years, and prices tended to be steady. Large local shops acted as wholesalers to the smaller shops and traders, often using travellers as go-betweens. Credit over several months was commonplace.

There was always the little problem of weights and measures, which varied from district to district, and sometimes on a very local scale. In one place you might buy by the pound, in another by the gallon. If you were buying a 'load' of wheat, it might be 40 bushels, but if it was of oats it might be 80. A 'stone' of meat in Sussex would be 8lb, not 14lb as elsewhere. In the village shop weights tended to be rounded, and if your joint of meat was a little short of the pound,

'*Up until the late 1950s the lanes were almost teeming with deliveries and quite a few of them were still by horse-drawn cart*'

▼ ITINERANTS PROGRESSED FROM PEDLARS *on foot or hawkers with carts to trading from vans and lorries that could offer a bigger range and carried a larger stock. 'Hardware' covered everything from tools and nails to pots and pans and oil stoves, and F Munday & Son in Buckinghamshire in the 1930s also sold the fuel for heaters and cookers.*

a few sausages would be thrown in rather than entering into complicated calculations of fractions of a pound.

In the 1920s, village tradesmen could still survive almost entirely on a system of barter based on exchange, or 'contra accounts', settled every six or twelve months when the two parties would compare what each had given the other and then settle the difference – coals for meat; milk and cheese for tea and flour; a funeral for horsefeed or bread; building repairs in exchange for household commodities, and so on.

The Victorians, ever worthy in social matters, created all manner of societies and clubs to help people in paying for this and that. Village benefit clubs were among them, and they often chose fair day for their own club day, when the members would unfurl the club's precious silk banner, with its logo and motto, to process around the village to the houses of prominent residents, who would contribute to the club's funds. Then the members could enjoy a good dinner among the fairground booths or at the local inn. The benefit clubs were the forerunners of the 'friendly societies' and Orders of this and that, which also liked a good parade in those days.

Advertising

The spread of advertising radically changed a lot of old buying habits. Combined with improved transport, it created not only a far wider choice of goods but also much more interest in trying them. Like everything else, the pace of change was quickening – alarmingly so.

In the national press and the journals, villagers could read about the latest fashions, the latest urban tastes in food, the latest gadgets for this and that, and all the modern conveniences they had not been aware they were missing. In the village street, enamelled

◀ RATIONING WAS INTRODUCED on January 8, 1940, beginning with bacon, butter and sugar, but this was soon extended to other basic foods. The shopkeeper would be supplied with enough goods for his registered customers, who would bring their ration book on every visit so that the coupons could be stamped. Basic foods could be sold in only very limited quantities to each household; for example 2 oz butter, 1 egg and 1 oz cheese per person per week. Rationing was later extended to clothes, soap and petrol, and didn't formally end until July 4, 1954.

advertising signs began to vie for attention – great big outdoor ones that could not be overlooked, window ones in the shops, more of them on the counters, folding boards outside the shop; so much colour, so much boldness, so much reading to be done, so many goods to be coveted. People began to demand goods with brand names: instead of the loose-sold goods of old they wanted things already packaged, emblazoned with names they had seen in the advertisements.

How could the countryside resist? If the village shop didn't stock it, the town did, or you could find your heart's desire in mail-

▼ THE ENTIRE VILLAGE OF ASHOPTON vanished when the waters of the massive new Ladybower Reservoir gradually flooded part of the Upper Derwent Valley after the dam's completion in 1943. The village's small stone buildings were soon buried in silt, though parts of the neighbouring village of Derwent can still be seen when the reservoir levels are low.

▼ MANY VILLAGES HAVE RECORDED THE MEMORIES *of their older generations. Florence Radley, who was a student teacher in the early 1900s and would have known the grocery shop in this photograph, recalled an 'old chap' who had kept a shop when Florrie's father was a lad. Her father's family was too poor for him to have any schooling and the old shopkeeper would call him over and generously add a bit of cheese to his dinner bag, which sometimes contained no more than bread and a scooped-out turnip filled with wild blackberries.*

order catalogues. The catalogues have been coming through the letterboxes of rural homes for decades, but increasingly are a way of life for those who either cannot or will not traipse to the towns in search of what they need. It keeps their cars off the roads, replaced by delivery services that can bring an order to the remotest farmhouse within 24 hours of a telephone call. And now there is shopping by Internet too. In the country the wheel is turning its full circle back to doorstep delivery, and there is the opportunity for country dwellers to become isolated again at their own volition.

Vanishing village shop

Mobility had brought the heyday of the village shop in the 19th century, but conversely the greater individual mobility of villagers by bicycle, bus and train or, later, by car became one of the biggest threats to village shopping. People enjoyed the excuse of going to town now and then, pennies carefully counted, making a family outing to do a week's shopping on market day or on a Saturday evening (even when this meant a journey on foot) and meeting their friends in town streets for a chat and a drink at the Crown. With luck there would be a railway station within two or three miles of home and they could take a cheap return ticket to town, piling their goods into the carriage for the homeward journey.

The demise of the village shop is not a new problem. Even in 1891, a sixth of the rural parishes in Oxfordshire (for example) had no village store. There was a gentle revival in the 1940s, when petrol rationing reduced mobility and food rationing encouraged people to shop locally. If they were lucky, the village shop could supply them with under-the-counter country-fresh local luxuries such as cream, eggs, ham and cheese. For a while there was a trend for mobile shops, visiting villages in rotation with a range of goods.

◄ THE VILLAGE SHOP AT LOXWOOD *was established by the Society of Dependents, founded by John Sirgood in the 19th century. To liberate women from the tyranny of service, the sect also set up shops, starting with Loxwood in the 1870s. Sect members lived communally and worked in the shops; they pooled their resources to build the shop and were shareholders in it. They also acquired farms in the 1880s, selling farm produce in the shops.*

▲ **BUTCHER'S SHOPS ARE RARELY SEEN IN VILLAGES TODAY** *or even in towns, where they and the greengrocers have been shouldered out by supermarkets. A few enterprising villages run their own monthly farmer's markets, where local farmers and smallholders can sell their produce.*

In some places village shops continued to thrive after the war, with family businesses such as grocers, general stores, newsagents and even betting shops. Sometimes customers could also buy tomatoes at the bakery, fresh lettuce at the chemist, pork chops at the grocer's, bananas at the butcher's and antiques at the newsagent's. The fact that these were family businesses gave them individuality; it meant that future generations would hear tales of old Jones the Grocer, and how Mother Heath would don a leather helmet and jump on a motorbike to deliver the meat. In many places today, village shops have lost that individual touch and become anonymous; the continuity of stories has been broken.

'If they were lucky, the village shop could supply them with under-the-counter country-fresh local luxuries such as cream'

More recently taxes, increasingly stringent public health regulations and other government decrees and, of course, the overwhelming competition from supermarket chains in and outside towns have almost sealed the fate of the village shop. The demise has been swift. In 1961, throughout Britain, there were about 147,000 grocery outlets; only 15 years later there were 39,000, and of these only about 9,000 were in rural areas. In 1999 the

▲ **MANY VILLAGE SHOPS HAVE STRUGGLED TO SURVIVE** *in recent times, and have often relied on running a post-office counter to eke out their income. Despite government criteria stating in 2008 that 95% of the total rural population should be within three miles of a branch office, the Post Office has now withdrawn its facilities from a large number of villages in a county-by-county programme, replacing them with mobile services once or twice a week for an hour or two or, where agreed, a 'hosted' service within another premises such as the local pub, again with limited hours. Pensioners (especially those who have to rely on public transport) the smaller village shops and the growing number of self-employed and small village businesses are the greatest losers.*

already been a movement towards community shops: in several places, the whole village formed its own cooperative to buy the shop when it was about to close for lack of profit, which meant that everybody had a vested interest in keeping the shop going by buying their groceries from it on a regular basis. In some villages there have been informal arrangements to use the village hall as a twice-weekly shop and post office. In at least one instance the man behind the counter is the vicar, who has extended the concept by serving tea, coffee and homemade scones so that shoppers can sit down and have an old-fashioned gossip – which is what village shops are all about.

During the 1990s there were the beginnings of a return to home deliveries, when various entrepreneurs began to sell fresh and frozen fish, readymade frozen meals for gourmets and so on. But very few of the old regulars such as bakers, butchers, grocers and greengrocers continued to deliver. Only the milkman persisted, extending daily doorstep deliveries to include soft drinks, bread and potatoes as well as a wide range of dairy produce. He certainly no longer comes with fresh milk from the farm carried in pails on a yoke, and you no longer see children carrying jangly milk cans on their rounds, with eggs and butter in their baskets, as would have been common in the 1920s. Nor does the milkman come with a horse that knows which door to stop at while the milk is ladled into the householder's own receptacle, and he certainly no longer brings the milking animal itself to be milked on the spot, fresh from the udder!

More ambitious villages have persuaded the enemy to help them out. Some of the supermarkets now open satellite shops in the village, thus keeping a few more cars off the roads and keeping the heart of the village pumping. Socially and environmentally, this is better than the home deliveries that some supermarkets are prepared to make (which in itself is a welcome return to an old tradition): the village shop is almost more important as a social centre for public information and informal encounters, discriminating against no one, than as a source of goods. Without a shop, the centre of the village is hollow.

National Federation of Women's Institutes produced a report in which it listed the closure of 474 village post offices, 178 pubs, 196 butchers, 71 greengrocers, 70 bakers, 58 grocers, 36 hardware shops, 29 mobile shops and 24 newsagents. The villagers' 'wish list' of improvements to village life numbered 'new shop' as high as fourth place, after improved public transport, slower traffic speeds and a higher police presence. In a similar NFWI survey in 1956, there had been no mention of village shops in the top ten wishes.

In the early 1980s there was a major campaign of support for village shops, with assorted agencies seeking to give advice and to publicise their importance. There had

5. Village Work

The choice of work in rural areas had been restricted largely by lack of transport, but this aspect would change radically during the 20th century. Traditional ways of earning a living in the countryside, other than in agricultural labour, included skilfully converting woodland and heathland materials into brooms, tool handles, walking sticks, fence palings and the like. A major source of income and employment for some was the wide range of village trades, working with leather (tanning), iron (blacksmiths and farriers), wood (wheelwrights and carpenters), clay (brickmaking and pottery) and also milling, cider making and the production of cheese. Women's cottage industries could also bring useful additional income into the home. There were other opportunities in some areas, such as mining, cloth making, milk processing and increasingly a range of factory work in a rural setting.

The nature of work in rural areas, or rather, the nature of the work of those who lived in rural areas, changed dramatically in the 20th century. In the Victorian village the great majority would have been working on the land and most of the rest in crafts and trades more or less directly connected with agriculture, or serving the needs of the immediate village. Paid work other than in agriculture became more of an option with the development of larger local industries and with creating the infrastructure of a modern world, such as building the railways. The latter, in turn, led to the opportunity to work beyond the village.

Today the proportion of rural dwellers whose work has any connection with the land has shrunk to a small minority in all but the more remote parts of the country. The urban spirit often prevails even in the countryside, because most people are divorced from the reality of land work.

Numerous rural communities in recent years have undertaken village appraisals, looking at every aspect of village life and making a genuine effort to listen to those who live there. The more useful of these appraisals, aimed at understanding villagers' needs, ask about the nature of people's work, how far they travel to it and what new job opportunities they would like to see in the village. Whatever the type of employment, in many villages the distance to work has increased considerably in the last 50 years, with often a high proportion of people commuting by train, bus or car to jobs in towns and cities.

The effects of the swing of the workers' focus from their own parish to the towns are far-reaching. Absent from the village for most of their waking hours, they cannot contribute fully to its economic and community life, however much they might wish to do so. They shop in town, as they happen to be there anyway, to the demise of the village shops and services; they take advantage of the town's recreational facilities and so the village ones wither; they add to lane traffic by their commuting and are very often in a hurry, late for work or for delivering the children to school, so they drive at speed; they are simply not around enough during the week to notice the small details of village life, the little local difficulties and joys; they are not there to

▲ BASKET MAKERS WORKED WITH LOCAL MATERIALS. *In Somerset, the wetlands of the Levels were used for growing basket willow (osiers, locally known as withies), but major areas for the large-scale cultivation of basket willow and for basket making were Nottinghamshire's Trent Valley and Lancashire's Mawdesley district. These areas also produced large quantities of woven wicker (willow) and (imported) cane furniture. In other regions, such as Suffolk, rushes, sedges and reeds (some of them also used for thatching, chair seats, hassocks or horse-collars) were used for weaving baskets and mats. Straw was another weavable raw material, especially for bee skeps. Sussex basket-makers specialised in using thin strips of oak for making trug baskets or 'spelks'.*

keep company with the old or the lonely or their own young; they have too little time at precious weekends to be involved in village activities, preferring to spend it at home catching up with the family or the mowing or household tasks or private leisure pursuits. In too many places the villages are almost dead during weekdays and then feel invaded by virtual strangers at weekends – strangers who are often highly articulate and tend to take over 'management' of the village, bending its ways to suit their own and sometimes claiming, somewhat patronizingly, that it is 'for the good of the village'.

Home industries

Smallholding is a way of life and a way of acquiring the basic essentials by sweat rather than cash, and it could be said proudly that smallholders were Britain's peasants. As well as growing crops and raising livestock for their own tables, smallholders generally needed paid work or turned to a range of cottage industries. They were ingenious at converting cheap or free raw materials into something that could be sold. They were also typical of the many Victorians who had fingers in many pies – not for them a single job that was the same day in, day out. They believed firmly in diversification.

Woodland and heathland crafts

For example, there was besom making – creating brooms from birch and heather on the commons where so often smallholders had grazing rights for their animals. The materials cost nothing, the brooms were quick to make and at the end of the 19th century they could be sold direct to the customer at three-and-sixpence a dozen for birch or half-a-crown a dozen for heather. In some parts besom making became quite a well-organised trade, with loads being carted to the railway station for shipment to

▼ COPPICE CRAFTS *were carried out in woodlands where species such as hazel and sweet chestnut, both of which would throw up many new stems if the original plant was cut down near the base, were carefully harvested in rotation so that the crop could continue to be cut over many decades without killing the rootstock. Many of those who had the skill to split rods by hand were versatile enough to make a wide range of 'underwood' articles, such as the tent pegs shown here.*

'... you might find specialist workshops where craftsmen snaked scythe handles by steaming the wood until it was malleable enough to be curved gently into shape...'

▼ CLEAR-FELLING OF TIMBER *could bring plenty of work to axemen, sniggers (men using horses to pull the felled timber out of the woods), carters and sawyers.*

other parts of the country. Broom 'squarers', or broom squires, made for themselves the simple equipment they needed and usually worked under a heather-thatched shelter.

Wood is a highly adaptable material and woodland crafts were numerous, all needing only simple homemade equipment along with cutting edges fashioned by the blacksmith or adapted from old tools. Some fashioned walking sticks or shepherd's crooks; some created clappers for scaring off marauding birds; some made oaken pegs for pinning tiles to the roof; some made oak shakes, skilfully splitting the wood for use as tiles; some made thatching spars from supple lengths of hazel; some were adroit enough to split long hazel rods for making barrel hoops, or to split chestnut poles into fencing pales, or twist split hazel to weave wattle hurdles. Others made simple pole lathes – springy poles with a string to turn a lathe which was used for making wooden bowls and spoons.

Among the more organised woodland crafts on a larger scale were bodging (turning chair legs) and clog making. Bodgers usually

worked in pairs and on pole lathes, setting up camp in the beech woods to supply the big chair-making industries. Clogging gangs were itinerant groups living in homemade shelters wherever they were working (generally in the northern counties and Wales); they made stacks of roughly shaped clog soles, usually of alder or sycamore, to sell to the village clog makers, who would smooth the blocks into shape and attach leather uppers and sole irons. Charcoal burners also travelled in gangs, camping in woods to mind their gently smoking kilns.

All around them, more serious timber felling was in progress. The act of felling large trees required considerable skill and also, for a long while, considerable strength and endurance as the work was entirely by hand, using axe and saw. The big two-man saws needed a good degree of teamwork (and presented something of a challenge when you cycled to work with the saw along your crossbar). Next you had to get the timber out of the woods, and this is where oxen and

▶ USING A LONG TWO-MAN SAW *was skilled work but very slow and physical. One man would stand in a pit and the other above as they worked in unison to pull the saw blade to and fro through the timber. This technique gave way to mechanical saws that could be set up on site, their circular blades driven by pulleys attached to portable steam engines and oil-powered tractors, making them a much faster solution.*

horses came into their own, dragging felled tree trunks between standing trees and wagon-loads of timber along the roads.

In the 20th century there were two major revolutions in the timber industry: the replacement of animal power, first by steam and finally by the internal combustion engine; and the invention of the chainsaw in the 1950s (though it was not in general use until the 1960s), which made the job a hundred times quicker and less tiring, but which also brought premature deafness to a whole generation of woodsmen before it was appreciated that earmuffs should be worn. As for traction, the wheel is gently turning (so to speak): heavy horses are once again working in the woods to drag out timber from places that tractors and other machinery find impossible to reach.

Much of the timber would be taken to estate sawmills, and again the type of power used to drive the saws that turned tree trunks into planks evolved through animal and steam to petrol-driven and electric engines.

In the villages you might find specialist workshops where craftsmen turned wood into rakes, or snaked scythe handles by steaming the wood until it was malleable enough to be curved gently into shape. The same system of steaming wood in hot sand was used to curve the backs of bentwood chairs and the rounded handles of walking sticks. Some of these woodland skills are still practised today, but the maker's income comes as much from demonstrating at country shows as in selling the items for use.

At a more basic level, the old skill of turning straw and hay into rope died out during the 20th century, though there was a time when most farms had throw crooks or rope twisters in the barn. In some parts of the country rope making was a more serious business and there were still some old rope walks dotted about the villages in the 1920s.

Another home industry was working with rush, in areas where the raw material was plentiful. The work included making

seats for chairs, weaving labourers' dinner baskets, making mats and so on. During World War I rush dinner baskets were hard to find in Hampshire and the women of Micheldever decided to revive the craft of making them, turning it into a thriving little village business.

▶ PEG MAKING *required a sharp tool and an accurate eye. The splitting tool, a billhook, was also used by hedge layers and broom cutters and there were regional variations in the shape of the hooked blade.*

Trades

Villages needed to be self-sufficient and, where there was a large enough population and thriving local agriculture or a large landed estate to support them, the village relied heavily on its own craftsmen.

All over the country there are villages that developed their own local industry and whose names became synonymous with their products. Some continued to thrive and became more organised than mere cottage industries, but others gradually lost their skills and trade to industrialised towns when mechanisation took over the manufacturing.

Most villages, within living memory though no longer, would have at least their own blacksmith and wheelwright, and no doubt a paper-hatted carpenter or two (often doubling as the village undertaker), several general builders and a well sinker; many would have had millers, tanners, brick makers, thatchers and masons; some would have a cobbler (or even a shoemaker), a clockmaker and winder, perhaps a potter, a saddler, a cooper and a tailor, as well as a wide range of skilled individuals making baskets or lace, spinning and weaving, knitting garments, making gloves and buttons, plaiting straw bonnets, braiding fish nets, making barrel hoops – everything of a practical nature, producing things that people used. Today villagers tend to offer services rather than goods.

CH Middleton could remember his small boyhood village as it was in the late 1890s, when the horse still reigned along with the squire and there was a village harness maker who took apprentices, a tailor, a shoesmith, carpenters working round the sawpit, and so much more. By the 1930s, he felt that the spirit of village life had departed – the saddler and tailor had gone, the golden harvest fields were down to grass along with the old village allotments, and the bus took people to buy bacon in town instead of having their own pig.

Middleton described the good old countrymen that used to inhabit his village, 'ripe old gaffers, most of them with clean-shaven upper lips and a fringe of whiskers round the lower part of their faces; hale and hearty, bubbling over with wit and wisdom, and capable of emptying a quart pot without taking breath or flickering an eyelid'. But above all they were craftsmen, and they took a pride in their work and in each other's.

Working with leather

Ollie Baker, born before World War I, was the son of a well-known harness maker in the village of Northchapel, where Ollie, a market gardener, had lived all his life. His home overlooked the village green and he was saddened at the demise of cricket there. The village team was once highly esteemed – Noah Mann, the first 'swerve' bowler to play for England at Broadhalfpenny Down, Hambledon, was landlord of Northchapel's

'… ripe old gaffers … hale and hearty, bubbling over with wit and wisdom'

◀ THATCHING A COTTAGE OR BARN *required special skills. Although many farm labourers could make a tidy weatherproof thatch to protect a corn rick or haystack, the roof of a building was a greater challenge and had to be longer-lasting. Thatching materials varied depending on what was available locally, but the main ones were straw and reed (more expensive but longer lasting than straw). In some parts of Scotland heather was used for thatching, and in Sussex they used sweet chestnut peelings for 'thatching' outhouses.*

▲ THE WHEELWRIGHT AND BLACKSMITH'S YARD *was immediately next to the Star Inn at Bulwell, on the edge of Nottingham, where timber was plentiful. Thomas Aslin was apprenticed here, and when he was born in 1813 it was an agricultural village with a population of some 1,500; when he died in 1908 it was a town of about 20,000.*

Half Moon inn during the 18th century. Ollie also regretted that employment opportunities within the village were limited after his retirement. In earlier centuries it had thriving glass and iron industries as well as agriculture, and in the 19th century a charcoal factory employed many local people.

In the 1960s, the Devon village of Colyton had a rural tannery where much of the work was done by hand and where they still used tapioca on bridles and stirrup leather after the leather had been stained.

Working with iron, wood and steam

In an intriguing study of countryside crafts published in 1958, WM Williams of Dartington Hall wrote about the organisation of rural industries in England. Since 1925 there had been official Rural Industries Organisers at large, and there was a Rural Industries Bureau, arising from the 1909 Development and Road Improvement Funds Act, all vaguely connected with the Rural Community Councils (first formed in 1921 at a time of rural crisis) and under the eye of the Development Commission. People really were trying to save rural industries.

Incidentally, that 1909 Act listed, among the many types of rural industry it supported, the cultivation and preparation of tobacco.

Williams, in 1958, was still able to assume that most people had seen a rural craftsman at work, 'a farrier making a horse shoe, a wheelwright building a wheel, or a weaver at his loom'. Yet even in the 1940s Michael Tilley spoke in the past tense of the time when most villages had a farrier, an ironmonger, a saddler, a carpenter and a wheelwright, and the larger places might have a tannery, a brewery and a builder's yard. He reckoned that these village trades had been hit very hard since 1900 because of the changing structure of agriculture, as much as general economic trends. Cheaper mass-produced articles made in the towns were flooding their markets and squeezing out the craftsmen who had been the backbone of the village and who had made it self-sufficient. You could still quite easily find a farrier or blacksmith and perhaps a

▲ OAK-BARK TANNERIES *supplied rural saddlers, harness-makers and cordwainers, and were once ubiquitous in areas where they had easy access to both oak bark and animal hides and a good water supply.*

▲ THE VILLAGE BLACKSMITH *did much more than shoe horses, but with the increasing use of factory-produced agricultural implements rather than those fashioned at the smithy, he became little more than a repairer rather than creator.*

▲ SOME SMITHS TURNED TO DOMESTIC ORNAMENTAL IRONWORK, *including making gates; others made wheeled iron hurdles that livestock farmers could move easily over the land. The hurdles were expensive but lasted a lifetime, in contrast to woven hazel and ash hurdles.*

thatcher in the 1940s, though it was more rare to find a wheelwright or a saddler, but nearly all of them were by then old men whose business would die with them, there being no apprentices or sons interested in continuing it. Farriers, wheelwrights and saddlers had to adapt if they wished to service the tractors that were replacing horses. There might still be a demand for their services for repairs in the countryside, but not for making something new, and they increasingly relied on the well-to-do and the connoisseur as their clients, rather than farmers and the village in general.

Williams interviewed craftsmen in several parts of the country in his 1950s study and found many of them disheartened. Farriers in particular seemed to be ready to chuck their horseshoes over the nearest hedge: it had become a low-prestige trade and many of them seemed to hate doing it anyway. 'You can keep it,' said one, who blamed farmers for no longer understanding their own horses. 'If I put the shoes on backwards most of the farmers round here wouldn't know the difference. You can't blame the horse. A live thing is a foot and I don't like it. Only on Monday one kicked my cap off. I'd be glad if I never did another horse.' To the young, farriery seemed to be a dead-end, dirty, smelly, sweaty and monotonous job and they didn't want to know. Blacksmiths fared better in terms of status, income and optimism, diversifying into making agricultural implements and repairing machinery, and often becoming full-blown agricultural engineers.

Even by the 1920s, most of the old village trades were already declining or gone. For the blacksmith, be he farrier or forger, the demise of the horse was one blow (though for a while he could fix bicycles instead of horseshoes), and the mass production of agricultural implements another (of old the smith and the farmer would have designed implements together to suit a particular purpose). But smiths were usually quick to find new niches: several took the trouble to understand the workings of motor vehicles when they first came into the countryside, and developed a new trade for themselves.

Wheelwrights usually set up shop not far from the blacksmith as their skills were complementary: red-hot iron bands would be fitted as wheel tyres and shrunk tight to the wood in a steaming hiss of water, and

there were many other iron parts needed in making and fixing a wheel. Some of the wheelwrights were also wainwrights, making wagons and farm carts, and in due course turned their hand to making trailers and converting lorries and other vehicles for various rural uses in farming and the timber industry. Others developed a useful trade in making poultry houses, beekeeping equipment or ladders; many were general carpenters and often also coffin makers and undertakers. There was something very personal about having a handmade coffin tailored just for you by the village coffin maker who had known you for most of your life.

Wheelwrights, like blacksmiths, did their best to make the most of a changing world. Those who had coachbuilding skills could adapt to panel beating a car or repainting the sides of a motorised van or bus. In the 1920s they still had work to do on horse-powered vehicles – the vicar's trap, the farmer's wagon and the carrier's cart might still need attention, and gardeners still needed wheelbarrows. But as the car drove the horse off the roads, both wheelwrights and blacksmiths either gave up or turned themselves into village garages. Somehow villagers do not find the local garage as intriguing, skilful and romantic to watch as the old forge and the wheelwright's yard.

Iron, wood and leather were leaving the village workshops. What has happened to the village coopers, who used to make and mend all manner of essential everyday wooden containers – barrels and vats, tubs and bowls, casks and buckets, butter churns and barrel-shaped chairs? Once, casks were built to contain just about any commodity from butter, fruit and fish to beer, wine and gunpowder. Today, such coopers as remain are making decorative garden tubs and furniture and in most villages the art has

▲ THE FARRIER BECAME SUCH AN EXPERT *on horses that he was the forerunner of today's veterinary surgeon: he could treat equine ailments as well as making and fitting horseshoes. By the 1920s standards of shoeing were being raised considerably by farriery instructors working under county agricultural committees; farriers were encouraged to attend lectures and take examinations for a Registered Shoeing Smith certificate. The instructors said that ironwork could be learnt traditionally but that the anatomy of a horse's hoof could only be learnt under scientific instruction. Also, knowledge of ironwork could become out of date, whereas anatomical knowledge of a horse's foot lasted a lifetime.*

been lost of hollowing out the staves, banding them together with hoops, steaming them and trussing them into shape until they fit together so perfectly that they are leakproof with not a single drop of glue or solder in sight.

Villages are much quieter and less colourful places since the passing of these old trades, and more introverted – people tend to hide their work indoors now, instead of spilling out into the lanes and street.

Working with clay

Many villages in the clay regions had their own brick-making industries and there are older builders who can still tell you exactly where your house's bricks were made, just from the look of them – not merely which region of the country but the very brickyard. In the broadest terms, certain regions specialised in types of brick that depended on the local geology: for example, yellow bricks based on London clay, or blue bricks from the iron-oxide coal clays of the West Midlands and Staffordshire. In addition to the base clay, colour could be added during the clay-mixing process by including minerals such as barium carbonate or manganese dioxide; colour was also affected by controlling the amount of oxygen during the firing process, producing greys, purples and ochres as well as a wide range of reds.

The oldest bricks give away their age because they contain ash: they hark back to the days when bricks were baked in clamps, such as when Eton College was first built in the 1440s. Brick sizes were variable until 1769, when legislation set the standard as 8¼ x 4 x 2½in, but because the government levied a duty on bricks per thousand in 1784, bricks became bigger until the government doubled the tax on larger bricks. Then in 1850 the brick tax was finally abolished; brick sizes became properly standardised at 9 x 4½ x 3in and they began to be mass-produced rather than handmade.

◀ A WHEELWRIGHT WORKSHOP *could be found in nearly every town and village until the 1920s. Many wheelwrights gave up when they could not afford to invest in power-driven saws to replace the old saw-pits. Changes from the big old farm and road wagons to motorised vehicles sounded the end for many a wheelwright, but some adapted and took up typical timberyard activities such as making wooden gates; others became general carpenters.*

As every child knows, the Romans knew all about brick making, but it seems to have become a lost art; no Saxon brick kilns have yet been discovered, though there were medieval ones here and there producing bricks for grander buildings. During the 16th and 17th centuries the use of brick began to drip down to vernacular buildings, spreading very slowly across the country in the same manner as most other 'fashions': downwards through the social levels, and fanning geographically from the Continent-influenced southeast of England, on a time scale that might be as long as half a century from southeast to northwest. In clay areas bricks were made on a very local scale, with many a village and estate having its own brickworks, so that the houses were made literally from local mud.

Even in clay areas local cottages were rarely made solely from brick until the 18th or 19th century – it was simply too expensive a material for a whole cottage, though brick might be used as quoins on a stone building,

straightening and strengthening the corners, door jambs and window frames. In London, the Great Fire of 1666 had led to the creation of byelaws stipulating that all rebuilding must be in brick, to reduce the likelihood of a similar inferno, and by then there were already various regional decrees that chimneys, even in small homes, should be made of brick or stone, not the traditional and far-from-fireproof wattle and clay. By the 18th century, most cottages had a good, solid brick or stone chimney, very often built on to the outside – partly because there was no space for a chimney breast indoors and partly so that the neighbours could see that you could afford the bricks.

Transport was the biggest problem; hence the need to make bricks locally. A horse and cart could carry only a few hundred bricks, and it was not until there was a good network of canals and railways that brick transport became more practical. Here again, 1850 or thereabouts was the turning point. The Victorians fell in love

'Victorians fell in love with brick; the railways enabled them to be transported all over the country'

▼ **POTTERY BECAME A DECORATIVE CRAFT** *rather than a rural necessity once the essential items that used to be made in the village became mass-produced by the factories. Local potters often could not afford to keep up with new types of kilns and fuel, and were also limited by the type of local clay, though in practice many began to buy in clay from other parts of the country.*

▲ IN CLAY COUNTRY, *some villages had their own brickworks. These might be family firms, or might have been set up by the local big estate initially to make land-drains for the fields. The works usually also made roofing tiles, chimney pots and paving bricks. The brickyard had long, low 'hack houses' (drying houses), with horse-driven pugmills to soften and work the raw clay, and a shed in which the worked clay was pushed by hand into moulds before being turned out on trays to be loaded into the kiln for firing.*

with brick; the railways enabled them to be transported all over the country, and it rapidly became cheaper to use mass-produced bricks from elsewhere than to produce them by hand locally. So all over the country harsh red bricks began to dominate, ousting even the local bricks that had reflected the nature of the land from which the clay was dug; and the origins of the Victorian mass-produced bricks became meaningless.

Milling

Mills always seem to appeal to the romantic in people, be they watermills or windmills. The father of the painter John Constable was a miller, and probably one of Constable's best-loved paintings is *The Hay Wain*, with its horse-drawn wagon fording the millstream by Flatford Mill. Constable painted it in 1821, at a time of agricultural depression (those times have been many in recent centuries) when the farmworkers of his native Suffolk were rioting and burning ricks and being confronted by troops – hardly the peaceful scene of the painting, but then Constable was probably recapturing the better times of his boyhood. The mill was built in 1733 and its working life ceased about 165 years later; today it belongs to the National Trust, who have preserved the building since 1943 and try to maintain the original view, more or less. The miller's house, built about 1600 and unoccupied for most of the 20th century, was in Constable's time the home of one Willy Lott, a farmer who was born in the house and died in it, and apparently left it for only four days in his lifetime of 88 years.

Watermills for grinding flour, once at work non stop in every valley in the country where there was a decent stream, were already falling into disuse in the 1920s, though during World War II some old mills were brought back into work, and some were converted to generate their own electricity. The old working mill would have been a scene of constant activity, with the noise of horses whinnying, wagons rumbling, men shouting, hoists creaking, all against the background sounds of the wheel turning, the stones grinding and the busy working water splashing and rushing over its wheel.

Today the sounds are but memories save for the chuckle of the millstream and the chattering of ducks on the millpond. Mills seem to be favourite targets for conversion into homes and that is their usual fate, but one old watermill has been rebuilt, stone by stone, at the Open Air Museum at Singleton in West Sussex, where you can watch the water driving the machinery and buy unadulterated wholemeal flour fresh from grinding. It is intriguing to see the cogged wheels turning and interacting, like the workings of some huge clock.

Windmills remain a feature in some exposed landscapes but not usually as working mills any more, unless they too have been restored. Most were corn mills, like watermills, but the wind could also be harnessed to pump up water, typically in the East Anglian fens. Watermills could also pump water and (very relevant today) they could be converted to generate electricity. There is an example in Sussex of an old watermill that was first converted into a

hydroelectric generator in about 1901, operating at 48 volts at that stage and controlled by a handsome switchboard with brass measuring instruments. In 1946 the dynamo was changed and the voltage increased to 110 volts. It supplied electricity for the mill house, the farmhouse (300 yards from the mill) and three cottages, producing enough for lighting and water heating and even running the radio and television set. The millwheel was also used to pump water from a well and from the river to a domestic storage tank in the farmhouse attic and to water the garden. But the mill had long since ceased its original role of grinding corn.

Wind and water were not the only powers that drove wheels and pumps. On the Isle of Wight at Carisbrooke Castle there is a huge treadwheel in which a donkey would trudge to draw large pails of water from the castle's deep well; other devices were treadwheel cranes used to raise chains of buckets to lower the water level in mines, or to hoist building materials and dockyard loads. In some farms, horses or dogs worked devices that were very similar to the running

▲ **EVERTON MILL IN NOTTINGHAMSHIRE** *was a four-storey brick-tower windmill, built in about 1820. It was sold along with a watermill to a farmer in 1848. Its miller John Marple is photographed here in the early 1900s, shortly after steam engines had been installed in a nearby engine house to work the mill. The sails were removed in 1930 and the mill finally closed as a working mill in about 1950, when the machinery was dismantled.*

'It is intriguing to see the cogged wheels turning and interacting, like the workings of some huge clock'

▶ **INSIDE THE FLOUR MILL** *a hopper stands above the paired grinding stones, which are protected by wooden casing. A chute allows the grain to pour into the hopper from the next storey (sacks of grain had to be winched up to it from the delivery carts outside). The flour was allowed to cool before the process of separating out the bran and grading through sieves began.*

machines you find in fitness gymnasiums, walking against a moving belt. Dogs also ran on treadwheels to turn roasting spits in the farmhouse (there was even a 'breed' of dachshund-shaped dog known as the turnspit), or to work the butter churn. Horses and donkeys might trudge in circles to soften the pug for brick making or work colliery winding engines or mint coins or saw wood or thresh corn or crush anything from ore and corn to gorse for fodder – or apples for cider.

Cider and cheese making

Cider making remained a rural industry on a very local basis (often farm-based) into the 20th century. In that century's early years it was still being made in old wooden presses. All sorts of apples, many of them muddy and bruised and certainly not washed, would be crushed by rollers in the cider mill, worked by two men turning the handle; on a larger scale the mill would be a massive stone turning in a solid stone cistern, powered by a horse plodding in a circle. The crushed apples were then put into coarse fibre bags, packed together in the press between boards and squeezed by screwing down the presser to extract the juice.

Farm cider was not made for sale but to whet the thirsts of farm labourers, especially as a reward during the peak activities of haymaking and harvest. Cider was one of the perks, and a daily ration of two or three litres would be transferred from the farm's barrels into wooden harvest bottles or firkins for the workforce. Often the men drank considerably more than that daily ration, sometimes three times as much, and it has been estimated that the farmers of Herefordshire alone were producing as much as 13 million litres of cider a year during the 1870s.

The thoroughly pressed bagged pulp during cider making is known as cheese, and indeed the pressing process is broadly similar

▼ PORTABLE CIDER PRESSES *could be brought to the farm or orchard to carry out all the work of cider making, from crushing the apples to squeezing out the juice ready for bottling or casking so that it could ferment. Although many farms had their own presses, in some areas the local squire used to provide a communal press for use by the villagers, who brought their own apples for squeezing.*

to that used for making dairy cheese. Cheese making was becoming increasingly important as a rural industry in the late 1870s, when Richard Jefferies noted the 'enrolment of a cheese show on the list of annual exhibitions in London'. Throughout the West Country there were cheese shows and cheese fairs, very well attended by both buyers and sellers, and cheese making on the farm was an increasingly popular diversification. Jefferies called it essentially a 'connubial occupation' – he doubted whether a widow or widower could ever make a good cheese, 'and as for an old maid, it is a maxim beyond dispute in the West Country that the milk would turn sour under her eye'! He thought that the duties involved in cheese making were divided naturally between a man and a woman, the one to do the athletic 'hard' work, the other to do the 'light or head' work, and the teamwork was only successful in the couple that was 'united in the staid and homely bonds of conjugal felicity'.

▲ SOME 29 MILLION BULK BARRELS OF BEER *were consumed in the UK in 1948, compared with 25 million ten years earlier. Brewers and distillers were using about 900,000 tons of barley – more than half the nation's total barley crop – and nearly 66,000 tons of sugar a year. The barley used in brewing could have produced up to 125,000 tons of pork and 1,000 million eggs for war-worn Britain had it been fed to livestock instead. There had been a heavy increase in the consumption of beer since the beginning of a large-scale and sustained combined brewers' campaign since 1933 advertising beer in general, as opposed to particular brands.*

▲ 'BLEDISLOE' IS A WELL KNOWN NAME *in agriculture and rural affairs in general. Charles Bathurst (1867–1958), 1st Viscount Bledisloe, was President of the Royal Agricultural Society and on his 90th birthday in 1957 he made a Deed of Gift of £3,000 for the occasional award of a Gold Medal to a landowner 'having done outstanding service in encouraging the application of science or technology to some branch of British Husbandry'. He also established the Bledisloe Veterinary Award for those who had made outstanding contributions to animal health.*

Cottage industries

Cottage industries were an essential part of life for many women throughout most of the 19th century and were often in addition not only to housework and child rearing but also working in the fields or other jobs. Initially the industries were based on raw materials produced by the cottagers themselves; later the materials were bought in and many cottage industries were dominated by agents, who brought the materials to the cottages and sold off their output in the appropriate market place at a substantial profit – for the agents. Sometimes that little bit of spare-time home work became the main earner for the household and developed into quite a thriving small business, especially where several women combined forces and were capable of marketing the goods themselves.

Spinning and weaving

There is quite a revival of interest, usually as a hobby, in spinning and weaving, which are skills that have been practised in Britain for several thousand years. In medieval times the woollen industry was dominated by town guilds but during the 16th century it came out into rural areas on a big scale. Clothiers employed home-workers but the Industrial Revolution snatched back the looms from the cottagers and centralised the industry in places like the West Riding of Yorkshire during the 18th century, creating new towns such as Huddersfield out of what had once been hamlets.

In 1849 Angus Reach visited the West Riding and moors to see the cottage weavers:

High up on the hillside above Delph I counted from one point of view a couple of dozen cottages, in each of which the loom was going, and around each of which the kine were grazing. It was a glorious sunny afternoon, and amid the fields and by the roadside, the weavers with their wives and children were many of them stretching out their warps upon a rude apparatus of sticks to dry in the genial air. The gay tinting of many of these outstretched meshes of thread, glancing along the green of hedges or the cold grey of stone walls, made quite a feature of the landscape.

The weavers were unhappy; power looms threatened to take the work away from them. Yet they were a lot better off than their counterparts in the town factories, especially in the terrible shoddy mills where the workers permanently wore bandages over their faces to save themselves from breathing in lungfuls of omnipresent dust.

Knitting

Most women could knit by hand. Many cottage women used knitting as another means of earning money at home; you would see them knitting as they gossiped, on their way to market, or in the evening gloom without needing to see the stitches.

◄ SPINNERS GENERALLY USED SHEEP'S WOOL *but many other fibres have been spun. Here, the fibre is from the Angora rabbit. Originally angora fibre was from the coat of mohair goats in Turkey. The Angora domesticated rabbit was deliberately bred for long, fine, lustrous fur.*

It was not confined to women; many a shepherd became an expert knitter, for example. Hand knitting continued as a well organised industry into at least the 1870s in the north of England, with children attending knitting schools and cottagers knitting underwear, stockings and jackets for fishermen and also caps, gloves, stockings and clothes for a more general market, but village hand-knitting industries had generally died out by the late 19th century except in the more remote coastal and fishing villages. Across the country knitting groups were formed to provide a range of garments for the armed services in World War II – in Dorset alone, thousands of pairs of

▲ **SPINNING WAS A SERIOUS INDUSTRY** *that brought essential income into the home. Cottagers could undertake several of the different processes involved in converting a sheep's fleece into woven cloth, such as dyeing (using wild plants or those grown in their own gardens) and combing (disentangling the wool). In some villages evidence of an old weaving industry can be seen in the long windows designed so that weavers could see their loomwork more clearly, or in the 'spinning galleries' – cottage roofs extending over an open area where women would group together at their spinning wheels.*

'... you would see them knitting as they gossiped, on their way to market, or in the evening gloom without needing to see the stitches.'

gloves were knitted every week. Each group would follow Government-issued patterns in specified colours. In Leicestershire there were still many village stockingers working in the 1920s, though by then they were using steam-powered rather than hand frames.

Stitching

One of the most treasured inventions was the sewing machine. Singer sewing machines were invented in the United States in 1850 and were first used in cottages by glove makers, who would hire or hire-purchase treadle-operated machines to speed up production in their cottage industry. Home

glove makers, still stitching by hand earlier in the 19th century and ruining their eyes by candlelight, had supported whole families during times of agricultural depression. With home machines the industry continued, and new cottages were being built for glove makers in Oxfordshire as late as 1926.

By the end of the 19th century sewing machines were also being used by another cottage industry – that of stitching plaited straw into bonnets and hats. Plaiting was an industry in itself and required no equipment other than your fingers; you could plait straw anywhere, at any time – people around Luton were still plaiting straw in 1930.

▼ REGIONS DEVELOPED THEIR OWN STYLES *of knitwear, most famously the Fair Isle, Shetland and Orkney patterns of Scotland, the creamy jerseys of the Aran Isles off the west coast of Ireland, and the fishermen's robust dark blue Guernsey sweaters. Several centuries ago, in areas of the country where wool was produced, hand-knitters were knitting enough to export not only to other parts of the country but also overseas.*

Cottage hat makers continued to use treadle machines into the 1920s and country women who were accustomed to making the family's clothes gleefully adapted to sewing machines.

Smock making was a local industry in some places. Smocks were at their peak in the mid-19th century in both popularity and complexity. In the 18th century they had been rather plain working overshirts, sometimes described as frocks, but during the 19th century women began to embroider them and some became highly rated specialists in the art of smocking. At the Great Exhibition at Crystal Palace in 1851, nearly 800 agricultural labourers and other countrymen from Godstone, Surrey, turned up in force in their smartest smocks, with their women in best Sunday dresses.

By the end of that century smocks were largely going out of fashion, though some men wore them into the 20th century in some counties, and wore them with pride. Working smocks, usually produced in factories, were in shades of beige, or locally blue in the Midlands, or dark grey for shepherds, or black in some places, brown or green in others. White smocks, heavily stitched, were usually worn on special occasions and for Sunday best and were made by family members (typically a girl for her sweetheart) or by a woman in the village who was an expert. In some places families took the industry a step farther: they grew and spun their own flax as well as making it into smocks, and then sold them through a local tailor.

Increasing industrialisation began to swallow up cottage industries, which simply could not compete with mass-produced goods unless they could make a virtue of being 'different'. The old Dorset button-making industry collapsed almost overnight in the early 1860s when button-making machines were invented, though it was revived artificially by the Arts and Crafts Guild for a while in the early years of the 20th century. The ancient lace-making cottage industry had virtually died before Victoria was buried, though here and there it continued: for example, there was a family of hereditary lace makers in East Sussex in the 1920s, but they no longer peered at their work by the light of a candle enhanced with a globe of water to concentrate the brightness. In West Dorset villages women were still braiding nets in the garden well into the 20th century.

'... they no longer peered at their work by the light of a candle enhanced with a globe of water to concentrate the brightness ...'

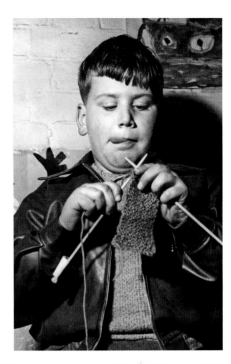

▶ **HAND-KNITTING** *could be carried anywhere and picked up or put down at will. As a cottage industry, hand-knitting was mainly a female occupation but many men, especially shepherds and fishermen, were expert knitters. There are old photographs of shepherds knitting while standing on stilts to keep an eye on their flocks!*

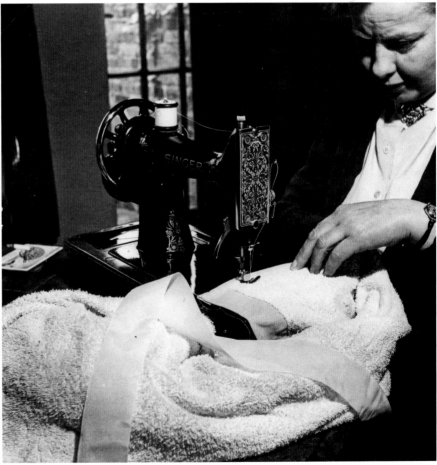

▲ **THE INVENTION OF THE SEWING MACHINE** *was an immense boon for those who stitched to make a living and also for those who made clothes for the family. Isaac Merritt Singer, a trained engineer who happened upon a sewing machine being repaired in Boston, Massachusetts, patented his own sewing machine in the US in 1851 and started what became a series of patent wars between various inventors and companies. The Singer Sewing Company introduced the first electric sewing machines in 1889.*

Work clothes

Many trades wore distinctive clothes, such as the red caps of brewers' van men. Smiths were practical with their leather aprons. The traditional carpenter's outfit until about the 1860s was a short white jacket in thick baize or felt, an apron and a tidy paper cap (many other tradesmen wore paper caps). White was remarkably popular, considering the washing problems. Ploughmen and farm labourers at the beginning of the 20th century still sometimes wore the white summer 'slop' jacket that drovers had worn a hundred years earlier, and white corduroy was a favourite. Corduroy and fustian (another cotton-based material) remained the everyday standbys for most of the working countrymen.

White smocks were usually kept for best wear; everyday versions of these practical linen garments were in greys and greens and browns, and they were worn by most agricultural workers until the 1860s or 1870s, and by some even into the 20th century.

A typical outfit in the early 19th century for those who could afford it would be knee breeches under a longish coat and waistcoat, or a full-length greatcoat in adverse weather. Leather spats might be worn over the shoes but leather gaiters seem to have been worn by only gamekeepers and slaughtermen. Low shoes, stockings and knee breeches were commonly worn in the countryside until the 1820s or so; thereafter workers compromised on breeches (which had been thoroughly practical for working men) by tying their corduroy trouser legs below the knee with straps or string, variously known as lijahs (elijahs), yorks, whirlers and the like. The trousers generally had a front flap for convenience, fastened to the waist on either side, rather than flies. Waistcoats were usually worn and rarely removed, though they would be unbuttoned when working. Even in the hottest work, men never took off their shirts. A neckerchief almost completed the picture but the missing item was what no working man was ever seen without: his hat.

You could always tell a man by his hat. In the 18th century, farmers and gardeners wore something like a top hat, but gardeners adopted bowlers during the 19th century and some head gardeners still wore them into the 20th. Farmworkers and others usually sported soft felt hats with low crowns and a wide brim that could be bent in various directions to suit the owner; if you flung a

▲ SOFT FELT HATS *were commonly worn in the fields long before flat cloth caps became popular head gear. An all-round brim protected the back of the neck from the weather, unlike the front peak of a cap. The cape-like collar shown in this photograph kept the worst of the rain off the shoulders. Sleeve settings were generally loose and low to give freedom of movement. Long cuffs could be buttoned to keep out debris and weather; the gathered cuffs of a smock served the same purpose.*

▶ STRIPED DRESSES WERE POPULAR *among women butter-workers in the 19th century, protected by a bibbed pinafore or an apron. By the late 1920s cross-wrap overalls began to replace aprons and pinafores.*

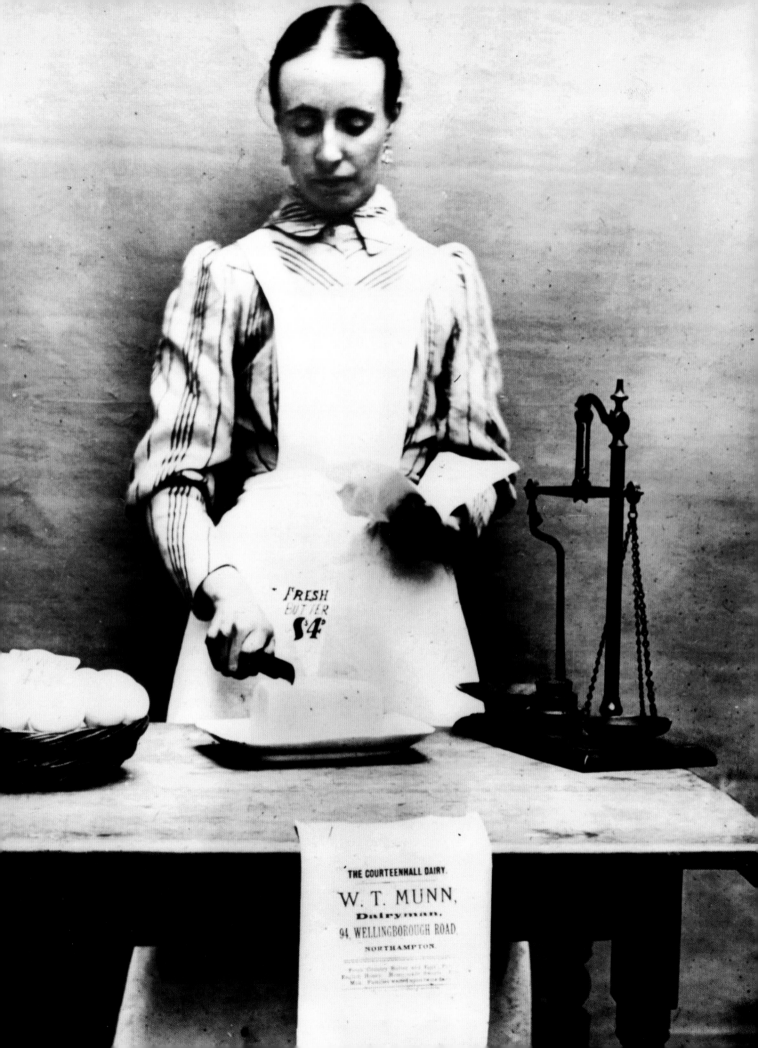

FRESH
BUTTER
¼

THE COURTEENHALL DAIRY.

W. T. MUNN,

Dairyman.

94, WELLINGBOROUGH ROAD,

NORTHAMPTON.

◀ SMOCK STITCHING PATTERNS *evolved in the late 19th century and varied from region to region. In Sussex and Surrey the patterning was limited, whereas in southern Wales and neighbouring English counties much greater areas of the material were embroidered and smocked, and the garments also had large collars. Smocks were often associated with shepherds but were worn as a convenient garment by other workers, shorter or longer according to need. For example, a milker's smock was likely to be shorter and lighter than that of a shepherd, who was out in all weathers.*

Once you had chosen your style of hat, you stuck to it. Middleton remembered a pair of old countrymen he knew well in the 1920s: one of them always wore a flat, clerical type of black felt hat with a small bone horseshoe on one side of it; the other always wore an old high-crowned bowler, green with age and with what seemed to be a rat-chewed brim. The local schoolmaster always wore a ridiculous square-topped bowler; old Bob Hall always wore an ancient top hat minus the flat part at the top, so that his crown was exposed to the weather (when he lost the hat, he found another and carefully cut the top out). Nobody would have recognised them in anything different.

Fishermen might wear woollen caps shaped like a nightcap. Rather than smocks, fishermen's waterproof canvas or oilskin overshirts were known as slops; along the east coast they were usually blue, unless you happened to be a Yarmouth herring fisher, in which case your slop was brown, though oilskins were at first black.

For women, clothes in the country were more for practical wear than for fashion and glamour (even today, except for town dwellers not yet fully adapted to country life) and in the 19th century you could still work out whereabouts in the country you were by the type of clothes people wore.

In the north, rather than the south, women tended to wear a shawl and kerchief; in the south-west they sported pinafores. Market women always wore white aprons; older women continued to wear their frilled caps inside their bonnets in the early decades of the twentieth century and sunbonnets for working in the hayfield.

By the 1820s many working women were wearing out-of-fashion clothes handed down by mistresses to their servants and then sold on, but country women still wore

wet felt hat of this type on to a peg as you came home, it would dry into interesting shapes and became a very personal item. The hard felt billycock hat (said to have been named after William Coke, nephew of the Earl of Leicester) had become standard wear by the mid-19th century. Cloth caps were not worn until the end of that century, but became universal in town and country by the 1930s and are still worn occasionally by elderly farm workers even now.

a shift, petticoat, leather stays and kerchief until the mid-19th century. Others wore cotton print gowns and used the offcuts for making patchwork quilts. Gertrude Jekyll remembered that in her youngest days the typical outfit was a print gown and apron, with either a cotton print sunbonnet (usually in pale lilac) with a deep curtain, or a plain straw bonnet with a ribbon under the chin, and kerchief shawl over the shoulders. Women wore mob caps, indoors and out; outside the cap would be covered with a straw hat, and by the 1850s both had been discarded in favour of a stiff, ruched and frilled sunbonnet that covered the neck, shoulders and head. There would be a flat black felt cap over the top on market days or a black satin bonnet for church.

Indoors, working women continued to cover their hair until the 20th century, but it was not until World War II that women took to wearing headscarves. The women of Llangwm, in Wales, wore tall steeple hats – that had been seen in other parts of Britain in the 17th century – them as they walked to Tenby to sell oysters and prawns.

Working skirts were shorter than fashionable ones and generally showed the ankles; skirts were frequently bunched up out of the way – women cocklers would pull their underskirts between their legs with string, almost forming culottes. Women always had aprons, whether indoors or out, and often wore two at once, generally without a bib. In the 20th century the aprons were replaced by flowered cotton overalls or pinafores.

In the 1890s some of the older women farmworkers took to wearing trousers, and during World War I trousers became common, as they and dungarees were among land girls in World War II. By 1900 most of the country sunbonnets had been cast off in favour of hats to keep off sun and weather.

Feet would be shod in boots or stout shoes. Women also wore pattens (clogs with a wooden sole, leather toe piece, leather bands tied over the instep and an oval iron hoop fixed underneath on two short legs) to keep their feet dry and clean of mud in the days before rubber galoshes became useful in the 1920s.

▼ THE TYPES OF HAT WORN IN THE FIELD *had a little more variety by the 20th century. One old carter in Sussex in the 1920s always wore a bowler hat – and he also wore it in bed 'to keep the rain off'. He used to sow wheat on his cottage's raggedy thatch to keep the wild birds busy and thus away from his peas. When the wheat crop ripened he moved his hens on to the thatch to clean it up.*

▲ MINING AND QUARRYING *could provide an alternative to agricultural work in some regions, and brought new economic life to rural villages. These industries also increased the wealth of local landowners, who in turn would often reinvest in the village by building homes for the workers.*

New rural industries

Industry was what kept many villages alive. One major industry that sprang directly from agricultural produce was the conversion of wool into cloth, an industry that involved many skills and many stages, which were often carried out in hamlets and villages. In several important wool regions this led to the setting up of rural fulling mills, especially in hilly districts where there was adequate water power to drive the big hammers for thickening and cleaning woven cloth.

Then there were all the mining industries on which so many villages depended – coalmines in County Durham and South Wales, for example. Elsewhere there were brickworks that extracted local clay, glassworks and cement works that depended on local minerals, or ironworks that depended on local iron ore deposits and the power of the streams to drive the iron hammers. The Sussex Weald, now so rural, was once the centre of charcoal-fuelled

ironmaking in the 16th century and right up to the end of the 18th, when it ceded its position to the coal-rich Black Country. All of these industries were situated in 'the countryside', not the towns, and provided alternative employment for the villages.

The history of the small parish of Highley, in Shropshire, has been described in Gwyneth Nair's study of the development of its community from 1550 to 1880. Highley is situated in an area that provided coal, ironstone and building stone but is mainly agricultural. Farming was virtually the only occupation until the local mineral resources of Highley and neighbouring parishes began to be exploited in the 1780s, leading to a more than doubling of Highley's population by the early 19th century and considerable changes to the social and economic life of the village. New stone cottages were built for the influx of those who worked in the mines and quarries. The building of canals in the 1770s had

increased the river traffic and new jobs were available to wharfmen and bargemen, along with the trades needed to sustain the boats. By 1811 more families were engaged in manufacture and trade than in agriculture, though there was a major hiccup in this trend when a local colliery closed and from the 1840s to the 1870s most men were once again working in agriculture and in services related to it such as milling and tree felling. In the 1861 census there was a new category of worker: the railway navvy, with a large number of men helping to construct the Severn Valley Railway (opened in 1862). Twenty years later the majority were working in the mines and quarries again. The women, meanwhile, continued to go into service as domestic servants (the younger single women), and in the second half of the 19th century more and more women had jobs as nurses, housekeepers, charwomen, lacemakers and dressmakers (one of the latter was described quaintly as a 'mantua maker'), as well as teaching, shop keeping and inn keeping, quite apart from part-time and casual field work.

Throughout all these fluctuations in the main source of work, various trades could flourish: Highley had its own glazier, plumber, joiner and bricklayers in the village's building boom during the early years of the 19th century, and the increase in population at that time meant there were also shoemakers, blacksmiths, a tailor, a weaver and several seamstresses. After 1815 there was a butcher and a chandler; three pubs opened in the 1840s and a small grocer's. In the 1850s, in spite of mines and quarries, Highley could still be described as a pleasant rural village 'noted for its extensive orchards and the excellence of its cider'.

For much of the 20th century, villages all over the country have been crying out that their economies are slowly dying and that they are increasingly peopled by those who work elsewhere. In some villages the trend has been reversed deliberately. Between the two world wars, for example, new industries were set up in the countryside, such as sawmills, agricultural engineers, joinery shops and milk-processing centres, usually in larger villages. They gave the villagers better wages and working conditions and brought new money into the village's existing trades.

▲ **BULK MILK TANKERS** *could collect the milk from many farms and transport it to milk processing factories. The tankers began to replace the old system of individual churns, collected from the end of the farm track. Farmers had to change their ways and install their own refrigerated bulk milk tanks in the farm dairy, so that their new automatic milking machines could take milk straight from the udder via pipes to the bulk tank and the lorry driver could take the refrigerated milk straight out of that tank into his refrigerated bulk tanker.*

▼ **DEMAND FOR QUALITY MILK INCREASED** *between the two world wars, and milk began to be tested for bacteria and impurities on the farm on a regular basis, along with levels of butterfat and protein. In 1950, after several decades of tuberculin testing of on-farm milk, there began a major campaign to eradicate tuberculosis entirely in dairy cows, as humans could be infected from their milk. This led to mass slaughtering in infected herds.*

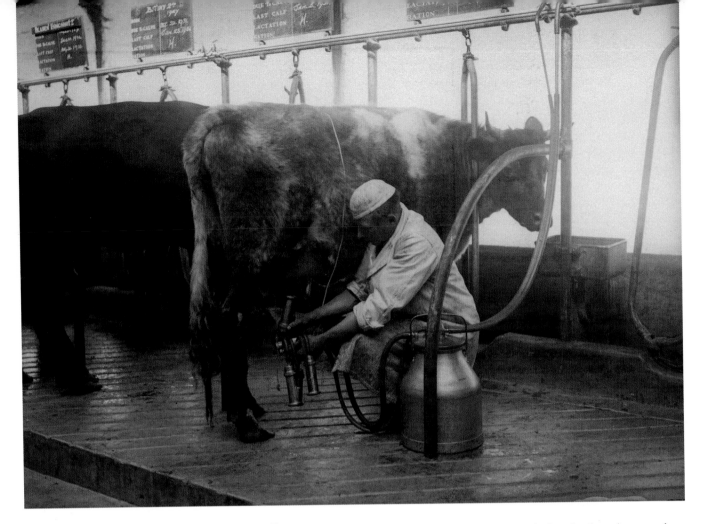

▲ **AN EXPERT HAND MILKER** *can milk ten to fifteen cows in the morning, and the same again in the evening. A machine-milker can deal with hundreds, rather than a dozen. In 1939, eight years after this photograph was taken, just 15% of the UK's dairy cows were being milked by machine rather than by hand. Today all commercial dairy cows are machine-milked.*

Milk processing

Lapford is about ten miles north of Exeter. It was a farming village, with Crediton and Chulmleigh as its markets, and most of its young either went on the farms or left the village as there was no other choice of employment. Even when the railways and, later, buses made local travel possible, agricultural wages were inadequate for more than the very occasional journey. There was nothing in the village to attract tourists or anybody else. Then in 1927 the Ambrosia Milk Company established a milk processing factory at Lapford, in spite of many initial local objections as people anticipated some smoke-blackened factory in their midst, or that the new factory would lure all the men off the farms and all the girls too. When the company offered to supply the whole village with electricity it was refused ('Oil lamps are good enough for us!') and when they offered to buy milk from the farmers many of them refused too – 'I've never sold milk, and butter will always be made on this farm while I'm still here!'

But the factory was duly built, and it employed 90 people, about half of whom were born within ten miles of Lapford. It set new standards in local employment: the working day was eight and a half hours and there was a half-day holiday each week and a fortnight's paid holiday as well – unheard of in such a rural area. The men earned as much as £2 to £2 10s a week, and the women about £1 7s 6d, which meant that girls could often take home more money than their fathers who were working long hours on the farm. The 50 per cent of the employees who were not immediately local, the 'foreigners', came to live in the village as householders or lodgers, all of them spending some of their wages in the village and boosting its economy in general. New houses were built; farmers had a market for their milk right on their doorstep and farm rents rose. The company provided various welfare schemes for its employees, including a social hall, which was made available to the rest of the village as well, sparking off several new activities and interests, especially for the young. The girls began to wear smart clothes instead of their habitually dull and dowdy ones; the boys owned bicycles, motorbikes and occasionally an old car. Lapford had come alive, and would remain so as long as this single major local employer survived.

Dartington

In the 1920s Dartington Hall, also in Devon, was derelict and roofless and its estate of some 2,000 acres was thoroughly run down. But Leonard and Dorothy Elmhirst had a dream, and took the estate in hand and created something unique. They wanted to develop all the resources of the estate (not just agricultural ones) and they wanted to discover if rural resources could yield a reasonable return on capital invested, given adequate capital and efficient organisation. To do this, they worked under normal industrial conditions, sold on the open market and struggled through ten years of disorganised international trade. They did not expect immediate returns: for example, they had 200 acres of woodland doing nothing in particular and had problems in finding adequate information about exploiting this asset without impoverishing it. The first ten years were exploratory in this respect and this was the same for the many other small industries that they wished to locate on or near the estate – weaving, pottery, woodland crafts, poultry breeding and so on.

Social values were as important as economic ones in their vision and they created an experimental coeducational boarding, day and nursery school and developed schools of art, drama, dance and music that extended their services to local villages, several of which developed outstanding drama and dance groups of their own. Then they thought about the many people working on the estate, initially as builders: should they be brought to live within the estate? Should trade unions be encouraged? Should wages be higher than elsewhere in the area? Should they organise 'welfare work' for the employees? They worked through the ideals and the problems and by the late 1930s Dartington Hall had reinvigorated a declining rural area and was influencing the cultural and economic life of local people in many different ways. Its story continues to this day.

▼ GLASSMAKING *is usually done on too large a scale to be described as a rural industry, but before World War I a Yorkshireman opened a glass works near St Ives in Cornwall. In 1921, when the works reopened after the war, they used broken bottles from chemists as their raw material to make new bottles. A lump of molten glass from the furnace was put on the end of a long tube and the worker blew to hollow out the lump as the glass began to harden, turning his work all the while. The outside shape of the bottle was created by pressing it into a mould while the glass was still soft.*

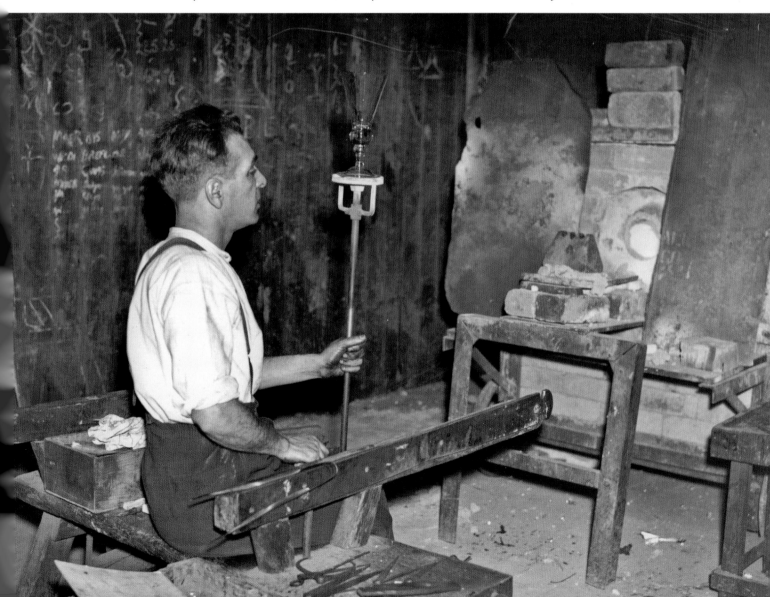

6. Work on the Land

Agriculture was the main source of employment in rural areas but with increasing mechanisation the size of the land labour force dropped dramatically. A major influence on farming was the effects of two world wars. Before then, traditional agricultural work relied on a large labouring force in arable fields, with crowds of extra workers brought in from the towns for casual work as needed. Farm workers also included those who worked with the horses that provided most of the power for agricultural machinery and for carting loads from field to farmyard and from the farm to the markets. Others were specialists who worked with livestock – stockmen, milkers, shepherds. With World War II demanding a rapid increase in production, farmers switched quite suddenly from horse power and mass labour to tractor power, and everything began to change in the countryside. Intensification became the master; but fast-changing circumstances in more recent times have demanded adaptability and diversification on the farm.

In 1851 there had been 1,778,000 farm workers in the country; in 1901 there were 1,399,000; in 1961 there were only 220,000 and the National Economic Development Plan of 1965 anticipated that the level would, and should, reduce even further: 'By continuing to improve its productivity, agriculture would continue to release substantial manpower resources to other industries.' In 2003 1.8% of the UK's total employed workforce was in farming, compared with 2.8% in 1984.

Farming fluctuates wildly in the public estimation of its importance. During wars, when these islands are so vulnerable to blockade, people suddenly realise that if they don't eat, they die, and they want to plough up everything in sight. In times of peace, they decide that manufacturing or services are far more important than agriculture and the whole country should be one big factory instead of one big farm.

The effects of war

World War I had a rebound effect in the countryside. After a huge effort to feed the country in times of war, in peace agriculture crashed. Among those who were hit hardest by the agricultural depression of the 1920s and 1930s were, sadly, the war heroes who had started a new life on the land with small farms and smallholdings. They often lost everything, and quite a few became tramps, trudging the lanes in ragged clothes and sleeping in farmers' barns.

Farmers in general abandoned intensive arable farming, dumped their implements and returned to pasture and animal husbandry, the old dog-and-stick way of farming, or set up their own milk rounds by pony and cart, or left the land for good. Three million acres went out of production in England and Wales between 1918 and 1932, half of it simply deteriorating to virtually derelict rough grazing land. Wages for farm labourers had been fixed during the war at quite a good rate, but after the war the farmers could not afford to pay them and simply shed their staff. One advantage of farming for meat and milk was that you could do much of it yourself, with the help of a cowman or two, instead of the dozen men who had helped with the crops. So it was back to unemployment in rural areas and, all around, hedges and stone walls and cottages became neglected and derelict.

On top of the postwar agricultural depression came the devastating economic downturn that hit Britain in 1931. There were 3 million unemployed and a coalition National Government was set up to sort out the mess.

'One advantage of farming for meat and milk was that you could do much of it yourself, with the help of a cowman or two.'

◀ ANOTHER STEP IN MECHANISATION *for agriculture was the baler, which packed hay or straw into manageable oblong bales bound with wire (and later string). Previously, hay had been pitchforked loose into stacks and forked out again as and when it was needed, while harvested grain crops had been tied in sheaves with the grain heads still attached to the straw, to be stacked until it was time to thresh out the grain in the barn. The baler shown here (c. World War I) is operated by a pulley, driven by a steam engine. It was still necessary to fork loose hay into the baling mechanism by hand.*

The new government's aims included rescuing agriculture from total collapse, by subsidising certain crops, controlling food imports under certain circumstances, subsidising the cost of land improvements and giving limited protection to pig farmers, market gardeners and hop growers. The aim was to halt the decline in farming, just enough to keep it going, rather than boosting agriculture into a healthy condition. World War I had taught a lesson: if it ever happened again, Britain needed to grow her own food and the land needed to be kept ticking over ready for that. The policy was to store up fertility in peacetime so that it could be cashed in time of war.

By 1937 rural areas remained depressed, farming was regressing, land prices were rock bottom and workers were leaving the land for better prospects. But another war, always the saviour of agriculture, was looming and farming's 20 years of depression in the face of national indifference were nearly over. For a while. As George Martelli explained in his story of the Elveden estate: 'On 2nd September 1939 agriculture in Britain was

▲ THE TRADITIONAL METHOD *of broadcasting seed by hand persisted here and there in the early 20th century. Jethro Tull invented a horse-drawn mechanical seed drill in the 18th century but most workers were still resisting mechanical methods a hundred years later, though they might use a hand-pushed 'drill barrow'.*

▲ **MECHANISATION MARKED THE END** *of large groups of farm workers in the fields and in the farmyard. This group, photographed in 1870, would today be represented by only one or two men. Agriculture is now a minor employer in many rural areas, whereas in the past the breadwinners of nearly every family in the village would have been working on local farms.*

still a relatively unimportant and depressed industry. By noon of the next day it had become a major element of national defence.'

The farmers' war

When the nation heard Neville Chamberlain's declaration of war on Germany at 11.15 on the morning of Sunday 3 September 1939 (and almost everybody did hear it, on the wireless), more than 60 per cent of Britain's food was being imported. Self-sufficiency in food production at home became crucial to the outcome of the war and the farmers became heroes. Quite literally, within 24 hours of the declaration of war, the future of British agriculture was transformed because it had become an essential industry in everybody's mind, including the government's. Once again, the ploughs came out, but this time most of them were behind tractors rather than horses. In the first year of the war, in spite of a severe winter and a severe labour shortage with so many men joining the forces, two million acres were ploughed

and cropped. By 1944 it was 6.5 million acres, reclaimed from pasture, derelict land and even from moorland, marshes and mountainsides that had never been cultivated before. The farmers did all that was required of them and more. By the end of the war, British farmers were the most highly mechanised in the world and were lapping up everything the agricultural scientists could tell them. The country's conservative farmers grabbed new ideas with both hands.

The British now thought highly of their farmers, who were of course delighted but wary, remembering what had happened after previous wars. Everybody loves a farmer when they are hungry, but then what? For several years everybody continued to love the farmers, partly because there was a world shortage of food after the war. The government promulgated a new programme of agricultural expansion, with guaranteed prices as long as farmers did what they were told. Confidence returned: businessmen who had made money in industry were now falling over themselves to invest in farms.

In 1941 Frederick Smith, advising those who wanted to live in the country, recognised that the world he had known before September 1939 had gone for good. He had come to the conclusion that:

> The land must play an increasingly important part in our lives. Many people who lived in towns prior to 1939 will find in the country the solution of at least some of their problems … We are many of us going back to the land. To my mind, country life today is an ideal life for better reasons than the worship of an antique but obsolescent rural England … I contend that the country life is a partial answer to reduced incomes as well as to war-weary minds.

The optimism continued for quite some time, even though there were no more wars during the 20th century except for those fought in distant lands. Then towards the end of the century things started to go wrong again and the endless wheel of good times and bad turned sharply downwards. Again, only the best or the luckiest, or the most determined, will survive.

This farming business

In the 1960s the agriculture industry was poised between two worlds and hesitating about which way to go. The decision in favour of mechanisation had been made by the time of World War II but the next decision was a matter of scale. The average farm was still a family one and the choice seemed to be to become large and specialised or to revert to smallholdings.

Increasingly it would be the former. Farming was becoming big business, run by those who were trained at agricultural colleges rather than those whose knowledge of farming was imbibed with their mother's milk. By the 1990s the family farm was almost extinct in many parts of the country.

Here and there they tackled it in a different way. In the Devon parish of Loddiswell in 1958 the local farmers and

those of adjoining parishes formed a cooperative as a non-profit-making company to reduce their costs and improve their marketing techniques. Within a few years the company was supplying 800 farmers throughout South Devon, turning over more than £600,000 a year. It handled feed, fertilisers, seed, sprays and any farm or domestic equipment the farmers and their families needed. It sent calves to farmers as far away as Lincolnshire and Kent and weaner pigs to the Midlands, obtaining much better prices than individual farmers might. Its buildings department employed 20 craftsmen and labourers. It was felt that tighter economic circumstances were changing farming into an industrial business rather than a way of life. 'The farm labourer

> *'There used to be an urban assumption that country workers were simple people doing simple work.'*

▼ THE WHEELED PLOUGH *being used here would have one wheel in the furrow and the other on the unploughed land. The number of horses in a ploughing team depended on the heaviness of the soil. Lighter soils would be referred to as two-horse land, whereas teams of three or four horses were needed to drag a single-furrow swing plough through heavy soils. With an average ploughing speed of up to two miles an hour, it could take a full working day to plough one acre.*

of the past is almost redundant, and staff with specialist knowledge is becoming essential.' With increasing mechanisation, farmers had to know about engineering as well as about crops and animals.

There used to be an urban assumption that country workers were simple people doing simple work. But in agriculture you need – and always did need – a complex level of skills and above all ingenuity. Many of the skills were and are highly technical, and there is also a much greater need for self-reliance than in many more 'intellectual' jobs.

Agricultural work

Melon Green lived on a smallholding near Liss, Hampshire, but would camp on the South Downs at Rottingdean. Here he got to know a ploughman with two heavy horses, a man who never took a holiday because he so loved his animals. Then, in the late 1930s, the farmer for whom the ploughman worked died. A younger man took over the farm but said that by the end of the summer he would have to use a tractor, not the horses. Well, you can't say 'Woah', 'Gee-whut-ah' or 'Mither-wee' to a tractor, can you? Melon Green met the distressed ploughman that summer on the Downs, looking as white as a sheet at the thought of losing his horses. A while later he saw a picture in the local papers of the same man ploughing on the Downs, with the story that a thunderbolt had come out of a clear blue sky and killed him and his two horses stone dead.

Gertrude Jekyll, writing in 1925, noted that 'mechanical traction' was taking the place of horse power: 'Perhaps a few years hence we shall no longer see the jolly teams of horses starting out for the day's work or see them at work in the field or carrying the loads of farm produce along the roads. Are we to expect the extinction of those splendid breeds of heavy horse? Is all this living strength and beauty to give way to dead contrivances of unsightly iron?'

How often do you see the ploughman as he 'homeward plods his weary way'? How often do you see whole families in the fields, helping with the hay or the harvest? Consider the changes between the 19th century and the 20th, especially since World War II.

Ploughing

In the 19th century, arable land was worked by oxen and heavy horses, at a slow and steady pace. The ploughman, his hand guiding the plough and his eye maintaining a straight furrow, knew every inch of the fields that he walked. With his boots tramping the soil (he walked on average about 16 miles a day), he was in touch with the land and part of it. He worked up a sweat under the sun, he felt the jaw-numbing icy wind in his face and the rain on his back; he smelled the earth, saw the worms, felt the wingbeats of the seagulls that followed him, heard the sudden twittering of flocks of sparrows and finches as they rose ahead of him, stumbled on the stones, slithered in the damp patches, and all the while kept company with the animals that helped in his work, their rumps methodically swaying and dipping in front of him. His eyes were always looking ahead.

That might seem lonely, but at least he had the animals and he constantly talked to them, in the traditional language that guided them to press on or draw to a halt, turn a corner, edge right or left. He was in touch with living creatures and his rhythm was their rhythm, the hooves plodding carefully and regularly, harness jangling gently, the occasional swish of a tail. Even if his thoughts were elsewhere, his whole being was focused on where he was, in the field,

▶ THE ROMANTIC SIDE *of working with horses continues to this day with competitive ploughing matches. These events have a long history and used to give a boost to the everyday business of farming. Horsemen would take great pains to present their teams immaculately groomed, with the harness and equipment in perfect order, and with jingling horse brasses polished to sparkle in the sun. Presentation was almost as important as ploughing the perfect furrow, as this 1935 photograph shows.*

◀ THE CHANGE FROM HORSE POWER *to oil power was gradual, and there was an interlude when steam power was seen on the farms. For ploughing, two steam engines would be parked at opposite ends of the field and a 'drag' plough on a cable would be reeled back and forth across the ground from one engine to the other. This system could plough at least a dozen times more land than a horse-drawn plough in a day. It evolved into cultivation with mobile steam-powered traction engines.*

◀ HORSE-DRAWN REAPING MACHINES *began to replace hand harvesting with hook and scythe during the 19th century, and by the turn of the century inventors had created self-binding reapers, which bound the sheaves as well as cutting the standing corn.*

fields. The wives and children of farm servants were allowed to glean on the fields of the father's employer before the sheaves were lifted. If anybody else came along, they were roped off into an area where the sheaves had already been removed: there would be a horse at either end of the rope to move the line down the field as the sheaves were taken off. The gleaners popped their bounty into apron pockets and kerchiefs, threshed what they had gleaned and then took it down to the mill for grinding, free of charge. They could gather enough to keep them in bread through most of the winter.

Gertrude Jekyll, who had been a rural child in the 1840s and 1850s, watched the changes in farming practice with interest. 'Nearly the whole of the change from hand labour to machine work in agriculture has taken place within my recollection,' she wrote in 1904. She could remember when hay was mown with scythes and made with forks and wooden hayrakes – you only needed these three tools to make hay, and they would hang in the labourer's back kitchen or outhouse. But for haymaking in late Victorian times they needed a number of horse implements: mowers, kickers and tedders to air the hay for drying, swathe turners for turning it and finally horse rakes. All of these mechanical tools needed plenty of maintenance, repairing and space for storage, on top of which you needed at least a pair of horses to work them. And all of this would be used for perhaps only three or four weeks in the year.

Jekyll wondered if the days of cheerful gangs of haymakers and harvesters had gone forever – all those lovely memories of well-earned meals eaten sitting under the shady side of the hedge or a large oak.

Today haymaking and harvest are of concern only to the farmer and the farmworkers. The village might watch, and perhaps complain, while the crop travels along the lanes; the children might thrill to the majesty of the huge combine harvester wheezing into life in the morning and then relentlessly moving up and down and around

in the furrow, behind the animals. In contrast, today the tractor driver rarely uses his legs. He is isolated in his cab, insulated from the weather and from the living world that surrounds him. He plugs his ears and links with the world of the radio, its music jarring against the birdsong and his tractor engine's rumble travelling across the fields.

Both men will be tired and grimy by the end of the day; both will have their resentments and their worries; but perhaps the ploughman will have had a richer life than the tractor driver, and he will have been surer of his place in the scheme of things.

Haymaking and harvest

The greatest contrast is at the culminations of the farming year. Victorian haymaking and harvest often involved most of the village – farm labourers, women and

children, granddads and grannies, aunts and uncles, school teachers glad to escape the school room on a summer's day, a few others deserting their normal work in order to join in with the hard labour and the good company of these great village occasions. There was a strong sense of communal purpose, an understanding of the rhythm of nature's seasons, a sense of urgency to make the hay or to harvest the grain before the weather turned, a sense of celebration and security when the crop was finally in and winter could be faced in the knowledge that there was fodder for the animals and corn for the mill. And then, of course, there was the harvest-home supper, highlight of the year and the chance to stuff yourself silly.

After the harvest came gleaning, with women and children picking up the often substantial quantities of grain left in the

the field to fell the head-heavy stems and devour them, spitting out the straw. They might hear the chunter of the baling machine scooping up hay or straw, packing it tight and tying it with brightly coloured twine as if there were a hidden gang of gnomes working within its bowels; or, today, wrapping individual bales each the size of half a stack in black plastic (how romantic is that?). They might watch the bales being loaded on trailers and carted away; they might watch a succession of tractors individually shadowing the combine to catch

▶ THE SYSTEM OF STACKING LOOSE HAY *and then forking it by hand into a stationary mechanical baler would in due course be replaced by mobile balers that could pick up sun-dried hay straight from the field rows. Straw baling became more efficient with the invention of the combine harvester, which in a single operation harvested the crop, separated out the grain, poured the collected grain into tractor-drawn trailers to be taken straight to the grain store, and delivered the straw in rows in the field ready for the mobile baler.*

▼ BEFORE THE INVENTION OF THE MECHANICAL BALER, *loose hay or bound sheaves of grain were stacked in the rickyard. Until mechanical elevators were developed, loading the carts in the field and then building the stack was entirely by hand with pitchforks.*

▼ NOMADIC GROUPS OF CASUAL WORKERS *were essential for the labour-intensive work of harvesting in the large market gardening areas. Peas needed to be picked and transported to market rapidly while they were in their prime. The workers stripped the pods off the plants and put them in bags and hampers; the remaining foliage was uprooted and left to dry on the ground before being carted for animal fodder, but peas for canning factories were delivered still on the whole plant.*

cascades of grain in their trailers; they might watch trailers loaded with wilted silage haring along the lanes in busy convoys. But they would only watch; they would not take part. The men in their machines would be working more or less alone in the landscape. The community spirit is no longer at work in the fields; hence it is hardly surprising that much of the community is divorced from the farms and no longer understands or sometimes no longer sympathises with them.

Field workers

Farmers now employ very few workers. A farm that might have had a team of a dozen men now has only one or two. In the parish of Bedingham in Sussex at the end of the 18th century, there were 25 households.

One farm maintained 23 labourers from the parish (all but three of them married, with 41 children between them); another maintained two labourers, both married and with a total of eight children; at another it was 16 labourers supporting 38 children. The farmers themselves had in their own families 11, 5, 24 and 20 people. Three men, four women and 18 children were maintained by the poor-house, which was a very small proportion of the total population of 252 people – everybody else was on the farms.

Women labourers were common in 19th-century fields, although they earned much less than the men. By the early years of the 20th century the sight of women field hands was growing increasingly rare, except in times of war when land girls took

on the work of men serving in the forces. In Northumberland you would still see women bent over their hoes in the turnip fields and here they were known as bondagers. In the old days labourers who had the benefit of living in tied farm cottages were bound to bring an assistant with them to work in the fields. The assistant would usually be a woman, traditionally dressed in kerchief and big straw hat; there would be gangs of women at work in the mud.

Hops and gangs

The towns sent casual job seekers out into the countryside at certain seasons. In particular there was the great annual exodus of hop pickers, with whole families from the cities coming out to the hop-growing areas for what was a combination of fresh-air holiday and the chance to earn some money. These crowds of women and children came by rail on 'Hop Picker Specials' and camped in fields and barns at the farms. The work was hard (they were paid by the bushel, monitored by a tally man with his wooden tablets) but good-natured, and many hop

pickers look back wistfully to happy times in the field, despite the very basic amenities of their living quarters. Ernest Pulbrook waxed quite lyrical in 1922: 'When dusk has fallen and the evening mists begin to rise the twinkling fires breaking out in lines and groups turn a Kentish valley or a Hampshire hillside into fairyland; the smoke billows upwards, and the children pass to and fro in the flicker like elves in a garden lit by glow worms.' Glow worms? Now there's a sight that has become rare in the countryside.

Hop picking in this traditional style died out during the 20th century. In the 1960s, in the Kentish village of Pembury, only one farm still used its oasts for their original purpose of drying hops, and only one family came down from London: the hops were picked by machine and the family joined about 14 local women merely to do the final checking for quality and the absence of leaves. Local orchards of cherries and plums had mostly been grubbed out by 1960 and replanted with apples, mainly Coxes, which were sprayed perhaps 14 times in a growing season.

▲ **WHOLE FAMILIES OF HOP PICKERS** *poured out of the cities in large numbers during the season for the chance to earn money by hard work in cheerful company. Hop picking had a high labour requirement – you needed two or three times as many casual workers to harvest hops as to harvest potatoes – and hop growing also had high capital costs in the network of poles in the gardens and setting up hop-drying kilns.*

'By the early years of the 20th century the sight of women field hands was rare, except in times of war where land girls took on the work of men serving in the forces.'

▲ ORPHANED LAMBS *and the weakest of triplets, or other lambs whose mothers could not suckle them adequately, would be cared for by the farmer's or shepherd's wife. The lambs needed bottle-feeding and warmth, and a temporary home in front of the range or even the inglenook fire was ideal.*

'She would rise at five in the morning to bring in the 17 cows and milk them before getting the children ready for school; then she would clean out the cowshed and feed the pigs'

Much less happy than the hop pickers were the gangs of casual workers, many of them women, who came to dig potatoes and harvest other vegetables in the huge market gardens that were so often found on the outskirts of the cities. They worked in the cold and the wet for very low wages and often at the mercy of unscrupulous gang masters; their countless untold stories would make miserable reading. This system continued well into the 20th century.

The farmer's wife

Where women gained full equality was in marrying the farmer. Farming was necessarily a partnership – in the good and the bad of it – and the woman's role was just as important as the man's. Quite apart from the shared physical work, she was frequently entrusted with the finances, chasing creditors, paying bills, paying wages and so on. Quite a few women were farmers in their own right as well, even as long as several centuries ago.

The life of a farmer's wife could be tough. Marian Atkinson, born in Cumbria, married a farmer in 1924 and raised 15 children with him, while at the same time helping with the farm work. She would rise at five in the morning to bring in the

17 cows and milk them before getting the children ready for school; then she would clean out the cowshed and feed the pigs. Perpetually pregnant, she thought nothing of heaving hefty bags of cattle feed or digging sheep out of snowdrifts, or bringing in 600 sheep at lambing time and helping them with difficult births. She naturally cooked for her huge family, kept the house in order, did the laundry and all the other countless unpaid jobs that women did; she never had time to go anywhere else, never had time to be ill, never had time to rest before or after giving birth, but she always made time to picnic in a field with her children, eating bread and jam, singing songs, telling stories and making daisy chains, and she always had time to notice the seasons, especially the beauty of autumn. She subsequently had 50 grandchildren, 82 great-grandchildren and five great-greats, and her life was typical of many country women in the earlier part of the 20th century.

Today family farms remain one of the few industries in which husband and wife work in partnership, and most of the women have such shrewd business sense that they could succeed in running any other business they choose. Equality for women came to the farm a long, long time ag

Land girls

So many men (and women) were called up during World War II – the thatcher, the rat catcher, the best bowler in the village cricket team, the squire's sons. The fields were emptying of men, as they had in World War I, though for World War II agricultural workers were generally exempt – they were crucial to providing food at home. The absent men were replaced by teams of land girls, volunteers in the Women's Land Army, often straight out of school and out of the town. More than 80,000 women became land girls and sometimes they brought a breath of fresh air into the country, with their different ways, their different attitudes, their sense of fun in spite of the hard labour to which they were put, their new faces and new stories. In some places they were mocked for their inexperience and their horror at many of the discomforts of rural living; but generally the men who worked beside them came to admire their guts.

▲ SOME OF THE LAND ARMY WOMEN WERE 'LUMBER JILLS' – *members of the Women's Timber Corps. Like the WLA land girls, the lumber jills received no recognition until at last medals were distributed in 2008, more than 60 years after the war had ended.*

▲ THE WOMEN'S LAND ARMY WAS FORMALISED *by the government in 1917, taking over from the Women's National Land Service Corps formed a year earlier. The Corps had been confined to educated women; the Army placed much less emphasis on a good education, but the women had to be prepared to work wherever they were sent and to sign up for as long as the war lasted.*

Land girls worked extremely hard: they drove tractors, loaded trailers, humped bags of potatoes, planted and weeded, pruned and harvested, milked cows, cleared out cowsheds and pigsties, caught rats and sometimes found themselves regarded as virtually slave labour by some farmers. After the war they were gradually demobbed over the next few years and the WLA was finally disbanded in 1951. Among many of the volunteers there was a sense of deep disappointment at the lack of official recognition for their contribution to the war effort.

Prisoners of war

Many of the land girls (and their woodland counterparts, the lumber jills) found themselves working alongside gypsies on piecework and also prisoners of war. Occasionally they had to fend off unwelcome advances from handsome Italians, but usually the men only flirted mildly. Many prisoners, though far from home and desperately missing their families, appreciated that it was better to be a PoW on the farms and in the woods than to be dead on the battlefield or lying seriously injured at a field station.

In the late 1940s, on the whitewashed walls of the extensive cellars under Grittleton House in Wiltshire, you could still see pictures 'painted' with candle smoke by the PoWs who had been billeted there. Others were housed in Nissen hut camps in various parts of the country. Locals did not necessarily have much contact with them, though they saw the work parties in the fields and woods or mending roads and bridges, but there was more of a sense of pity for the men than anger or hatred against an 'enemy'. Sometimes a parson or squire would extend hospitality to the prisoners in many small ways, to make them feel less homesick. In return, prisoners often made little gifts for village children – charming small baskets fashioned from bark and twigs, for example, filled with woodland violets and primroses. At Osmington in Dorset some German PoWs who were clearing mines made toys

◀ **THERE WERE HUNDREDS OF THOUSANDS** *of prisoners of war in Britain during World War II, and those in camps in rural areas became valued as part of the farm workforce. Many were from farming stock and only too glad of the chance to work on the land. Members of the British and Allied armed forces also helped out on the farms from time to time.*

▲ PUMPKINS WERE RISKY PRODUCE *for smallholders, as the season for selling these big squashes was a short one and a poor growing season could jeopardise the whole crop. Pumpkins need warmth and water to grow to any size; and they need bees to fertilise their flowers (which open for just a day). They could be stored for several months over the winter in the right conditions.*

'*... the Board of Agriculture declared that all would be well in the rural world if every family had "three acres and a cow".*'

for every child in the village, and this much appreciated gesture has been commemorated in Osmington's very personal 'Parish Map', created under a scheme inspired by the environmental charity Common Ground in the 1980s.

After the war, a few of the prisoners made Britain their home; they had married local girls and set up as smallholders or builders or used other skills to make a living and a new life in the countryside.

Smallholders

A smallholding cannot really be defined. To governments, it is generally a farm of less than about 50 acres and often as little as just a couple of acres. In 1801, after the enclosures of the 18th century had deprived many of access to grazing land, the Board of Agriculture declared that all would be well in the rural world if every family had 'three acres and a cow'.

That phrase became well used, and was adopted by Eli Hamshire, born in 1834 as the seventh son of an agricultural labourer at Ewhurst Green, near Cranleigh, Surrey. Eli was a great one for writing to politicians

and the like and had grown up on his father's smallholding of three acres; at the age of only 14 he rented a field for himself (a little less than three acres) at £4 per annum, though for the first year all he managed to grow on it was horse mint and clover. Three years later he had become a chicken dealer as well.

Eli was a wily young man. For example, he also traded as a carrier and had a useful ruse for passing through tollgates: he would unhitch his horse from the cart, take the horse through on its own (for free) and then pull the cart through himself for a charge of only a halfpenny, instead of the sixpence it would have cost for horse and cart to go through together. Then he would give what he had saved to the first poor fellow he met on the rest of his journey. And if he decided his load was not worth putting the horse between shafts for, he simply packed the goods into a wickerwork frame strapped on his own back and walked the nine or ten miles to Guildford, bringing back in the same manner whatever the local shopkeeper needed from town, which was often a hundredweight of sugar. This was a man destined to do well in life (despite always wearing a short slate-coloured smock) and by the time of his death in 1896 he was a man of property who owned four houses, including a five-bedroomed bungalow he had built for his wife when she became wheelchair-bound after giving birth to a 14lb baby in 1881.

Above all Eli Hamshire became an author (and self-publisher), writing under the pseudonym 'A Carrier's Boy'. He was a man with strong political views that have variously been described as Liberal, Socialist and Communist. In numerous pamphlets and in his books *The Source of England's Greatness and the Source of England's Poverty* and *The Three Great Locusts*, he wrote about machinery, he wrote about vaccination, he wrote about the agricultural labourer and the oppressed in general, and threw in his views on nicotine, 'young women pinching their waists in', intermarriage, labourers' cottages, illegitimate children, homes for heroes, the game laws, pollution, the cost of fish, drinking, swearing, hunting, the workhouse, allotments, stepmothers … This particular smallholder had a very active mind indeed.

In the New Forest, it is still possible for smallholders to thrive, as the Stride family continue to do. They have commoners' rights, which not only keep the family tradition going but also help to maintain the forest in its familiar form. There have been Strides exercising those rights for at least 650 years and its ways are in their blood. Outside the cottage they have a few pigs, cows and calves, and of course they all ride and help in the annual round-up or drift to check the state of the free-ranging ponies and mark them to show that the grazing fee has been paid. In the New Forest and on many commons of old, rights included grazing for specific numbers of specific animals (ponies, cattle, goats, geese and so on), pannage for swine, and the right to collect firewood or to dig up turves (turbary) for fuel.

Donkeys and mules

The New Forest became a centre for mule breeding when the animals were much in demand in the United States (Southampton was a convenient port for shipment). During wars, mules became highly regarded by the Army and played a crucial role even in World War II, when they were notably used in Burma to carry weapons and other equipment over difficult terrain. After both world wars many a soldier remembered his experience of mules and recreated the partnership on the farm, using mules as agricultural animals.

Mules and donkeys (or asses) were essential to the rural economy, and to that of the towns, for several centuries. They were ideal for itinerant hawkers, for all manner of farm work, for drawing carts and, in the case of mules, even aristocrats' carriages. Mules could stand 15 hands high or more and the landed gentry liked to breed teams of milk-white mules for their carriages. Mules are donkey/horse hybrids, bred by putting jackasses to mares; they cannot reproduce and so any mule breeder must always start again with a jack and a mare. Hinnies are the other way round: the sire is a horse and the dam a jenny. You can tell which species was the father by looking at the hybrid's head.

Farmers used pannier-laden asses to carry turnips to sheep in winter, to pull light

▼ DONKEYS OR ASSES *were the common beast of burden in the English countryside until the 20th century. At one time fish carts would be pulled by large dogs rather than donkeys, taking fresh fish from the coast to the city markets and covering the distances many times faster than any donkey.*

carriages on the roads and even to haul canal boats. Droves of 30 or more donkeys, each loaded with three bushel-bags of sand, would travel from the Wiltshire village of Cherhill in the late 19th century for journeys of 50 miles; one of the donkeys would be laden with pots, pans and blankets as the drovers slept rough along the way. The teams belonged to Old Aaron Angell and Levi Brittain, and when they died the donkeys were replaced with horses and then motorcars.

In Devon mules and asses were in full-time employment carrying sand from the shores to other parts of the county. The poor, patient donkeys would be given loads that were no smaller than those on the accompanying big mules and horses. They could be bought for about 25 shillings and seemed to live on thistles and whatever else they could glean from the verges, hedgerows and fields, but lived to a considerable age even on that regime. Mules, on the other hand, would cost about £15 to buy.

Donkeys were the cottager's friend as well as the itinerant's, but were all too often abused with overwork and neglect. In some centuries they had unexpected periods of being in demand when wars requisitioned horses from farmers and they turned to the reliable old donkey instead. They probably reached their peak in Britain during the 19th century, both on farms and country lanes and as town pack animals. They were ridden by miners, they pulled lawnmowers, they worked treadmills, they drew rubbish carts, they delivered the milk – and in London there was a substantial number of milch jennies, which were taken to the houses of rather wealthy Londoners and milked in the street for the sustenance of their children. They became costermongers' beasts of burden and cart pullers, and would take the family for outings on Bank Holidays. In Ireland they seemed to be everywhere, laden with goods on their backs or pulling carts. In England they found a new role on the beaches, giving rides, and they still do now, though much less so than 50 years ago.

The donkey's dramatic decline was really brought about by motorised vehicles. In the 1920s there were said to be only 100 donkeys in the country (patently untrue, as there were more than that on a handful of beaches). For some 40 years the donkey world went rather quiet, until in the 1960s donkeys suddenly became in demand as pets. They are rarely worked in Britain today, except by enthusiasts; they more often find themselves keeping lone horses and ponies company. Abuse through ignorance of their real needs persisted and countless numbers of donkeys ended up with rescue centres every year. For an animal that is so patient, loyal and uncomplaining, that is not a good state of affairs, but it is improving and the future for donkeys looks brighter. Maybe there will be new work for donkeys one day.

Horses and oxen

The age of the working horse was surprisingly brief. The traditional working animal on British farms was the ox – a castrated bullock. Sussex was one of the last bastions of working oxen. The deep red, massive Sussex breed was ideal for the job and at least one pair of them was still being worked in the 1990s. Arthur Beckett, writing in 1909, described a ploughing match in

▲ TEAMS OF OXEN WERE USED FOR FIELDWORK *and roadwork in times gone by. They were slower than horses but cost less to rear and maintain and worked more steadily and with more determination. Their average speed was 2–2½ miles per hour, a rate at which they could plod on for seven or eight hours a day as long as they had ample time for grazing. They had the additional advantage of being good for the table when their working life was over.*

▲ **WORKING HORSES REQUIRED MORE ATTENTION** *and equipment than oxen. As well as the animals themselves, the harness and tack needed to be kept in good condition and the stable as well. This photograph of a Lakeland farmyard shows advantage being taken of the overhanging store to air some of the harness, blankets and other horse paraphernalia.*

which a team of six black bullocks yoked to a plough of the old type caught his eye on the South Downs. It was a fine sight but sadly he knew of only three teams of oxen even in Sussex by then: one at Chyngton near Seaford, one at Southover near Lewes and a team of 'dun-nut' coloured plough oxen on the Possingworth estate at Waldron. His description of the dignified black ploughing-match beasts with long, wide-swept horns, marching up and down the furrows at a leisurely steady pace, harnessed with heavy wooden yokes and guided by a boy directing them with the slightest touch of a long pole, is superb. They were competing directly with equally splendid teams of horses that were 'sleek, fat and of great strength', their coats gleaming, manes and tails plaited with bright ribbons, polished brasses reflecting the November sunlight and their gait proud. As you read his story, you can almost smell the freshly turned soil and the sweat of the ploughmen as they followed their animals.

In North Devon the cattle, like those of much of southern England, were blood red and stocky, ideal as draught oxen. It was claimed that the Devon breed was the best in the country for its 'docility, activity, and hardihood' as a working animal. But not just anybody could work a Devon ox. The local ploughboy had 'a peculiar mode of cheering

▲ **AN ESSENTIAL PART OF A WAGONER'S JOB** *was the extra hours devoted to feeding, grooming and generally caring for the horses, quite apart from the actual working of them between the shafts. A wagoner's day might start as early as 4am to prepare the horses for their work, and end with cleaning each animal thoroughly, rubbing them dry and feeding them again, before bedding them down in the stables and heading home as late as 8pm in the summer months.*

them on, with a song he continually chaunts in low notes, suddenly broken, and rising a whole octave. The ceasing of the song is said to occasion the stopping of the team.' On flinty soils the oxen were properly shod: the smith would shackle the animal and throw it down on its side and accomplish the shoeing within the hour. The shoes lasted several months, as long as there was not much roadwork, and the price of shoeing was up to 20 pence per animal.

Oxen were quite rapidly giving way to horses on the farms and the local roads as the 18th century rolled into the 19th. By the end of the 19th, about 2.6 million horses (out of the British total of 3.3 million) were working in either agriculture or trade. But after that war there was an agricultural depression and to cap it the combustion engine was in direct competition with horse power. On the roads it was motorised lorries; on the farms it was tractors. In 1920 the government census revealed that there were about 1.4 million draught horses in Britain, half of which were working in agriculture. After World War II the victory of engine power over horse power was virtually

▲ **THE HORSES ALWAYS CAME FIRST.**
In the field, the ploughman would ensure that his team had their nosebags and a good drink mid-morning before he settled down to his own field meal. Watering was more often from a pond or stream than from a trough.

▶ **A GOOD HORSEMAN** *would ensure that his charges were given a little work even when the weather was frosty or snowy, to keep their feet and legs in good condition. To prevent slipping in frosty conditions the shoes were 'roughed', usually by inserting special 'frost nails'. An alternative was to remove the shoes and alter them by turning down and sharpening the 'heels' (the outer heel being turned across and the inner one in the direction of the shoe) before replacing them.*

complete, and the heavy horse was pushed firmly into the sidelines. By the 1980s the total number of all types of horse in Britain was probably somewhere between half and one million (nobody really knows); of these, at a guess, perhaps 8,000 were heavy working horses, with these numbers decreasing.

'Carthorse', incidentally, is not a good name for these big animals. The big draught horses were perfectly capable of pulling hefty great wagons with at least four wheels.

Livestock farming

One of the big revolutions in the countryside has been the change from mixed farming – the family farms that grew a bit of this and a bit of that, generally in small fields, and had animals as well as crops, partly for sound husbandry reasons, partly in order to be self-sufficient and partly from a dislike of putting all your eggs in one basket.

The feeling, and experience, was that if cattle prices were disastrous, corn prices were likely to be good; if pigs crashed (as

they often did and do) then sheep would see you through. Today, mixed farming is rare; most farms are either arable or livestock, and the latter specialise in either cattle or sheep, pigs or poultry, but not usually a combination of them.

As for the animals themselves, they have changed hugely during the past three centuries or so. Before the 18th century, farm animals were just farm animals, and the breeding and management of them was something of a hit-and-miss affair. It was a matter of 'Four stiff standers, four dilly-danders, two lookers, two crookers, and a wig-wag'.

Then in the 18th century along came the 'improvers', remarkable individuals who revolutionised British agriculture, including its livestock. Britain was way ahead of the rest of the world in the latter by the end of that century.

In the 20th century, for the first time in Britain's history, the great majority of people have no knowledge or understanding of

livestock. Those who have moved out of their towns and into 'the country' may take offence at the everydayness of the animals – the dawn crowing of a healthy cockerel glad to be alive, the bawling of a bulling cow looking for a mate, the raucous squealing of pigs at feeding time, the braying of a donkey. Then there are the country smells of sweet silage and of slurry spread on the fields to manure them and of acrid chicken litter.

Livestock farming has always been less labour-intensive than the work of growing and harvesting crops, but even so the advent of mechanisation has reduced the number of stockmen in relation to the number of

▼ SHORTHORN CATTLE *were the major breed in Britain, spreading out from their original bases in Durham and Yorkshire to become dominant as a dual-purpose milk-and-meat animal, and also becoming hugely influential in many countries overseas, including in tropical regions. Their popularity began to wane from the 1950s.*

▲ DAIRY COWS ARE CREATURES OF HABIT, *and when villages and lanes were free of traffic, the cows would wander home from the fields to the milking parlour at the usual time with very little need for guidance from their keepers.*

'The milkers no longer have jobs; the cows no longer have names, but numbers; the cowman has a computer and the cows wear transponders around their necks'

inhabitants, and the countryside became a factory for urban areas. It has remained so ever since, with subsequent governments encouraging more intensive production of cheaper and cheaper food, putting the producers on a treadmill that they cannot escape. This has had enormous ramifications in the countryside – for its landscape, for its social structure, and for its attitudes.

Milkers

Ma Snooks, born in Dorset in the first decade of the 20th century, was fond of harking back to her girlhood, when she milked cows by hand. She could manage seven cows an hour (if they behaved

animals they tend considerably, so that here again the number of people employed to work in the industry has been slashed.

Stockmen

With animals, you can form a relationship, whether of mutual respect or affection, dominance or distrust; it is a two-way affair. Because it is a living relationship, good stockmen cannot be clock watchers: they are responsive to the needs of their charges as they arise. Animals need to be fed and watered every day of the year, including Sundays and Christmas Day – days when they invariably create a crisis by escaping from the field, falling ill or dropping dead. All that is changing, of course.

Mechanisation is distancing the stockman from the animals. It might be making the daily work easier, but it has also meant the loss of many jobs among those who used to look after the animals, so that in turn there are fewer agricultural families in the countryside. Their individual voices are becoming fainter and fainter, and they feel increasingly isolated in rural society.

With two world wars, Britain looked to its livestock farmers to produce more and to produce it quickly. In fact this intensification began during the rush from country to town during the Industrial Revolution, hence the great interest in scientific breeding of livestock in the 18th and 19th centuries. Farming methods changed in order to produce large amounts of meat and milk to meet the demands of towns and cities that could no longer produce them for their own

themselves) and she loved it, but to the end of her life she would drink only tinned evaporated milk; she was too well aware of what else had gone into her pail.

Those of us who have hand-milked house cows appreciate how hard on the hands it must have been to milk at Ma Snooks's rate, but there are far fewer of us now. Fifty years ago there would have been countless villagers able to turn their hand with practised ease to milking.

Things have changed for the dairy farmer. In Ma Snooks's youth, the herds were still small enough for a family to manage – often no more than a dozen. Those of an older generation can certainly remember a time when every local farm and most smallholdings had a few milking cows, even after the last war. Today the cows are milked by machine in herds of at least a hundred, often twice or three times as many, managed by one person. In the old days it would have taken a person about 15 hours to milk one hundred cows, non-stop, or eight milkers to do what one machine can do in two hours. So the milkers no longer have jobs; the cows no longer have names, but numbers; the cowman has a computer and the cows wear transponders around their necks so that their allotted rations are delivered automatically – in some parlours today the cows are even milked by robots. Cowmen usually work

▼ WOMEN MILKERS *would always cover their hair when milking, partly because the technique of the expert involved pressing the forehead into the cow's often muddy flank, but also because any unwitting tickling would provoke an instant lash of the tail to swat away what the cow believed was a fly.*

alone, with their robots and machines, and you'll never see the likes of Hardy's singing groups of milkers again. It is a much lonelier job now than it ever used to be.

Shepherds

Sheep were once the source of many fortunes, in the long-ago days when they were farmed for their fleeces or for their milk. It all changed, and instead they were farmed for meat – initially good old-fashioned mutton but then lamb. The sheep industry is now carefully stratified: you have hill ewes in the uplands where not much else can be done with the land; you draught older ewes down the hill a bit to cross them with meatier rams for meatier lambs; and you take some of those lambs down to the lowlands to fatten or to be crossed with what are rather alarmingly known as terminal sires – nice stocky breeds like the Southdown and the Hampshire, for example, to make even meatier lambs. Wool is now almost irrelevant in the UK, although sheep are still shorn.

Among stockmen, shepherds have always been held in higher respect by their employers and regarded more romantically

by dreamers. Shepherding has changed much less than dairying. There isn't the scope for mechanisation and the old dog-and-stick method often persists in the hills except that, now, the shepherd often rides a quad bike. He (or increasingly she) relies on well-trained dogs but has a mobile phone to summon help in remote areas (if he is lucky enough for the mobile to get a signal there) and he probably practises preventive medicine on his sheep to a far greater degree than even 30 years ago.

Most of the old remedies have been cast aside or forgotten in favour of antibiotics and suchlike. Young shepherds today would look at you blankly if you asked them about bleeding sheep when there had been a case of pooke, or dosing sheep with turpentine for fluke, salting their hay to prevent 'the rot', grinding up hellebore for scab, using a mixture of train oil and brimstone or of sulphur and lard for fly strike, or chalk in milk for scouring and, better, a glass of gin with ground pepper for colic. But shepherds remain better stockmen on the whole than cowmen, because they remain closer to their animals, with no machines to distance them.

'Sheep washing was a tiring, cold, wet job and required several helpers'

▼ SHEEP SHEARING *was originally done by means of hand clippers, like outsize scissors. By the 1940s hand clipping was giving way to machine shearing, the example having been set by the Australians where shearing was a specialised occupation and where the sheep were shorn in huge numbers at speed. An early machine in the UK was powered by a hand-cranked wheel.*

A major controversy in recent years has been the regulatory dipping of sheep in persistent insecticides, which many claim are highly damaging to the health of the sheep farmer, let alone the sheep. In dipping, the aim is to ensure that the animals are wholly submerged, albeit briefly, in the dip mixture. The dip is deep enough to force them to swim, in which they need to be encouraged to keep going as sheep hate water, hate getting wet – hardly surprising when you consider the weight of a wet fleece.

Not to be confused with dipping was sheep washing, usually in the local river or stream. This took place in June about a fortnight before shearing, when the 'yolk' or lanolin grease had risen in the fleece. Washing was a tiring, cold, wet job and required several helpers. For example, two men might be suspended in barrels anchored to posts in midstream in a tidal river, rising and falling with the surge of the tide. The sheep were driven into the water and urged by the rest of the team, with the help of poles, to swim between the two men, who would grab them and rub the fleeces with their hands, then dunk the animals under the water for a thorough cleansing. Many places had special sheep-washing pools, some of

▲ SHEPHERDS WOULD GO TO EXTREMES *in caring for their flock. In this case a lamb had fallen in the Scottish Highlands and crofter-cum-fisherman Murdo Fraser, along with fellow crofter Roderick Fraser, used a rope to reach and rescue the injured animal and then carried it home to the croft. Every lamb counted.*

▲ POWER-DRIVEN CLIPPERS *made shearing much faster and much less tiring, but older shepherds continued to claim that hand clippers made a much better job with fewer nicks and a neater finish.*

them complete with a huge stone plug so that the water could be drained away. After washing came shearing, and here there has been mechanisation in recent years. The older shepherds used hand shears to clip the fleece; modern shearers use high-speed machines instead. The older shepherds placed a high value on the fleece; today wool is usually a negligible proportion of the farmer's income.

Shearers now are as likely to be teams of migrant Australians and New Zealanders as local shepherds. The teams are also taking over other aspects of shepherding in some areas, hired for a month or two here and there, usually at lambing, and always on the move. They no longer live alone for several weeks in isolated wheeled huts at lambing time, or build temporary lambing pens by hand on the hills and downs with wattle hurdles and thatch. It is more likely that the lambing ewes will be brought indoors to a barn close to the farmhouse.

Flocks of sheep pouring along the lanes on their way to market or to fresh pastures are now a rare sight in much of Britain. They are more likely to be piled into double-decker livestock lorries, packed tight so that they do not topple over with every bend in the road, noses pressing between the slatted sides for fresh air and a few querulous bleats plaintive above the sound of the engine. Some farmers do still move their flocks along the lanes on foot now and then, to the outrage of motorists in a hurry; the flock might be preceded by children, checking that every garden gate along the way is closed to keep the sheep out of the flowerbeds.

But there is still plenty of variety among sheep breeds, and strong regional identification with them. The big problem now is that people are putting large flocks of sheep on land unsuitable for the poor animals – wet lowland fields that were once the kingdom of cattle but that now rot the feet of sheep and attract flystrike and the subsequent maggots that can eat a sheep alive. The market for British lamb crashed to

'... there is still plenty of variety among sheep breeds, and strong regional identification with them'

the point where in the late 1990s some farmers were forced to kill their lambs and bury them, or give them to rescue centres, as feeding them was costing more than they could ever recoup by selling them.

Pig and poultry farmers

Perhaps the saddest change in the countryside is the disappearance of the livestock that bring landscapes to life. The fields are emptier and dull. With intensification, many animals have moved indoors since World War II: beef cattle are finished in yards and barns, out of sight; pigs used to rootle the fields but for the past 30 or 40 years many of them have been confined indoors, hidden from the general public to such an extent that people are surprised by just how big a real pig can be; chickens that used to scratch in farmyards are now, notoriously, reared intensively in cages or, at best, on deep-litter straw in barns.

Both pig and poultry farming have become major industries. By 1990, for example, some 80 per cent of all breeding

▼ THERE WERE TWO TYPES OF SHEEPDOG: *the collie (both rough- and smooth-coated) that most today would associate with sheepdog trials and which had endless energy and speed for gathering sheep out on the hills and moors; and the more sedate bobtailed Old English sheepdog that has since become a shaggy pet or show dog, and which some whimsically thought must have originally been crossed with a bear.*

▲ **SHEEP HAVE A STRONG TENDENCY TO BUNCH TOGETHER IN A FLOCK,** *which makes the herding of them simpler. However, the more primitive breeds such as the Soay have a very different instinct: they tend to scatter, especially at the approach of a dog, and rounding them up is much more of a challenge.*

sows in England were on only 2,500 units, with an average of nearly 250 sows per unit. Thirty years earlier the average pig herd size had been eight animals and there were 110,000 pig farms, run by families rather than companies.

Pigs used to be just pigs. Any colour, shape or size, whatever you fancied or whatever you could get. Regional types developed, and there seemed to be a general trend for white pigs in the north, coloured, spotted and splodged pigs in the Midlands and black pigs in the south (a very broad generalisation). Pigs belonged to cottagers or were in small groups on farms.

It was after World War II that pigs went commercial in a big way, partly because pig farmers did not receive government subsidies and had to do something to save their industry. So they began to specialise. In the 1950s and 1960s some gigantic pig-development companies emerged and they were brilliant at breeding just what the market needed, which seemed to be white

pigs with long bodies and with no fat on their backs or on their bacon. The white pigs were more efficiently reared indoors, except in a few eastern regions where they remained out in the fields but in large numbers rather than small groups. Eventually the great majority of British pigs were white and long-bodied and based on only two or three breeds. The rest became rare or minor breeds.

Therefore, the pigman's job became very different from that of the traditional swineherd caring for pigs on pannage, or even of the pigman of the immediate postwar years caring for outdoor saddlebacks and blacks. Today the pigman is likely to work with a very large number of animals, probably all indoors and probably all white. In almost impossible circumstances, pigmen struggle to retain their husbandry skills – for husbandry requires a recognition of individual animals and their needs. With intensification come all the diseases of stress and of too many animals together in one place. Modern pigmen sometimes know

▼ THE SMALLHOLDER *would rear a few pigs from his own sows, letting the animals range and forage if he had space for them to do so. The system in this photograph is a compromise: the pigs are in a large strawed yard with ample space and plenty of fresh air.*

more about regulations and drugs than about what makes a pig contented, and rarely have time to stand and stare, which is such a crucial part of animal husbandry.

Some farmers are now fighting back, and a bit of colour is returning to the pig scene.

But, as in every other livestock sector, as the 20th century turned to 21st, pig prices crashed and for many it was no longer worth trying to continue in pig farming.

The poultry industry has developed along similar lines and for similar reasons. After World War II, in contrast to sheep and cattle farmers, poultry farmers (like pig farmers) were without subsidies and had to become supremely efficient to survive. Scientific breeding was the secret of that survival, combined with scale, and during the 1960s in particular some very large poultry companies began to develop, dominating the industry. They did so by producing hybrids, bred for maximum production in intensive environments.

Hybrid hens were developed for battery units, in which all the birds' energy can be channelled into laying eggs; meat birds were developed for equally intensive broiler units. Poultry farmers no longer needed to shift homemade wooden arks around the field, scattering food on the grass and dust to supplement what the birds could find naturally. They no longer needed to collect eggs warm from the nest by hand, or search for them under the hedges. Everything was mechanised and, as with pigs, the nature of husbandry altered radically. Pigs and poultry, in a very few decades, have changed from being essential backyard animals for feeding the family to being factory animals produced to provide the supermarkets with cheap food.

In the past it wasn't all backyard farming, of course. In the 1870s the Oxfordshire villages of Fencott and Murcott were famous for duck rearing. George Dew of Lower Heyford visited these hamlets and wrote: '... of all the miserable places I ever saw these two are certainly the most miserable ... All the land lies so low that during winter it is partially inundated ... and when the water has subsided the fishy smelling miasma is to strangers almost unbearable ... There is only one sight worth seeing in either Fencott or Murcott, and that is their ducks in the several muddy pools; hundreds of white Aylesbury ducks as white as snow and altogether beautiful creatures contrasting strangely with

▲ BATTERY HENS ARE NOTHING NEW. *An intensive system of rearing chickens for the table was invented in the late 19th century in which the hen house was partitioned into individual wooden compartments, each confining one bird so tightly that it could not turn round or stretch its wings. At the time there were about 12 million chickens in Britain, but the country was importing 2–3 million eggs a day.*

the surrounding objects.' These ducks were destined for Smithfield market, and the locals could earn good money from the duck trade. By 1914, some of the local rearers were making a net 11–15 shillings per pair, which was handsome money at the time.

Diversification

Despite the sharp decline in agricultural jobs, farming remains a way of life for many in rural areas and they have been fighting to preserve it. In the 1980s the new buzzword was diversification and, to survive, farmers had to jump out of the age-old rut of corn-and-horn and try something new. They looked at what they already had – buildings, land, skills with livestock and plants, and so on – and then thought laterally. Some

tried different livestock (everything from snails and trout to llamas and ostriches) or different crops (a sudden rash of pretty blue flax and a few stabs at hemp). Some created farm parks open to the general public, who came to look at rare breeds of farm livestock or to watch cows being milked and lambs being born. A few went further and became showmen, creating full-scale travelling sheep shows, perhaps with a collection of all the breeds, or becoming professional demonstrators of their sheepdogs' skills, or working up the theme of 'back to back' – from shearing a fleece to producing the finished garment, with all the necessary processes in between. Others simply let in the film crews to use the farm and farmhouse as a period set.

Many of the new enterprises were based on welcoming the public on to the farm, which for some was a radical change of attitude from keeping people off it by fair means or foul. Old farm buildings were converted into living accommodation that could be let out to holidaymakers and weekenders in ventures that demanded a much greater input of capital but were less onerous in terms of daily work and less intrusive in the farmhouse than the good old bed-and-breakfast business. Farm walks and trailer rides were devised; farmhouse lunches and teas were offered. Some opened farm shops, selling their own produce (fresh, or 'value added' by processing on the farm) direct to their customers and usually selling produce from other farms and craftworkers as well.

▲ 'ORGANIC' METHODS *are returning farming to its traditional roots and in recent years the high premium placed by customers on organic food has been to the benefit of farmers prepared to invest in the long term in organic farming. Riverford Farms in Devon is a prime example of organic thinking on a big scale: the farms deliver boxed organic produce all over the country.*

◄ MANY FARMERS DIVERSIFY *by inviting tourists to the farm, offering holiday facilities such as camping in the fields or bed-and-breakfast in converted farm buildings. An added attraction is to involve visiting families in day-to-day farming, 'helping' with the milking, bottle feeding the lambs or collecting eggs, for example. For many children this will be their first hands-on experience of livestock.*

Some started mail-order businesses selling their own farm-processed ham, bacon and cheese or frozen meat. Many started pick-your-own centres, again bypassing the retailer and also avoiding the need to pay wages to picking gangs. Others invited groups against whom in the old days they would have almost taken up their shotguns: they offered facilities to caravan clubs, or for trail bikers and four-wheel-drive vehicles to have a bit of fun; they set up clay pigeon shoots, or allowed businessmen to play paintball games in the woods. And one imaginative farmer's wife started a home-based millinery enterprise specialising in high-fashion handmade hats for special, posh occasions.

For those who continue to rely on livestock in particular, however, the future in the early years of the 21st century is looking very black indeed and many are close to

despair. The levels of suicide among farmers remain alarmingly high and the feeling of alienation from an urbanised nation has become acute. The beef industry is almost as dead as meat on the slab; lambs and weaned pigs have been selling for far less than it cost to produce them; dairy cows were slaughtered in huge numbers as a result of the BSE crisis, which has cost farmers (and to some extent taxpayers) some £3 billion. Foot-and-mouth disease continues to reappear from time to time, reigniting passionate arguments about vaccination rather than mass slaughter, especially when the general public have witnessed huge piles of burning carcasses. To add to the woes, bluetongue arrived in the UK for the first time and hampered the movement of livestock from one region to another.

Rules and regulations emanating from Brussels and London are tying farmers

▲ AFTER GENERATIONS OF RESENTMENT
*against outsiders, some farmers are positively
encouraging ramblers and horse riders to use
their land by extending and improving the
network of footpaths and bridlepaths, and
offering picnic facilities – though perhaps not
always to travellers needing rather more than a
one-off picnic.*

in impossible knots and ruining what
is left of their livelihoods; supermarkets
absolutely control the prices they receive
for their produce and lay down impossible
production standards, and farmers no longer
feel they have any control at all over their
own industry. It is even worse for small
producers, staggering under the onslaught
of bureaucrats that seem determined to
aggregate farming so that they do not have
to bother with the irritations of smallness
of scale. Everything must be big and
centralised. Countless local abattoirs have

been closed in favour of the very large ones
that can afford to meet new standards; the
result is that livestock, already under stress
in any abattoir, certainly cannot be
slaughtered in familiar surroundings and
have to endure much longer journeys
to the abattoir, with the added stress of
being handled with the necessarily greater
impersonality of a large concern.

Writing in *The Times* in the summer of
1999, Roger Scruton railed against what
was happening in the countryside. The
manufacture of fertilisers required far more

▶ PICK-YOUR-OWN *was an early diversification for fruit farmers and market gardeners lucky enough to be close to centres of population. As well as being able to sell direct to the customer, it was a means of obtaining free labour!*

energy than could be yielded by the crops on which they were used; even more energy was wasted by the centralisation of food distribution, which demanded the transport of food on already overcrowded roads over great distances (the average distance travelled by a food item on a supermarket shelf was 3,000km). Local economies were dying from the emphasis on centralisation and scale. The very landscape was under threat because family farming was no longer practicable in so many places and the personal interest of those families in their surroundings was beleaguered from every side; and because the cry had gone up that huge numbers of new homes must be built in what was once the green and pleasant countryside.

And there was more. With suburbs, new towns and motorways spreading relentlessly across the land, more and more farms found themselves too accessible and suffered from vandalism and worse in the late 1990s. Poachers and livestock rustlers had become professionally ruthless armed gangs whom no farmer dared to confront; thieves swiped whole rows of newly planted trees and stretches of dry-stone wall (they took the latter from old churchyards, too); children would burn barns for fun; joyriders would dump scorched-out vehicles, and lorry-loads of rubbish would be fly-tipped in the fields; gangs would steal expensive farm plant and machinery to order, for selling overseas (the Home Office estimated that vehicles and plant worth £66.25 million were being stolen every year) and then return to steal the replacements. It is little wonder that, here and there, farmers have resorted to paying for security companies to patrol their land.

Since then, the situation has become worse in virtually all respects, except for those who have managed to cash in on the sudden demand for 'farm' land from developers or, increasingly, wealthy hedgefund managers who see land as a large green moat and playground around their new country homes. And no one should be surprised if in the end the farmers give up altogether. Who, then, will care for the countryside?

> '... the cry had gone up that huge numbers of new homes must be built in what was once the green and pleasant countryside.'

7. Keeping in Touch

The physical ability to move from one place to another has always been crucial. At first it was on foot in the lanes, then (in a gradually rising scale of speed and comfort) with the help of four-footed animals, especially those that pulled carts, wagons and carriages. Ease of travel depended on the state of the roads, of course, and the whole subject of making and maintaining local roads is an important one. Road improvements opened the way for country people to move even more conveniently, perhaps in carrier's carts (before there were public buses) and independently on bicycles, then motorbikes and finally in motor cars. Motorised transport has had far-reaching effects on the countryside, and so too has the creation of a railway network.

Communication is about more than physical transport, and rural life has also been transformed by the introduction of postal services, telephones, radio and television and, finally, the advent of computers and the internet.

In 1922, Ernest Pulbrook described country lanes as white roads winding through the great solitude of the countryside, with only occasional figures appearing at long intervals 'as spectres which come from nowhere and thither vanish; the labourer approaches a wayside cottage and is gone, the wagon is swallowed by the leafage of the lane, the fleeting motor-car dissolves in a cloud of dust'.

Most of the lane's users were on foot, picking up and distributing local and regional gossip as they passed, chatting with friends and strangers alike. Some of the more familiar traffic was already beginning to wane in those years immediately after the First World War: the big four-wheeled wagons pulled by teams of heavy horses no longer rolled on their long-distance journeys of several days, and horse-drawn coaches were being replaced by motorised vehicles. Even the famous Minehead-to-Lynton coach had been ousted by the 'remorseless motor-bus' from the road it had traversed for so long, and only middle-aged travellers had experienced the discomfort and drawbacks of coaching in winter.

Ironically, Pulbrook saw the motorcar as awakening the road into life again in lieu of the vanishing figures that used to walk the lanes or plod on the backs of donkeys, or clip along on horseback. Today country lanes are dominated by motorised traffic – cars, lorries, vans, buses and all – to such an extent that those who persist in using their feet or their horses or bicycles feel they have no right to be there at all and are threatened by the killing power of motor traffic. But the lanes originally belonged to those on foot, be it two feet or four, and they seek to reclaim them.

On foot

The lanes were social areas, places where you could happen upon acquaintances and have a chat standing in the summer dust or winter mud, or casually at their garden gate; places where you caught up on local gossip and the philosophies and tales of passing strangers. Lanes were places where you could wander to harvest hedgerow berries for pies, or sloes and elderflowers for homemade wine, or pick a variety of flowers to plonk in a jam jar on the windowsill.

Before combustion engines, before steam engines, before bicycles and before horses, if you wanted to get somewhere you walked. Before the Second World War people still often walked – to work, to school, to the village shop, to visit friends and relatives, to fairs and dances, even to the nearest town on market day, albeit ten miles each way. Between the wars, in particular, hiking was popular – townsfolk strode the lanes in unaccustomed boots, struggling with maps, and very clearly tourists.

In the nineteenth century and the early decades of the twentieth, you might also meet walking itinerants of various kinds: people who could mend chairs, umbrellas, pots and pans, or pedlars (literally, those who carry their goods themselves) with their knick-knacks in a waterproof backpack, doom-laden bell-ringing almanac sellers with a gaudy poster decorating their hats, sheet-music vendors, gypsies who made wooden clothes pegs and bunches of lucky heather, one-man bands knocking cymballed knees together and banging a drum behind their back while they blew on a penny whistle, tramps (women as well as men)

▲ FOR THE FIRST HALF OF THE 20TH CENTURY, *each stretch of a country lane was the responsibility of one man employed by the county council to keep that stretch in good condition, digging out drainage grips, ensuring the verges and roadside hedges were kept in trim and passing the time of day with the locals. Road traffic at the beginning of the century (this photograph was taken in 1910) was minimal.*

with their bundle of worldly goods wrapped in a checked cloth on the end of a stick over their shoulder, roving fiddlers and ballad singers, beggars heading for holiday resorts in summer, sailors making their way to seaports, soldiers rejoining their regiments, and migratory agricultural labourers.

With luck, you might even pass the time of day with a padding, bare-footed, bent-kneed moucher, out in all weathers to collect anything he could possibly sell – bundles of briar roots as grafts for garden roses, moss and peat for flowerpots, small snails as food for cage birds, small squares of turf for those who kept larks for their song, primrose 'mars' and rooted ferns to hawk from door to door in town along with violets and other spring flowers, frogs and lizards and snakes as pets, watercress from the brook, birds' eggs complete with nest to remind townsfolk of the countryside they no longer had time to wander in themselves, dandelion and other weed leaves for townies' tame rabbits, worms and grubs as anglers' bait, young rabbits or squirrels as pets, fledgling goldfinches and linnets as cage birds, bunches of 'blue-bottle' (cornflower) to sell in London at amazing prices, groundsel as cage-bird food,

wild duck eggs for the farmhouse table, mushrooms of course and basketloads of blackberries. No tramp or thief was the moucher – just a man who knew his lanes and knew how to harvest them for a living. The lanes were so rich then.

In the late afternoon and evening, women would be trudging home after a hard day's work in the fields, trying to be back in time to cook for their families, or bent double under bundles of deadwood and fir cones for the fire, perhaps with small children clutching their skirts and toddling along with them as best they could. You might hear, as George Sturt described it, 'in the gathering dusk ... the buzz and rumour of manifold homecomings – tired children squalling, women talking and perhaps scolding, as the little chattering groups came near and passed out of earshot to their several cottages'.

Lanes were safe for children then. Richard Jefferies (1848–1887) remarked: 'As soon as ever the child is old enough to crawl about, it is sure to get out into the road and roll in the dust. It is a curious fact that the agricultural children, with every advantage of green fields and wide open downs, always

'Most of the lane's users were on foot, picking up and distributing local and regional gossip as they passed, chatting with friends and strangers alike.'

'Perhaps one day the cows will again wander down to the farmyard ... and lane walkers will once again find peace'

choose the dusty hard road to play in ... the younger ones sprawling in the dust, their naked limbs kicking up clouds, and the bigger boys clambering about in the hedge-mound bounding the road, making gaps, splashing in the dirty water of the ditches.'

Lanes are sensual places – so much to see and touch, and to smell. The smells have changed over the years, of course. Once, it was the smell of dust or damp soil, dew on the grass, the subtle scents of wildflowers and tree bark, lichen and fern, the richness of ripe berries, the musk of passing wild animals (you can always tell when a deer, fox or badger has crossed the lane), the

stable aroma of fresh horse droppings, the warm friendly smell of a sweet-breathed milking herd on its way from the meadow to the parlour. For several decades of the 20th century the smells have been masked by the throat-catching harshness of exhaust fumes, yet even this is changing: if you walk the lanes now you will find that the smell of those fumes is sweeter, gentler, far less offensive and, they say, far less damaging to the health of the walkers and the environment as a whole. The noise of the engines still wipes out the high song of grasshoppers and warblers, but perhaps that too will change in years to come. Perhaps one

▶ THE TYPICAL ENGLISH LANE *of memory had verges wide enough for grazing a smallholder's cows, untroubled by traffic. Today the verges are cut by the highways authorities on a regular basis, with little regard for the wildflowers that once flourished in these linear nature reserves.*

▲ THE VILLAGE STREET *used to belong to its villagers; it was where children could play, workers could 'commute' on foot to the fields, carts could creak gently by, drawn by ambling horses. Those who know the heavy traffic in the Sussex coastal strip today would be surprised to learn that this is a photograph of Shoreham-by-Sea in 1910.*

'Gypsies brought colour to the wastelands and commons with their romantic camps of brightly painted horse-drawn vans'

▼ **LOCAL FARMERS WALKED** *their market sheep to or from the railway station even between the wars, when the lanes were not yet full of speeding traffic. With a very good sheepdog behind the flock, it might need only one man to lead them to their destination.*

day the cows will again wander down to the farmyard unmolested by road-rage drivers, and lane walkers will once again find peace.

On four feet

Long gone are the days when herds of livestock filled the lanes on their way to market, often travelling huge distances. Droves of cattle from all parts of the kingdom gradually funnelled their way to the big cities and sheep streaming off the hills and downs jostled between the hedgerows. Small groups of wilful pigs were driven by agitated swineherds to woodland pannage in the autumn; large flocks of geese and other poultry walked for miles to market, sometimes with their feet shod in little leather boots for protection from the stones. Gone are the days when West Country farmers would bring their 'mobs' of cattle off the hills and drive them closer to the home farm along the lanes for the winter. Almost gone are the days when dairy cows wandered home along the lane at milking time, sampling the herbage along the verges, pausing to consider life in general and gaze about them, often in company with no more than a small child.

Otherwise, unlike the major coaching roads, country lanes were relatively quiet places where the clop or splat of hooves was heard only occasionally. Two feet were far more common than four but you might have met the doctor riding to a patient, or a team of plough horses ambling home at the end of a day in the field, or a drunk snoozing in the back of his cart while his horse found its own familiar way home, or a laden farm wagon on its way to market, or the nag-drawn carrier's van transporting household necessaries along its round and giving a lift to a housewife or two who wanted to get into town. The wise driver was wary of certain loads: carriers might have bundles of rod and strap iron (brought out from the town for the local blacksmith) sticking out from the back of their hooded vans and difficult to see in the twilight; and builders' vehicles would have long ladders and floor boards protruding, which tended to sway dangerously from side to side as the horses moved smartly downhill on uneven roads.

In many areas, especially hilly ones, goods were carried on the backs of packhorses: they could pick their way where wheeled vehicles would come to grief, and in

the 19th century trains of them were still heralded by the jangling bells of the lead horse. Many a bridge was designed for packhorses, with indented passing places.

Gypsies

The donkeys and shaggy-maned piebald and skewbald horses of gypsies were once so familiar in rural areas. Many people were quite fond of 'their' gypsies; they understood and wryly admired their way of life, and came to know them quite well. Others saw gypsies as furtive and dishonest, apt to poach and a general nuisance to be watched closely by the village bobby and the gamekeeper. Gertrude Jekyll, writing in the 1920s, said that a distinction should be made between 'the true Romany and the rougher van-dweller, who is by no means always a real gypsy. The right people have a pleasant address and manner much like that of the Italian peasant; they are generally honest, and have a good deal of self-respect. It is to be regretted that they have to so large an extent given up their distinctive dress; the bright handkerchiefs for head and shoulders, and the long gold ear-rings. Now they dress in any old clothes that may be given to them, and wear on their heads any battered old hat with draggled feathers.'

Gypsies were very much a part of country life; they brought colour to the wastelands and commons with their romantic camps of brightly painted horse-drawn vans or quickly made 'benders' fashioned from supple hazel branches. The smoke of a gypsy's fire, to some, meant a welcome pause for a chat and a hot drink, once you had made friends with the dogs. The gypsies were courteous, kindly and hospitable to those who respected them but sometimes took advantage of those who did not. Gypsies knew where to find whortleberries, blackberries, sloes, nuts, watercress, mushrooms and wild plovers' eggs

▶ SINCE THE 16TH CENTURY, *gypsies (thought to have originated in India, though the word derives from 'Egyptian') had been subjected to brutal vagrancy laws in England and Wales and also had problems with regulations concerning pedlars and hawkers – traditional occupations for gypsies. In the 18th century they tended to be lumped together with Irish travellers, but in the 19th century there was a growing new interest in gypsy folklore and the Romany language.*

to harvest and sell; their nimble fingers could make pegs and besoms, or repair pots and pans; and they were forever offering lucky bunches of heather.

The state of the roads

For nearly three centuries some of the local lanes were maintained by farmers, but many were not maintained at all. Under the 1555 Highways Act, the parish was made responsible for all the roads that ran through it, including the major ones. Every farmer had to fulfil a required number of man-hours each year, under the beady eye of the parish's highway supervisor. Various individuals were bound to provide a cart, a team of oxen, donkeys or horses, and the requisite labourers and their tools. If you look through old vestry minutes you will find mention of appointments to this unpaid supervisory post – one that most did their best to avoid. You

will also find deep resentment that the locals had to pay for the maintenance of roads used by outsiders passing through, and endless complaints about the state of local roads.

When the main traffic was on foot or on four feet (donkeys and packhorses), the system just about coped, but wheeled vehicles – whether two-wheeled carts or carriages and coaches – needed better surfaces and standards and also caused a great deal more damage by carving indelible ruts.

Travellers painted a vivid picture of life on the roads. The ruts were often so deep that coaches would sink to their axles in mud and water, making progress almost impossible. Country roads (and most town ones) were alternately mud or swirling dust, and for centuries it was the practice to 'lay' the summer dust by watering the road surface. As traffic increased, this simple routine was no longer adequate.

The series of county reports to the Board of Agriculture published in the 19th century always had a section on the state of roads. For Devon, Charles Vancouver in 1808 complained that the turnpike roads were not of the width prescribed by law, and being so

◀ MUD WAS THE MAIN PROBLEM *on the old country roads, and in some places regular use by horse-drawn wagons and carts created ruts so deep that the base of the vehicle scraped the surface of the lane. Some old carters were happy with ruts, which kept the wheels on track and the carter didn't have to concentrate too hard on where his horses were taking him. On hills, for example, if there was a big rut down the side of the road at the bank the wagon wheels could be tied and the wagon would simply stay in the rut, helping the horses to hold it back and prevent it from careering down the hill and overtaking them.*

Allestone hill Turnpike, Hereford.

narrow became 'so high in the middle, that without sides or bulwark to support them, they are, in a short time, by the traffic of the lime-carts, bilged, and forced out upon their sides, when the only passage remaining is confined to a narrow ridge on the top of the road, but which, from the excessive coarseness of the materials of which it is made, is soon broken into so many holes and unevennesses, as very much to endanger the knees of the horse, and the neck of its rider.'

Vancouver remarked on the very Devonian feature of high hedge banks along the narrow lanes, which created 'the idea of exploring a labyrinth rather than that of passing through a much-frequented country'. But the illusion was quickly dispelled, he warned, on meeting gangs of packhorses: 'The rapidity with which these animals descend the hills, when not loaded, and the utter impossibility of passing loaded ones, require that the utmost caution should be used in keeping out of the way of the one, and exertion in keeping ahead of the other.' Wheeled vehicles in these lanes were rare.

Lincolnshire was one of the counties surveyed by Arthur Young (1741–1820), an East Anglian farmer who became the first Secretary to the Board of Agriculture and was one of the earliest to turn agriculture into a science. In the 1780s Young had undertaken a 20,000-mile tour of the country for his *Annals of Agriculture*, riding a blind white horse. In his Lincolnshire survey, published in 1813, he said that the roads in general were 'esteemed below par' and he said very little more about them, except that in 'the hundred of Skirbeck to Boston, and thence to Wisbeach' they were generally of silt or old sea sand 'deposited under various parts of the country ages ago, and when moderately wet are very good; but dreadfully dusty and heavy in dry weather; and also on a thaw they are like mortar'.

In Sussex, the Reverend Arthur Young (a Sussex clergyman, and not the same Arthur Young as above) wrote in the same year that the turnpike roads were generally in good order and of excellent materials ('whinstone; the Kentish rag, broken into moderate-sized

▲ A 1663 ACT OF PARLIAMENT *allowed the imposition of tolls on road users passing through Hertfordshire, Huntingdonshire and Cambridgeshire, and the first tollgate (or turnpike – it was a spiked turnstile) was installed at Wadesmill in Hertfordshire. The turnpike network gradually spread over much of the country and new turnpike trusts were still being created in the early 19th century. The system faded out when the new railway network provided an alternative for the movement of heavy loads and the last tollgate closed in 1895.*

pieces'). Other roads in the coastal areas were kept firm and dry with gravel or sea shingle but on the claylands of the Weald the roads were 'in all probability the very worst that are to be met with in any part of the island' – indeed it was claimed that the women and horses of the Weald had the longest legs in the country, as they were always having to drag their feet out of sticky mud. The Wealden roads also bore heavy loads of timber and corn, which quickly made them virtually impassable for wheeled traffic in winter, and conversely baked so hard in summer that animals' hooves suffered badly.

Young drew the contrast with what he considered to be the best roads in England, especially the 44 miles of turnpike from

Bury St Edmunds to Huntingdon, and those around Newmarket; the splendour of these roads he attributed to the nature of the soil and the openness of the country. He also described the turnpike at Horsham, noting that 'the present road to London was made in 1756; before that time it was so execrably bad, that whoever went on wheels, were forced to go round by Canterbury, which is one of the most extraordinary circumstances that the history of non-communication in this kingdom can furnish'.

The Worcestershire report in 1813 claimed that the principal roads with tollgates that ran from town to town were generally in good repair, though rather stony and uneven in hilly districts. Some of the 'cross' roads were very bad, especially

▲ STEAM ENGINES PLAYED A LARGE PART *in agriculture throughout the 19th century, as did road steamers – traction engines that could draw heavy farm and woodland loads along the lanes. Steam contributed to road making and maintenance in the 20th century. For example, in the 1930s there were steam-powered rock crushers broke up road stone, but the major use of this source of energy on the roads was in traction engines (the large steel wheels were cushioned with solid rubber bolted around the rims for road use) and steamrollers. Highways authorities generally invested in combined engines that could be converted in a few hours from traction engines for haulage to steamrollers for road repairs.*

in clay areas, 'where little attention is paid either to plashing hedges, opening ditches, or mending roads; many of these are scarcely passable from Christmas to Midsummer, either on horseback, or with a loaded carriage'.

Road making

It took a blind man, John Metcalfe, to draw attention to the need for good drainage and good foundations in road making, an art known to the Romans but apparently lost in Britain thereafter. Metcalfe, of Knaresborough in Yorkshire, began to use bundled heather for drainage under his road stones, finishing with gravel and cambering the surface so that rainwater was shed into roadside ditches, and built his first successful road on these principles in 1753. But he was ahead of his time.

Three or four years later, two men were born in Scotland who would take his ideas further in the early 19th century: John Loudon MacAdam and Thomas Telford. MacAdam (1756–1836) and Telford (1757–1834) both understood the importance of

good drainage. Telford's rather more expensive roads were built on solid foundations: at the base were tightly packed stones up to about 10in long, covered by a 6in layer of broken stones, topped by small stones and gravel forming a slightly convex surface. There were drainage ditches along the side of the road, fed by culverts running at intervals beneath the foundations. MacAdam's principles were broadly similar but he used cheaper material, often recycling stone from earlier roads and grading it in size in successive layers.

Macadamised roads revolutionised transport, and steamrollers added to the improvements by consolidating newly made and repaired road surfaces. Travelling roadmen would camp beside their

'It was motoring that eventually brough tarmac to all of the lanes. Macadamisation had been a good start but it was not good enough for the rapidly increasing motorised traffic.'

▼ **MAJOR ROAD WIDENING** *and improvement was undertaken largely by manual labour and without the aid of pneumatic drills, even as the volume of motor vehicles on the road steadily grew. New village bypasses carved out of the countryside reduced traffic through the village but created large scars in rural areas. Where new roads divided a farm into two sections, footbridges would sometimes be built across the new roads so that milking herds could walk safely from their fields to the milking parlour.*

▲ **TAR SPRAYING TO LAY THE DUST**
on macadamised roads had been practised in the 19th century. In 1901 a barrel of tar fell off the back of a wagon and burst open; someone spread local slag on the sticky black puddle and a county surveyor noticed that this combination produced a dust-free, traffic-proof surface. Thus 'Tarmac' was born: by 1903 the surveyor had formed the TarMacadam Syndicate (the name was changed to Tarmac Ltd two years later).

steamrollers wherever they were working, spending the evening listening to one of their number playing a concertina or having a night out on the town or nearest village.

It was motoring that eventually brought tarmac to all the lanes. Macadamisation had been a good start but it was not good enough for the rapidly increasing motorised traffic.

Maintaining the roads

While the parishes were still responsible for the maintenance of local roads, gangs of local men would regularly repair surfaces, clear ditches and keep the roadside hedges in good trim. Hedge cutting remained useful winter work for farm labourers at a time of year when there was little else they could be doing on the farm. In those pre-mechanised days, hedges were trimmed by hand with the skilful use of sharp blades to keep the hedge dense and livestock-proof. All the cuttings were cleared up and heaped on a bonfire, which kept the men warm as well as disposing of the debris. Ditches were scoured out with ditching irons; and the 'grips' dug into the verges to channel water off the road and into the ditch were carefully kept clear.

When roads became macadamised, the top layer of small stones and gravel was the renewable part and many local people would be employed as stone breakers, sitting at the side of the road by a large heap of stones and laboriously breaking them into smaller pieces with a stone-hammer. Stone breakers remained a familiar sight in rural areas well within living memory, always ready for a chat with passers-by and generally opening the conversation by asking the time. They were eventually made redundant when tarmac roads became the norm. Tar spraying to lay the road dust was being widely used by 1910 in some places, but elsewhere many villages did not have the benefit of tarmac until the time of World War II. Many country people can remember the coming of tarmac to country lanes: as children they would be encouraged by their mothers to stand by the great steaming barrels of pitch at the crossroads, breathing in the harsh fumes, which were deemed to be good for the chest and for warding off colds.

When county councils were first created in 1888, they took over responsibility for main roads in their county; six years later

▲ THOSE WHO BROKE STONES *into different sizes for road maintenance sometimes protected their eyes from flying chips by using walnut shells with a small viewing hole carved out of them. The shells were fastened around the head with string.*

other rural highways became the responsibility of the new district councils. Later, county councils took over responsibility for the minor roads as well.

For a golden while, county councils employed lengthsmen or linesmen. Each man was responsible for a defined length of local lane (perhaps 15 miles) and it was his job and pride to keep it in good condition, and to make sure that local landowners did their bit by cutting the hedges. Everybody in the village knew him and would pass the time of day when they came across him by his little laneside bonfire or working close to the small handcart or wheelbarrow in which he carried his spades, forks, shovels, brooms and faghook. These familiar characters continued their responsibilities well within living memory, until councils began to replace them with mobile road gangs whose areas were rather wider. The last of the

lengthsmen had retired by the 1970s. Even after mechanisation, council road gangs were local enough to know their patches well and be known, and they continued to take a personal pride in keeping the grips and ditches clear as well as dealing with potholes before they became a problem to traffic. Locals who noticed a problem would simply mention it to the foreman and it would be dealt with then and there.

Such is progress that, in the interests of 'efficiency' and economy, most councils centralised their operations during the 1980s and 1990s and their gangs became roving ones with no particular interest in a village or parish. In some council areas the gangs no longer know where the grips should be or care to maintain them – a small detail, but it leads to water lying where it should not and early degradation of the surface.

Budget cuts also mean that the grass

grows freely down the centre of narrow and less used lanes, fed by the mud washing down from the hedgebanks that has been dislodged by vehicles too wide for the lane but persisting in using it. Increasingly, local lanes are hammered by ever-larger lorries that are sometimes delivering locally but equally often are simply cutting through on their way to elsewhere, choosing what might look on the map like a short cut but which on the ground is unable to carry them, or is so narrow that invariably they must reverse on meeting other vehicles (the innovation of satellite navigation systems made the situation even worse). Lane surfaces and especially old bridges are rapidly crumbling under their impact, and locals are frustrated that there seems to be no way of deterring the intruders. There is rebellion in the air.

Bicycles

Roads essentially liberate people: they enable you to travel from one place to another, by various means and at various speeds. In the country, your travels were generally limited by the endurance of your own legs; you went as far as you could walk. Then in 1817 Baron von Drais of Karlsruhe invented the hobbyhorse, which was the forerunner of the bicycle. And it was the bicycle that truly liberated country people, opening

'Several coastal regiments had their own Cyclist Battalions, who patrolled their areas to prevent an enemy from landing'

new horizons of independence and choice. On your bike you could travel to work far more quickly than on foot, you could travel to town, you could travel to meet new people, you could find marriage partners who were not simply recycled from the village gene pool.

The hobbyhorse was not for country lanes; nor, realistically, were the four-wheeled and three-wheeled cycles of the 1820s or the

▲ TANDEM BICYCLES *were popular for courting and married couples and could be extended into a three-seater 'Triplet', with sidecar attached for the children. Sidecars were more commonly seen with motorcycles and in some arrangements, with pillions as well, could carry (precariously) as many as six adults.*

◀ MOTORCYCLES WERE CHEAPER THAN CARS *– cheap enough for young people in rural areas to afford – and gave a sense of adventure as well as a practical means of getting somewhere else quickly. They could even be ridden across the fields and commons, making a trip to town much more direct.*

'boneshaker' velocipede of the late 1860s, nor indeed the 'Ordinary' bicycle of the early 1870s, with its outsize front wheel. Tricycles of the period became quite popular with more sedate cyclists, and as delivery vehicles, but it was not until the safety bicycle was produced in the mid-1880s that cycling for the ordinary country dweller began to become truly practical. In 1896 there was a great boom in cycle production, and once the fashionable folk had got over all the excitement, the ordinary working folk, be they in industrial or rural areas, claimed the bicycle as their own essential steed.

During World War I, bicycles were pressed into service for more serious matters. Several coastal regiments had their own Cyclist Battalions, who patrolled their areas 'to prevent an enemy from landing unobserved and unreported'. Bicycles were

ideal for the purpose: they were silent, swift and versatile, and you could sling your rifle along the crossbar.

Then came the motorbike – especially ones with sidecars in which you could carry your wife or your tools or your pig.

Wheeled vehicles

In the relatively brief heyday of the horse, you might have met all manner of horsepower in the lanes, especially agricultural and dray horses pulling carts and wagons. Sometimes you would meet fancy carriage horses and heavy 'machiners' (which pulled omnibuses and vans at a spanking six to eight miles per hour), or a fast trotter hastening past between the shafts (though more likely in town). You might have seen children in a small governess's cart pulled by a trotting pony; you might have leapt into

▲ LONG-DISTANCE COACHING *had dwindled rapidly in the face of competition from the railways in the 19th century, and its fate was sealed by the introduction of motor buses and cars in the 20th. This photograph was taken in about 1885, and the passengers are on a pleasure outing from Penzance to Lands End. It would have been quicker and more comfortable by train!*

▲ **SETTING UP AS A CARRIER** *required greater investment and organisation than setting up as a carter (which only really involved painting your name on the side of your open two-wheeled cart and offering your services). A carrier's cart (as seen here) was usually a four-wheeled wagon and had to have seats for occasional passengers, preferably under cover. Carriers often progressed from simple canvas covers to something more solid in wood, made by the carpenter or wheelwright.*

the ditch to avoid a careering rector driving his gig hurriedly between his multiple churches, parking it during the service in a convenient church-side gig shed.

Quite often, the barking of every local dog in the neighbourhood would herald the approach of another kind of draught animal altogether. Teams of large dogs, especially of the Newfoundland type, would pull yellow carts of fresh fish and salt bound for the London markets. A team of four dogs could carry three to four hundredweight of fish, plus the driver, who would ride with his legs cocked up along the shafts. The dogs were generally left to roam freely about the village to scavenge for food while their master downed a pint or two at the inn; then he would blow a horn and his team would reassemble for harnessing. A dog team could

travel as fast as a coach but there were so many complaints about the noise and nuisance they caused that a law banning the use of draught dogs came into effect in 1854.

The carrier's cart

Long before the railways, a nationwide network of carriers served country areas. The horse-drawn carrier's cart took goods to isolated communities, and some would deliver right to the doors of remote farmhouses. The carrier also took a few passengers, if you wanted to get into town or, more importantly, needed help in carrying goods home again from the market. (Anybody could walk to the market – five or ten miles was nothing – but with a load you needed help.)

The earliest form of the carrier's cart was the enormous road wagon drawn by six horses: this would take cattle and sheep over long distances to London markets, and come back with loads of groceries or whatever else people needed on the way home. Many carrier services had started as a sideline to a main trade that already involved the carrier in transporting his own goods to market; he had a vehicle that would otherwise be empty on the return journey. Perhaps his goods were flour if he was a miller, or livestock and grain if he was a farmer, or he might have set

up a coal delivery service, collecting coal from the railway depot and taking it round the houses. Trade directories also reveal carriers' dual roles as shopkeepers, publicans, blacksmiths and the like.

Carriers' carts were not exactly a comfortable way of travelling. They tended not to have shock-absorbing springs and bounced about heartily on the rough country lanes. You clambered up the steps at the back and sat on wooden benches along the sides of the cart, with no upholstery to take the bumps. Some were open two-wheeled tilt carts; some were more solid wagons covered with canvas in the style of the Wild West. Other carriers fashioned a cabin on top of the vehicle, perhaps with dusty curtains between driver and passengers and usually with old paint peeling from the sides.

The horse knew where to go and where to stop as well as its driver, who was one of those invaluable characters, a mine of local information and gossip. Typically he would extend his job well beyond carrying market goods and people; he knew his customers well and often did small favours for them in town such as collecting debts. The older carriers could not read or write but always remembered their many commissions; a later generation needed notebooks. By the 1880s there were at least 200,000 carriers in the country, and they were still offering their services in the 1920s. But as World War I broke out the system began to change: carriers' carts became motorised vans, or even buses packed with passengers and with hardly any room for the goods that were once the carrier's main trade.

Motoring

In 1930 *The Field* gave details of 'Mr Norrison's new Code of the Highway'. The Code was aimed at motorists but applied equally to all road users, be they cyclists, horse-driven vehicles or people in charge of animals on the road.

'It is of the most vital importance, for instance, that everyone should know that, in future, all animals, ridden, led, or driven, must keep to the left, or near side, of the road, except when overtaking. Hitherto, of course, they have kept to the right, facing oncoming traffic. Use should be made of grass or other verges where these exist, and, when approaching a corner, drivers of flocks or herds should send someone on in advance to warn approaching traffic.'

So by 1930 two and four legs had already been pushed to the verges by motorised vehicles. The article continued: 'But why should not the carrying of a lamp or lantern by the drover or shepherd be made compulsory? Nothing is quite so invisible as a black horse or bullock on a wet night.' In 1909 *The Times* had warned car drivers that many horse drivers travelled with no lights at night, on the crown of the road, with the driver confidently sleeping in the knowledge that the horse could find its own way home.

In the early years of the 20th century, the battle for supremacy between horse power and motor power had been in full swing. Steam traction had had its brief moment of glory, with steam engines chuntering at walking pace along the lanes as the 19th century became the 20th, and they continued to be valued by farmers for threshing for several decades to come.

But horses and steam had met their match. For the transport of goods and of people, the petrol engine won, even though there were still a few horse-drawn deliveries still being made as late as the 1950s. While the general public seemed to welcome motorised goods vehicles and

▲ WILLIAM RICHARD MORRIS *began his career by repairing motorcycles in Oxford, and progressed to become the wealthy Baron Nuffield by designing and manufacturing cars. His first was the 'Bullnose' Oxford in 1913. Morris concentrated on the mass market with his Morris Eight in the 1930s, followed by the equally popular Morris Minor. His family version of the Minor was the Morris Oxford, shown here in its first year of production in 1948 and designed by Alec Issigonis (famously later the designer of the Mini).*

▲ MOTORING TOURISTS BEGAN TO VISIT THE COUNTRYSIDE *and they included foreign visitors. The village of Sulgrave, for example, photographed here in 1910, drew in American tourists eager to visit Sulgrave Manor, the home of George Washington's ancestors. In 1914 the house was purchased by the British Peace Centenary Committee, who restored what had become a farmhouse and opened a Washington Museum there. Today most of the village's cottages are no longer thatched.*

public transport, such as cabs and omnibuses, the private motorcar was not popular, especially in country areas. It was too noisy, it frightened the horses, and it went too fast. The old 4mph limit had been increased to 12mph for vehicles of less than three tons in 1896, which was also the year in which motor cars were first legalised as road vehicles.

In 1903 the speed limit for motorcars was increased to 20mph. All over the country villages deplored the danger of 'fast' cars and begged for lower speed limits, but their pleas went unheeded.

In 1905 there were 15,800 cars on Britain's roads. By 1914 this had increased to 132,000; by 1920 it was 200,000, by 1924 it was more than half a million and in 1939 there were already more than two million private cars on British roads (and more than 400,000 motorbikes and 488,000 goods

vehicles). Virtually all of them, of course, were black. By the early 1970s there were 17 million vehicles on our roads and today there are more than 31 million, including 20 million cars – very few of which, incidentally, are black.

Harking back to his youth in what is now the traffic-clogged Surrey village of Chobham, Frank Burningham recalled: 'There was no vehicles in the village, there was no traffic of any sort. If you saw three carts go through the village, trundling through with gravel on them from up on the Common, it was about all you saw all day long.' And there are many photographs from all over the country to prove the lack of traffic: empty village streets, perhaps a pony and trap, or old Tarry Jack walking beside his donkey, or children playing with hoops in the road, or a dog lazily scratching itself at the crossroads.

▼ VILLAGE GARAGES OFFERED EMPLOYMENT *as well as petrol and vehicle repairs. The young lad who happened to be billeted at this garage in 1939 quickly took the opportunity to get some basic training as a mechanic.*

Motoring for pleasure was in full swing in the 1930s, especially on Sundays and Bank Holidays. Beauty spots within motoring distance of the cities were eagerly visited by people in double-decker omnibuses, people on motorbikes and in sidecars, and richer people in their cars. In 1931 petrol was 1s 4d a gallon; the 20mph speed limit had just been abolished and the 30mph limit in built-up areas would be introduced in 1934. Proper signposts were being introduced so that you knew where you were going.

Garages

In cinemas across the land in 1950, Pathé News reported on a little local story. A black London taxi drew up outside a blacksmith's shop. The back door of the cab was opened, and out stepped Joey, a small pony. He stood patiently while the smith gave him four bright new shoes, then he climbed back into the taxi and rode home. Joey's owner, cabbie Les Brockhurst, ran his own garage and so he knew all about horsepower.

Garages began to spring up in every village. Some had started out as the village smithy – it was a natural progression from hammering iron on the forge to welding bits of car together. In the very early days of motoring, fuel would be purchased from oil shops or ironmongers and so journeys needed rather careful planning. When cars broke down, it was generally a matter of do-it-yourself (or get the chauffeur to do it, as most early motorists were rich enough to employ staff) or asking a passing horse to drag your crestfallen vehicle to the nearest bicycle shop for help. Many such shops

▲ THATCHING THE PUMPS *was popular in rural areas in the 1930s, in an attempt partly to be less of a blot on the landscape but more to attract tourists by including a thatched tearoom or shop. This petrol station at Blashford in Hampshire has managed to attract a French vehicle (a Renault).*

developed into garages for motor vehicles, and one or two of them combined with local coachbuilders whose experience with horse-drawn vehicle bodies was readily transferred to those of motor vehicles.

At first these businesses were in cities and larger towns, accessible to the richer folk who were able to afford motor cars and as close as possible to railway stations, as fuel and spares would be delivered by rail. The word 'garage' was eventually adopted for these new ventures. Apparently the word originally applied to the wide passing places in French canals and was then used on French railways to refer to train sheds, thence to places for motor cars. The term was in use in Britain by 1900.

After World War I, mass production of motor cars and commercial vehicles boomed and village garages began to open at crossroads, or on a field that had become dirt cheap during the agricultural depression. They provided cars for hire, with or without chauffeurs; they ran taxis and they often provided bus services; they towed fire engines, they carried the mail, and they could fix anything that needed soldering. Some of

them even generated electricity, using oil-powered generators, for the locals to recharge their batteries.

Filling stations began to pop up – scattered roadside pumps in the middle of nowhere along busier roads, often to the horror of locals at these blots on the landscape. In 1927 there was legislation for the licensing of roadside petrol pumps, and a year later county councils were given powers over the appearance of garages in general, many of which strongly featured corrugated iron. Some entrepreneurs, especially on tourist routes, developed their filling stations with tearooms and other attractions for the weary traveller. Others began plastering the area with signs – not just on site but along the road to catch your eye as you approached them.

As agriculture became increasingly mechanised between the wars, country garages built up a steady business with local farmers, repairing implements as well as tractors, to tide them through to the age when cars became essential in rural life. Otherwise they had lean times in the 1920s and 1930s, when poverty in the countryside

▼ MOTORING FOR PLEASURE *was all the rage in the 1930s – and then came 'nouveau camping'. In 1934 you could even buy a tent with an awning that stretched out over the car, acting as a covered way between tent and vehicle. In the 1960s there was a tent that could be incorporated into a roof rack, which acted as the frame; the telescopic legs were drawn out until they reached the ground, the rack was unscrewed and the car was driven away, leaving the frame tent in position. A 1960s design was a small tent erected in seconds on the roof of the car, and reached by a metal ladder.*

put cars well beyond reach of most. And World War II had a severe effect on country garages: their mechanics were called up and petrol was rationed. But many family businesses did survive, and continued to play an important part in the life of the village.

The country bus

Another great liberator for rural populations was the country bus. By the early 1920s it had more or less replaced the friendly old carrier's cart but genuine buses were limited in their routes. More common was the motorised van, and typical in rural areas was the cheaper-to-run open lorry, with padded seats, a roof for storing packages, and canvas sides that could be dropped down to keep out the rain (they had celluloid portholes as windows). Others were converted furniture removal vans, with a drop-down tailboard for easy loading of goods and folding seats for a passenger or two; or you might go to market in a small van fitted with benches, where you would be joined by livestock and packages.

Such a journey could provide considerable entertainment as the passengers exchanged conversation, shouting loudly above the rattle of the van. As on any country bus, this was where you heard the local gossip, exchanged witty remarks (usually rather personal), aired unusual or prejudiced views on topics of the day, discussed prices and the state of your crops and everybody else's, and let your imagination run wild about the new tenants of the local farm.

During World War I many men were trained as mechanics and drivers, and those who returned from the killing fields often put their new skills to good use in civilian life by setting up village taxi or bus services. Their vehicles would be highly individual, converted from all manner of motors, and many of the men worked indefatigably, on the road all day, going wherever their customers needed to go and providing a service in the true sense of the word – meeting people's needs. They knew that half of the young would want to go the town

▲ THE MOTORISED CHARABANC, *nearly always open-topped, was popular for day-tripper outings of all kinds (especially between the wars) and could be hired for taking groups of workers, members of friendly societies, teetotallers, school groups, extended families and even whole villages to the seaside, the towns or scenic beauty spots.*

▲ **COVERED CHARABANCS** *were used for more serious outings, although the cover was rigged up quickly and provided rather basic shelter from the elements. The men here are taking a break after searching for a missing person – hence the sensible clothes, sticks and dogs.*

cinema or dance hall by a certain time, and that they also wanted to be brought home afterwards, so the bus would be there for them. ('Nobody ever left behind!' was the slogan.) They knew that the women wanted to go to town on market day, and needed the bus to be parked conveniently nearby so that they could leave some of their packages (including baskets of live poultry and the like) safely on the bus while they completed their shopping. They knew where people lived and would drop you right at your gate.

Sometimes a bus would take the whole village on a day's outing. Such buses were often 'sharrybangs' (charabancs – open vehicles fitted with rows of benches), which also brought tourists into the countryside. The tourists brought money with them, and wily locals soon learned to take advantage of their desire to spend it on teas and meals and bed-and-breakfast.

By the 1930s buses were comfortable saloons with pneumatic tyres (a decade earlier many buses had iron wheels, which made the ride far from easy). The new buses still carried everything their passengers wished to carry and became greatly loved as well as essential to village life.

But with the increasing popularity of the private car, rural bus services were already deteriorating in the late 1940s.

'The tourists brought money with them, and wily locals soon learned to take advantage of their desire to spend it'

Companies found that they were running at a loss and began to reduce their timetables, exacerbating the situation. Bus services gradually became too few, and the revised times no longer suited the needs of the passengers. Yet it is in rural areas that a good bus service is the most essential. The small minority in rural areas who do not have access to a private car now experience considerable difficulty in meeting their most basic needs.

It is a problem that has resulted in many rural families becoming multiple car owners, to ensure that people can get to work and to the shops, children can get to school. The lack of good public transport is one of the many factors that have been slowly undermining village life.

Canals

There was a period when transport by water was seen as the solution to the eternal problem of avoiding impassable lanes when getting heavier goods from one part of the country to another. Quite apart from existing rivers and the sea, it made sense to create a system of artificial waterways so that there was a proper network for waterborne goods.

▼ THOMAS HENRY BARTON, *born in 1866, founded what would become the biggest independent bus operator in Europe. In the 1890s, though not actually able to drive, he bought his first bus and it took him three days to get home with it. His bus business started with a charabanc service between Long Eaton and Nottingham launched in 1908 (a route that Barton buses still use today). He was a pioneer in running buses on gas (stored on the roof in a bag) and was working on a diesel engine several years before the eponymous Rudolf Diesel.*

Canals were built extensively in the 1770s and 1780s. Sussex, for example, was a rural rather than an industrial county, with the main products being corn, timber, charcoal, chalk, lime, marl, iron, marble, limestone, cattle and sheep – all of them bulky goods for which transport could be very expensive. It was much cheaper and easier by water than by land. In the old days, huge loads of timber had been sent laboriously by land, over the terrible Sussex roads, to the coast for export; lime, likewise, was carried from the Downs by land; corn was sent in large quantities to Portsmouth, and so on. The rivers Rother and Arun were partly navigable, but the network was greatly improved by cutting new canals in the early 19th century.

The net result of these waterway improvements was that far more timber was accessible, thus land values increased considerably in that woodland previously left untouched because of transport problems could now be felled and exported. Not only could Sussex export its products; it was also now easier to bring in coal from other parts of the country – initially to replace locally grown furze used by farmers to fire their lime kilns, and thereby releasing furze land to the plough for growing more grain. Another bonus was in local employment in cutting the canals. In many parts of the country, however, canal-cutting gangs were dreaded: they tended to be mobile teams, not of local men but of outsiders and foreigners whom nobody trusted and who caused riots and general mayhem wherever they went.

In Devon, the Reverend Coham of Black Torrington described how, instead of a 'most forbidding wild, and in a manner uncultivated desert, calculated only for the grazing of lean bullocks, and horses of the smallest and hardiest kinds' in the country that was surrounded by the circuitous course of the River Torridge, there were by 1808 extensive cornfields, luxuriant pastures, sheep-covered uplands and the continual creation of new enclosures and improved drainage and grazing on the moors. All this was apparently due to the improvement of the roads, which allowed wheeled vehicles to bring in large amounts of sea sand as manure. However, Coham felt that far greater improvements could yet be made

with the help of canals, because 'oxen do not possess strength and agility sufficient for heavy draughts and long journies' to bring in the necessary manure; while horses, which some were at that stage advocating to supplant oxen, would have to be kept as expensively large teams. If everything went by canal instead, the horse teams could be reduced, road repairs would be required less often (and travel on them by others would be more pleasurable) and everybody would be happier!

In Lincolnshire, of course, they knew all about waterways and there were canals aplenty. The complaint was directed at the canal engineers themselves, 'for after giving their plans, they leave you to yourselves; and then difficulties arise in which the people are ignorant, and upon application to them, and ready to pay, cannot have their attention'. Nevertheless, a very fine canal from Grantham to Nottingham, 33 miles long, had been completed in 1796 at a cost of £100,000 and it was expected to bring in 'very great returns'.

> 'If everything went by canal, the horse teams could be reduced, raod repairs would be required less often … and everybody would be happier!'

▶ **TRANSPORT OF HEAVY GOODS** *was not the only use for canal barges. The barge plough worked on the same principle as land-based steam-powered cable cultivation, dragging a plough across the land on a winding cable attached to one or two stationary steam engines, but the barge plough could give access to pieces of land isolated between waterways. The apparatus shown here in 1865 was one of the many inventions of John Fowler, the first man to make cable cultivation practicable (in 1852) with his steam-driven winding engines. By the early 1860s, Fowler had more than 1,000 employees producing his agricultural implements. He died when he was only 38 but it would not be until the next century that his ploughing system was gradually replaced by tractor-drawn ploughs.*

► MEMORIES OF CANAL VESSELS *generally involve them being towed by horses trudging along the towpath. But when the barge had to go through a tunnel with no path the 'leggers' took over, walking the vessel through by pushing their feet against the sides of the tunnel. The famous Dudley Tunnel, opened in 1792 and passing under the town, was more than 3,000 yards long and only 9ft wide, and it took more than three hours to leg a boat laden with iron and steel through it.*

Railways

The impact of the rail network on rural areas was far greater than that of canals and far more sudden than that of road improvements. The building of the railways brought local employment aplenty, and money in the pocket of many a landowner whose land was required by the railway companies. It also brought fast, cheap public transport – initially of goods but very soon mainly of passengers – so that the countryman who had never travelled much farther than his legs would take him found he could take the whole family, indeed the whole village if you booked an excursion train, for outings to the seaside or anywhere else they fancied. The railways were not just escape routes for pleasure; they were also a means of finding work in new areas; and they would eventually introduce the concept of the commuter. Village life would never be the same again.

The railway companies also introduced the concept of national time. Time had been a relatively unimportant and slow-moving local matter. The church bells let you know when it was time for certain important things like coming in from the fields or turning up for a church service (they also let you know when there had been a death in the village, and whether it was man, woman or child; and gave news of battle victories and suchlike) but there was no need to know what time it was elsewhere in the country unless you were one of the few to travel by the mail coaches that had begun to race from London to Bath and elsewhere in the late 18th century. Otherwise, all you needed to know was what the church bells told you, and rural time revolved around natural phenomena. Each town had its own time, based on the sun's local noon, and each village often decided its own time too.

The railways were more demanding: trains ran more or less to a timetable

▶ **LOCAL BRANCH LINES** *transported all manner of agricultural items, and both farmers and smallholders would make good use of the nearest 'halt'. The closure of so many of the branch lines was a severe blow for rural areas, cutting off villages from a cheap, fast means of public transport to the nearest market town.*

and in 1840 the Great Western Railway instructed all its stations to synchronise their clocks with London time. The other railway companies soon did the same and in 1849 an electric clock was installed at Greenwich Observatory, which by 1852 was transmitting a time signal to Lewisham station and thence via the railways and telegraph stations to post offices and public clocks all over the country. Even the remotest rural villages came to accept that their time should be the same as that in the rest of the country, that is, London time, which made catching the right train much simpler.

Time was not the only rural horizon broadened by the coming of the railways. In the 1861 census for the Shropshire parish of Highley, a quarter of those registered were railway navvies and their families lodging temporarily in the parish, and their own places of birth included 23 different counties. Highley had become almost cosmopolitan overnight. Some of the navvies' children had even been born in France, while their fathers were building French railway lines. Imagine the effects of such an influx into villages whose inhabitants had often travelled no farther than ten miles from home in

their entire lives, and who had not even read about foreign lands. Villages on main coaching routes were more wise in the ways of the world; they had seen all sorts passing through and had heard many a traveller's tale over a pint at the local inn. But for villages in more remote parts of the country, the coming of the railway was a major and life-changing event.

The first main railway routes had been created in the 1830s. By 1850 far more freight and long-distance passengers travelled by rail than by canal or by road. The spread of the rail network continued throughout the rest of the 19th century, and by the 1870s there were cheap fares for workers, enabling them to find work wherever they pleased. The chains of village life had been broken.

And then the town and city dwellers discovered the countryside through the windows of their railway carriages. Theirs were usually through-trains, but there soon developed a system of country trains that stopped at every station and wayside halt, sometimes by request. For example, a large landowner might flag down the train at his private halt, perhaps to load on horses,

◀ **DALMATIANS WERE HISTORICALLY KNOWN AS CARRIAGE DOGS.** *Familiar with horses, these muscular and loyal dogs used to run alongside coaches and when necessary would run ahead to clear the way. In America this role was carried out for horse-drawn fire engines and they became known as firehouse dogs.*

▲ MANY VILLAGES HAD A GOODS YARD
*at the station where local produce – ranging
from minerals and timber to livestock and crops
– could be loaded for rail shipment to various
markets all over the country. The station-master
knew all his regulars and would make sure a
wagon or farm lorry could park slightly uphill
from the railway truck so that the men could
offload more easily by hand.*

riders and hounds for the local hunt. Funnily
enough, if was often these same landowners
who had financed the building of rural
branch lines in the first place.

Initially the railway was designed for
the carriage of bulk freight, and instantly
brought new markets for rural goods
wherever there was a country station.
Relatively few villages had their own railway
depot and these ones often began to grow
quickly with this new asset. The station was
sometimes a mile or so outside the village,
and the village began to stretch towards
it. Farmers soon began to accompany
their livestock on the trains and found it
a convenient way of getting into town for
other business. All sorts of farm workers
and tradesmen joined in the fun, and to find
work elsewhere. Increasingly the country
train became a passenger train, though with
far less profit to the railway companies than
freight. Rail travel became cheaper and
faster, wages increased with the scope for
choice of work, working hours decreased and
more and more people had time and money
to take a train journey for leisure as well as

for work. Huge numbers of people would
flock to events all over the country by train,
such as race meetings and seaside visits.

It was boomtime for the countryside,
and it lasted quite a while. It brought
new buyers for country homes within
commuting distance of the cities; it brought
new businesses to cater for those buyers; it
brought goods and ideas and so much more.
And so the boom continued, until that black
day when Dr Richard Beeching, Chairman
of the British Railways Board (1963–
1965), wielded his axe and peremptorily
severed a large number of what had been
essential arteries feeding the countryside,
all in the interests of 'economy', with no
comprehension of the far more important
social role of public transport. It was to prove
a devastating blow for many villages, though
the effects were slow to be recognised.

The deserted stations were converted into
dwellings and the now silent tracks reverted
to nature and became artificial greenways
for walkers, riders and cyclists. At Lavant,
in Sussex, the parish council was informed
in 1986 that 'a "gentleman" together with
a "lady" are residing in a tree house built
in an evergreen oak on the Railway Track
near Oldwick Meadows.' The gentleman's
presence was causing some concern to locals,
as he was sometimes the worse for drink and
he frightened people. But surely he was just
another rich character, so many of whom
have disappeared from rural areas in an
increasingly uniform world?

Aircraft

The two world wars brought another
new presence to the countryside. At first
it was fun, watching planes made of brown
paper and string cavorting in the skies,
manned by ex-cavalry officers who, for
World War I, were told that because they
could ride a horse they could fly a plane
without being taught. Rich young men
began to buy private planes that they landed
with dangerous imprecision in grassy fields
when attending country house weekends, but
that was an enjoyable spectacle for the locals.

With World War II, aircraft became
threatening instead. Many rural areas were
used by homebound German aircraft as
dumping grounds for their undelivered
bombs – almost more frightening than the
regular drubbing suffered by some of the
big cities for which those bombs had been
destined. In many places people had ringside

*'Many rural areas were used by homebound
German aircraft as dumping grounds for their
undelivered bombs'*

▲ PILOTS 'SCRAMBLE' TO THEIR SPITFIRES
*in May, 1939, as a practice for what would
soon became all too familiar. Rural children
during World War II could identify different
RAF aircraft as much by the sound of their
engines as by their shape and features.*

views of the dogfights in the skies. New
airfields were built, not only for British craft
but also for large numbers of American and
others, which had a considerable effect on
many small communities. But still people
were basically on the side of aircraft, and
after the war one of the more pleasant
sounds of high summer was the background
drone of friendly propellers across a blue sky
above the meadows.

Then came the rapid growth of the
commercial airlines and the new mass habit
of spending holidays abroad and getting
there by air. Jet engines replaced props and
the sound became intrusive rather than
soporific. Military jets began to scream very
low over the fields, terrifying animals and
people alike (hot-air balloons, so innocent,
also stampede the animals); the heavy
vibration of military helicopters throbbed
menacingly as the big bugs loomed suddenly

▲ THE EPSOM DOWNS *is a favourite area for flying model aircraft (as well as for horse-racing).
In 1902 Mr Guillion was attempting to fly a full-size biplane that appears to be patched together
from a tricycle, balsa wood and paper. Newly recruited Royal Flying Corps pilot Archie James
had memories from World War I that the early planes were indeed 'made of string and paper',
as far as he could tell, and he had to fire at the enemy with his own pistol, aiming between the
blades of his own propellor.*

▲ **THE VILLAGE POST OFFICE** *was usually a general store as well, or at least a grocery shop. At Rustington in Sussex in 1910 the village veterinary surgeon had his surgery next to the post office, as it was the centre of life in the village.*

over the horizon and skimmed farmhouse rooftops. Flying became a hobby for more people, and light planes flitted about the skies in increasing numbers.

Communications

The whole of this chapter has been about communication – keeping in touch – and its dramatic effect on life in the countryside. It is appropriate, therefore, to include a section about the forms of interpersonal communication that have had an even greater and more direct effect.

For centuries, those who lived in rural areas were isolated and introverted. They knew little about the world beyond the village, or beyond the nearest market town. It was really only within the 19th and particularly 20th century that their eyes were opened, first by education, especially learning to read, so that books, journals, political pamphlets and advertisements became accessible to all.

Postal services

The ability to read and write opened an immediate line of communication through letters. A countrywide penny post was

introduced in 1840 and contracts for running village post offices were first offered in the 1840s and 1850s, but by the 1870s most villagers still so rarely received post that when something was delivered, be it a letter or a mail-order circular, it would be read time and time again, carefully folded and kept in an apron pocket or on the mantelpiece in the meantime. About half of all village post offices in the 1850s had been connected with a shop of some kind, and these shops were the ones that would survive when the heyday of the general village shop began to wane in the early 1920s.

The mail usually came by rail and with the railways came another new and exciting form of communication in the 1840s: the electric telegraph. It was based at the local railway station because originally the system was used to pass messages concerning only railway matters down the line. Soon the station-master found himself also acting as an agent for postal telegrams on behalf of the post office. The railway system brought national newspapers and weekly journals into the countryside as well, hot off the city presses, opening more eyes to the rest of the world.

Postmen have always been popular in rural areas, where for some isolated dwellings the 'postie' is the only person they see for days on end. Postmen and postwomen have quite an important social role in rural areas: they tend to know a lot about what is going on in most of the households they visit, and are often the first to notice that someone is ill, or depressed, or in need of help. They can scan faces as they deliver the mail and are generally aware of whether an envelope contains a bill or a love letter. In times gone by the postman would blow on his whistle as he passed a house, to give the occupants a chance to send a parcel or buy some stamps from him; today you cannot help but hear

▲ POSTMEN AND POSTWOMEN *often walked many miles in rural areas, in all weathers, and had to be physically fit. The luckier ones might do their deliveries on a bike or a pony, and in the 19th century some postwomen had the use of a donkey cart.*

the familiar sound of the red van bouncing up the track and are relieved to be able to hand over outgoing post without having to walk two miles to the postbox.

Telephones

Next came the magic of the telephone. At first only the select few installed them in the home – people like doctors, who needed them, and city weekenders, who were used to them. In the 1930s farmers began to find them useful, and various tradesmen. Between the world wars those familiar red telephone kiosks began to dot the countryside. Private phones were still limited mainly to the middle classes and it was not until after World War II that they generally found their way into cottages. By then, every part of the countryside was delineated by stout telegraph poles, their multiple wires singing in the wind as if with the hum of the countless voices that chattered across the land, and dark green GPO lorries wandered the lanes with new poles protruding over their cabs.

There were many complaints about the presence of these festooned dead trees in the landscape, but in general they followed the line of the roads and were accepted more readily than the dominating rows of huge electricity pylons that eventually marched menacingly across swathes of open countryside, destroying the view forever.

Radio and television

By the 1940s the wireless was well and truly ensconced in every home. Radio particularly proved its worth during World War II, when ears would be intent on the sound of the news that reached the homeland almost simultaneously with the actual event. The BBC had begun its radio broadcasts in 1927. In due course programmes such as *Mrs Dale's Diary* seemed to reflect a life people recognised; and *The Archers* really did help farmers, always an isolated group, to learn about current farming practices. But there were those who were wary even of radio. In 1951, for example, a study of English life and leisure, begun in 1947, warned severely about the effects of 'continuous radio'. The report's authors stated that one woman had suffered a nervous breakdown from her husband's prolonged and loud playing of the radio, so that the family doctor instructed him to sell the infernal machine. In other cases, students had abandoned their studies, unable to concentrate when their parents had the radio on; wives almost divorced husbands for 'sitting by that blessed radio' and listening to whatever programme was broadcast, however dull; family arguments over which programme should be heard were frequent.

Next came television, with the BBC's first broadcast as early as 1936. Television brought new blots on the rural landscape – not just masts but forests of aerials on venerable country rooftops. It offered an even wider scope for new knowledge, though many distrusted it for 'doing away with family life', fearing that children would sit silently in front of the set rather than joining in with the rest of the family to play musical instruments, play games, read books and chat. Television sets were still rare even in middle-class homes in the 1950s, when several families would cluster round the only set in the village and peer at its tiny black-and-white screen.

The new revolution

And then came a new type of screen. With the advent of computers, and particularly with the Internet, not only is the village linked easily with the rest of the world but also many individuals can work from home in whatever part of the country they prefer. They are no longer tied to the workplace, no longer obliged to travel daily to their jobs, no longer forced to live in an area simply because that is where the jobs are. They can choose to work from home, and that means they can also choose to take part much more actively in the everyday life of their community.

It is perhaps this above all that will revitalise rural areas, though back in 1965 Paul Jennings had expressed doubts about its coming: 'Is there now a tide before which even those protecting Welsh mountains will crumble, will the electronic village, in an irresistible process, worldwide, a mechanical and electronic culture, endlessly universal and homogeneous, obliterate the diversified life of villages as we have remembered them, all rural and all different?'

Will the man who stood outside in the moonlight to watch and listen to a nightingale singing on a television aerial still see the real bird and hear its real song, or will he only see the virtual reality of it on the screen?

▼ COMPUTERS *did not come into the home until they were small enough not to take up an entire room and were affordable. Farmers were sceptical about their value but the so-called portable Osborne computer, developed in 1981, did find some agricultural applications in the UK and the equipment was deemed tough enough to be taken out into the fields and cowsheds. The machine was the size and weight of a full suitcase and its screen measured a mere 5in. It had 'floppy' disk drives, was very slow and with limited capacity (64k RAM), and the bundled software depended on WordStar, but it never crashed – unlike the manufacturer.*

8. Growing Up

Those who lived in towns might mock country children for their rusticity and lack of sophistication. They might sneer at the lack of modern amenities such as mains water and electricity, which tended to reach rural areas several decades after they had become common in urban areas. Even as late as 1940, a quarter of rural parishes had no piped water, and half had no sewage disposal systems. But country children were rich in their knowledge of the natural world; they were wise in the matters of birth, life, death and procreation among the animals that surrounded them; they were self-sufficient in supplying the family table with home-grown vegetables, hedgerow fruit, wild meat and produce from the backyard animals. They were hard-working and disciplined, and they learnt rural skills that would ensure them a job for life.

rowing up in the countryside was, for most children, a combination of idyll and hardship. They had an exhilarating freedom to roam and explore the diversity of their extensive surroundings; but they often experienced poverty, appalling sanitation, epidemics, hard physical work from a young age, limited horizons and choices, and perhaps isolation.

Swimming in secret ponds, paddling in streams, tickling minnows and sticklebacks, gathering frogspawn and blackberries ... so many golden memories of childhood in the country. Frank Burningham grew up in the Surrey village of Chobham, and most of his memories from childhood involve being out-of-doors – watching the 'thrashing' machine, tagging along with the village band as it marched down the village street on the evening of Armistice Sunday carrying acetylene lanterns for the bandsmen so that they could read their music, carol singing

'... they often experienced poverty, appalling sanitation, epidemics, hard physical work from a young age and perhaps isolation.'

with the band ('I remember we played one foggy night in front of a haystack thinking we'd been playing in front of a house!').

Percy Heath, whose father was a shepherd in the 1940s, roamed the countryside with his brothers when they were young and knew tree, hedge, ditch, pond, cow, pig, path, birds' nest, fox den and rabbit hole. He remembers his very deaf old granny: 'Used to have to talk to her through a rolled-up newspaper tied with bits of string – you had to get it up to her ear. She used to sit us up on the old copper edge and get hold of your hair to wash it, and scrub your face hard.' He also remembers the pranks he and his brothers would get up to, and playing

▶ **CLEAN-KNEED AND DRESSED IN HIS BEST** *for granny: this was a rare occasion for a small country boy. Usually he would have worn clothes that suited his everyday lifestyle – out and about in the fields and woods, playing in the dusty lanes, poking about in ponds, getting muddy and nobody minding.*

▲ **THE BICYCLE WAS A TREASURED AND WELL-USED POSSESSION** *and the luckiest would get their first bike at the age of 11. Once they left school they relied heavily on two wheels to escape the village or to work on delivery rounds in the area.*

football among the cowpats in the meadow. Dad had Dexter cows and an old mule when Percy was little; the boys would gather big bundles of bracken as bedding for them, and would drive the two-wheeled mule cart to get firewood and sheep.

Little ones

Harking back to the building of the railway network, an old man said that the area was 'chock full o' navvies, very near every 'ouse 'ad lodgers ... and there was more babbies in the place then than there ever 'ad been afore, or ever 'ave been since, an' I could name a few wot come in the Pig's 'Ead of a night now who 'ouldn't be 'ere at all if it 'adn't been fer the railroad.'

Richard Jefferies – a renowned writer on natural history, rural life and agriculture in Victorian England – described the labourer's child of the 1870s. He had noted that the style of walk of the Wiltshire labourer was caused by 'following the plough in early childhood, when the weak limbs find it a hard labour to pull the heavy nailed boots from the thick clay soil. Ever afterwards he walks as if it were an exertion to lift his legs.' He talked about a typical boy of three or four years old, dressed by his mother in the morning but then turned out of doors to take care of himself. Wearing his father's greasy old hat (well over his ears and down almost to his shoulders), a jacket that used to be white, a belt, and a pair of boots like his father's in miniature with iron at the heel and toe, his legs bare and sturdy, he would toddle off to the nearby farmyard to watch the big horses being harnessed, hiding behind a tree or rick so that he was not spotted by the carter. Then he would watch the steam engine, or the shovelling of grain in the great barn. Soon his morning-scrubbed skin was boyishly grimy. In due course he might go home for a slice of bread and dripping; his little sister would be trying to look after the crawling baby.

Jefferies marvelled how 'those prosperous parents who dwell in highly rented suburban villas, and send out their children for a walk with a couple of nurses and a "bow-wow" to run beside the perambulator' would be eaten up with anxiety should their darlings have ventured where the little labourer's son played – under the hoofs of carthorses in the field, or floating twigs in the stream to pretend they were boats, or mingling with the cows and the bull in the meadow, the big sows with their young, the carts rumbling to

▲ HIGH BUTTON BOOTS *and ankle-high lace-up boots were worn by many country girls in the late 19th century. For younger girls, frocks were usually covered by a loose pinafore. Boys had ankle-high lace-up boots and often wore guernseys or round-frocks over loose collarless shirts and loose calf-length trousers.*

and fro, the steam engines ploughing the furrows: the little boy, all by himself out in all weathers, the freezing wind whipping tears from his eyes and reddening his skin, the rain plummeting on him as he splashed happily in the puddles, the sun blazing down on him in the fields.

Yet he not only survived; he seemed to thrive and be happy out there, happier than the sister already burdened with household work. The little girl, like him, would be locked out of the cottage during the day but she also had to be in charge of her younger siblings as they played outside. In summer her life was

'Open to the elements, knees were constantly cold, grazed, grass-stained and muddy, but these were badges of pride.'

pleasant enough, sitting by the brook with the toddlers around her, picking flowers to make dandelion chains, plaits of rushes and cowslip balls. Later in the year she would take them to forage for wild fruit. All the while she would be alert for suitable pieces of fallen wood to drag home for the fire – even in London children in the 19th century were constantly scavenging for bits for the fire.

Frocks and bonnets

In old pictures of small children it can be hard to tell which are boys and which are girls. In their younger years, their clothes were often interchangeable; or, more precisely, small boys wore their sisters' cast-offs. To add to the confusion, girls up to about eight years old usually had their hair cut short like the boys and wore similar round black felt hats.

Most small girls in the late 19th century wore frocks that were short-sleeved, whatever the weather, made of cotton in summer and 'stuff' (coarse woollen cloth) in winter. Helen Allingham's paintings show the typical cotton print frocks with long pinafore and plain sunbonnet worn earlier in

that century. Those pinafores could be quite a problem if you were in a hurry to get to school: they had countless fiddly buttons down the back. Buttons also featured on boots for both girls and boys – horrible things to deal with when your fingers were cold and wet.

At one time country boys often wore 'gabardines', which were short round-frocks (like smocks), over corduroy suits. Gertrude Jekyll was amused when an aged and long-retired schoolmistress, pondering her pupils, said, 'Let me see, which boy was it that used always to speak of his gabardine – was it Jushingto Earl? No, it was Berechiah Gosling.' Many a child had an extraordinary Christian name in the 19th century, and even in the 20th; typically the parents would open the Bible almost at random and pick a name from it, and in the late Victorian period they might also choose fancy names from novels.

In the 20th century, there was the ritual of the trousers. Small boys wore short trousers until a certain age – usually about 13 – when they graduated to long ones. They considered themselves to be tough in their shorts; long trousers before your time were wimpish. Open to the elements, knees

▲ OUTINGS TO THE SEASIDE *were a memorable occasion, although for those who lived far from the coast the journey could often be long and uncomfortable. Here, young members of a country church choir enjoy their annual break from busy church duties.*

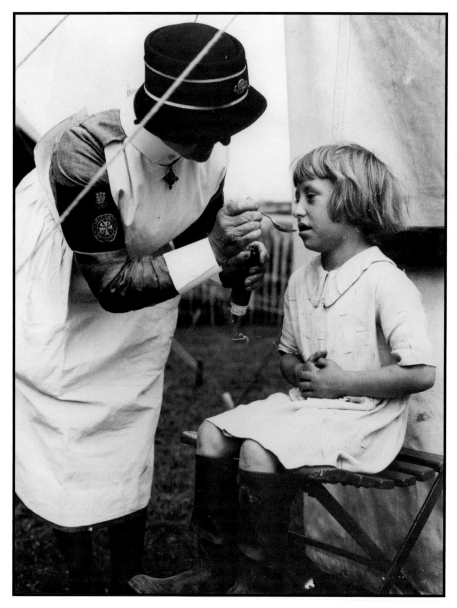

▲ CASTOR AND COD LIVER OIL *were both popular remedies for a wide range of ailments. Castor oil was used above all for the relief or prevention of constipation, and many children were given a weekly dose to ensure regular bowel movements. The oil was processed from the seeds (castor beans) of a tropical plant from which the deadly poison, ricin, is also obtained.*

were constantly cold, grazed, grass-stained and muddy, but these were badges of pride. The shorts were baggy and generally just down to knee level; often over-large hand-me-downs, they would be held up by braces or string, or by those adjustable striped belts with an S-shaped metal 'snake' clasp that had so many other uses as well. In many a household a boy would have only one pair of shorts, but that didn't restrict him from forgetting to keep them clean and not to rip them when he climbed trees and scrambled through hedges.

Coughs and sneezes

It is heart-rending to visit old graveyards, or go through the parish registers, and discover just how many children died very young. Sometimes you will find a succession of children in the same family grave, their

names gradually added to the headstone and their deaths ranging from a few days to three or four years old. In the church register of one small rural parish it was recorded in the year 1836 – the year before Victoria ascended the throne – that one family lost three children on 10 January (aged seven, four and nearly three); within the next two months five more toddlers and babies in the parish were dead.

Scarlet fever was one of the killers that led to frequent fatalities in children. Florence Brooks remembered catching 'a fever' at the age of three or four and going to hospital, where her parents were only allowed to look at her through the window. Another woman remembered catching scarlet fever in 1901 and being bundled into the enclosed black horse-drawn 'fever cart' to be isolated at the fever hospital. All of her clothes were burnt. The children would be incarcerated for six weeks, and could only wave at their families on the other side of the road for what must have seemed like a lifetime. Even in the early 1950s scarlet fever was still around: anyone who was thought to have the illness was rushed to hospital immediately. Anyone who was thought to have been in contact with a sufferer was put in quarantine for what would have seemed like an eternity to a small child. They would be separated from the rest of the world by a curtain of disinfectant-impregnated sheets, and only allowed out to play when no other children were around.

Smallpox was another highly contagious killer. It was realised early on in the 18th century that vaccination might protect the young against smallpox, though many distrusted the whole idea. In spite of this, the smallpox vaccine was the first successful vaccine ever developed. George Dew of Lower Heyford, Oxfordshire – one of whose many local roles in the 1870s was to keep a register of vaccinations and to try to persuade village families to vaccinate their children against smallpox – was empowered to take out summonses against parents who failed to do so. His diary noted the case of a journeyman painter by the name of Prosser who was sent to Oxford Gaol for seven days for not having his child vaccinated; in the meantime the Anti-Compulsory Vaccination League paid his fine. The league had been formed in 1866 when it realised that the arm-to-arm method of vaccination in use at the time presented a high risk of cross-infection, and many parents believed that healthy babies could become fatally infected through the vaccination process. There was much heated correspondence in journals such as *The Field* about the dangers and advantages of vaccination.

The third major killer was typhoid fever, usually due to appalling sanitation and contaminated drinking water. Whole families were dying of typhoid in the 1870s. Then there was influenza, especially the terrible 'flu epidemic just after World War I. The church bell would be tolled once for the death of a man, twice for a woman and three times for a child. Cruelly, many of those who died in that epidemic were soldiers who had managed to survive the trenches.

There were other childhood ailments, of course – measles, mumps, 'German measles' (rubella), chickenpox, whooping cough, diphtheria and the like – but on the whole the attitude, right up to the 1960s, was that these were simply what most children were likely to catch anyway as part of growing up and in most cases parents did not worry unduly about them: you got the rash, ran a temperature, took a welcome break from school and recovered without the aid of antibiotics or anything other than some soothing calamine lotion. There was certainly no vaccination for such common diseases; a measles vaccine, for example, was not introduced in the UK until the mid 1960s, followed by a separate vaccine for rubella, and for mumps eventually in the late 1980s.

Epidemics of measles and whooping cough in 1838–1840 did kill up to 50,000 people throughout the UK. In 1887, Blyth in Northumbria suffered firstly a miners' strike and then, when 'misery, starvation and hunger' were rampant as a result, along came

▶ EVERY CHILD IN THE 1930s *had to have a daily gargle to ward off influenza. The gargle solution would generally be warm salt water, diluted TCP (a mild antiseptic introduced in 1918) or plain water, but none would have been much deterrent against viral disease.*

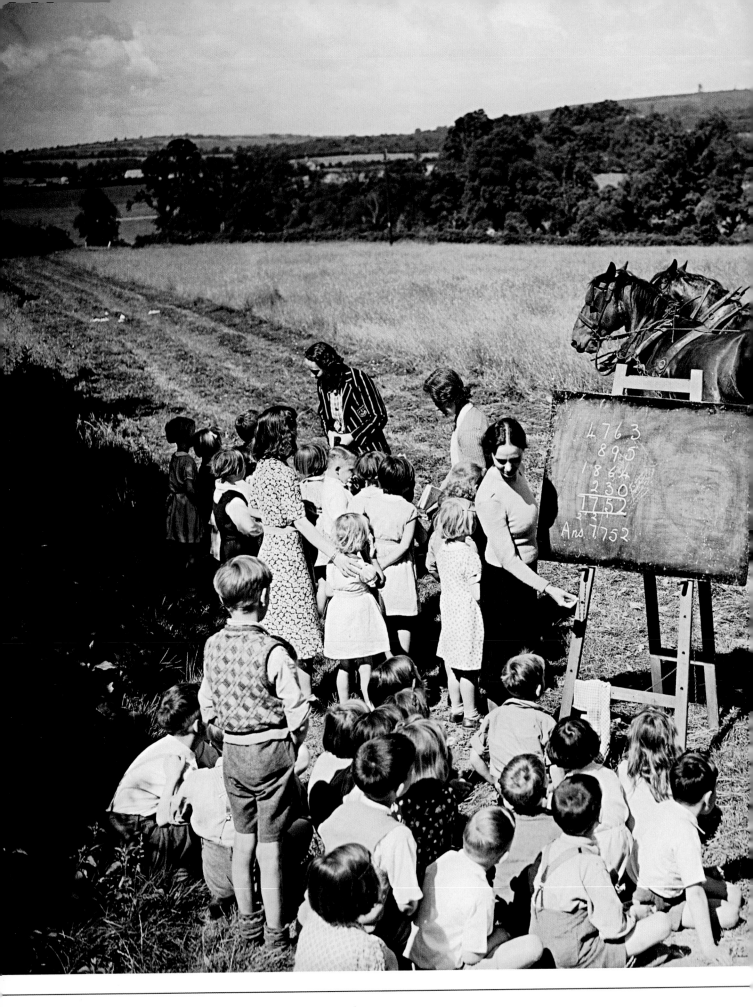

TIMES PAST IN THE COUNTRYSIDE

a measles epidemic, with up to 300 cases and with infant mortalities on a daily basis, but this was largely because the children were weakened by being grossly undernourished.

In 1891 a school log book for the Staffordshire village of Bushbury recorded that a local measles epidemic had caused the annual school treat to be deferred, but nobody seemed too concerned about the epidemic and the death rate from measles in children under the age of 15 dropped dramatically nationwide from about 1900. By the 1930s it was known how to treat any secondary complications, so that mortality was at a low level long before the national immunisation programme began. This huge improvement was due to generally better health as a result of clean water, improved nutrition and better living conditions. The same was true of whooping cough. As for mumps, it was usually rather a mild disease and quite often parents and their doctors didn't even realise when their children were suffering from it.

The three Rs

As soon as children were capable of walking the distance, they would be off to school in the village, in groups coming together from various cottages along the way and playing as they went.

'I be'ant no scholard,' the old folks would say, meaning that they could neither read nor write. But book learning is what schools taught. William Cobbett – 19th century political pamphleteer, farmer and prolific journalist – said that the very act of growing your own food and raising your own livestock was 'the best possible foundation of education of the children of the labourer'. Many parents throughout that century agreed with him, and felt that their children would learn much more of value by working in the fields or at the family's cottage industry, contributing to their income, than sitting at a school desk learning by rote. The farmers agreed too: children should be available on demand to help with the harvest

◀ **CLASS SIZES IN RURAL AREAS** *increased during World War II, often beyond comfortable capacity. The chance of an outdoor lesson was rarely missed, and evacuated city children remember the novelty fondly, often learning more about countryside work than the lesson at hand.*

and haymaking, sheep shearing and poultry plucking, not glued to their books in a dusty school room, growing pale out of the sun.

In early Victorian times, school was voluntary and for most country children that meant no school. Villages were free to choose whether or not they would have a school, and if so what sort of a school and how it should be run. It was not until 1876 that attendance at what were still voluntary schools became compulsory, and it was not until 1891 that free education (no more paying a penny or tuppence a week to attend school, and twice that if you failed to turn up) became available to all, up to the age of 14.

Finally, the 1902 Education Act put the State in control of local education so that everybody had to conform. No longer could children take the day off because the travelling circus was coming through the village or there was a local farm sale to be enjoyed. In theory, the employment of children in agriculture had been regulated since the 1870s anyway, but in practice it was a different matter in the villages and even the village worthies often felt that children benefited from starting work as young as seven, much more so than going to school.

To school you had to go, sitting on hard planks with nothing to lean back against, scraping a pencil across a slate or scratching away with an inky nib, dashing across the yard to stinking earth closets when nature called, shivering with cold in the classroom unless you were next to the stove, which steamed, being draped with everybody's wet clothes. Dire penalties were issued if you arrived with dirty shoes or boots, despite the fact that you had been walking miles along the muddy lanes and fields to get to school.

Lessons were the three Rs and the parson's scripture class; later you might learn a little history and geography, needlework and basic science. In the villages you would

'Dire penalties were issued if you arrived with dirty shoes or boots ...'

▲ **FLOODING IN THE VILLAGE** *meant that schools would have to shut, which was a good excuse for the children to enjoy themselves (as here at Langport in 1935). In Victorian times flooding often led to serious outbreaks of disease: foul water would lie stagnant for days, contaminating drinking supplies and carrying diseases such as typhoid fever and cholera.*

probably learn something more relevant to your life as well – nature, weather, agriculture, practical gardening and poultry keeping. In the early 20th century practical lessons included handicrafts, cooking, laundry, butter making and woodwork, but the range was hardly adequate to meet Cobbett's ideals.

Every country child of yesterday has their own school memories: the separated playground with a wooden fence between the boys and the girls; walking to school along main roads that were so empty the children ran along the middle of them (stopping along the way to play with the goats on the common); eating home-packed sandwiches at dinner time while you watched the big mill wheel turning and water rushing down the slip, or lingered to see the blacksmith's flying sparks and hear his ringing hammer; then spinning out the long walk home by playing hide-and-seek

among the trees, looking for mushrooms and berries or collecting returnable bottles so that you could make a few pennies, or just generally mucking about with your friends.

In the classroom

The school in the small Wiltshire village of Biddestone was built soon after 1844, the year in which a piece of land was conveyed as the site of a school and schoolhouse. The exact date of building is unknown, but it was clearly well established by the time of the first log books in 1873. Six years later there were more than 60 pupils, and at some stages in its history the numbers rose into the low hundreds. However, if there were more than 108 pupils the children had to take turns to attend, as there simply wasn't room for all of them. In 1884 several children were 'obliged to go to Hartham on Thursdays for soup' (there was no explanation in the log book as to why this was so, but perhaps a charity was

involved). Alan Hayes attended Biddestone in the early years of the 20th century, when the schoolroom had two rows of desks, then a screen to separate them from another class with its own two rows of desks, and so on. This was typical of village schools, many of which were simply one large room in which children of all ages were taught, the older ones often taking turns to teach the younger.

School punishments were usually beating, detention, black marks or standing in the corner. Many a village school's old punishment books record the stroke of the cane, generally on the hands, for what today might seem petty misdemeanours – careless work, dirty hands, 'idleness during singing', 'running out of lines', being cheeky, not paying attention, dawdling into school after the bell had rung and so on. One poor young lad could not read out the word 'signed' properly; he always pronounced it 'sig-ned', which was perfectly logical. Eventually his

▲ THE ELEMENTARY EDUCATION ACT *of 1876 obliged all parents to ensure that their children received elementary education between the ages of 5 and 14, and stated that no child should be in employment under the age of 10. The 1902 Education Act brought the control of schools under the jurisdiction of local government, creating local education authorities. Timetables and term times applied to town and country alike, and children could not be released from their desks to help in the fields. Times were changing: the farming calendar was no longer the dominant one in the countryside.*

▲ SCOTTISH SCHOOLS IN THE 1940S *adopted the general rule that girls had to wear their hair short enough to be 'off the collar', as demonstrated in this photograph from Kinlocheil.*

teacher's patience snapped and the boy was 'caned on the bum'. His mother was furious and marched round to the school to tell the teacher exactly what she thought of the punishment, loudly and threatening violence. In the 1870s the master of a village school in Oxfordshire was summoned before the magistrates and charged with excessively beating a small girl, but the case was dismissed as she had evidence of only one stripe of the cane across the shoulders 'although she swore she had four'.

Village schools have suffered over the years with instructions from on high altering the curriculum, dictating how the school should be run and the lessons taught, and being closed down because numbers have dropped too low. The loss of a village school can destroy a community; no wonder people have fought so hard to keep their schools. At

times teachers have come close to despair. In the 1960s a primary school at North Kelsey in Lincolnshire expressed its frustrations in the local scrapbook, organised by the Women's Institute to record local life. The teachers wrote: '... primary education is in a state of flux. This is considered by "educationists" to be a sign of virility. It is to be hoped that by the time this report is read in 25 years' time thoughts and actions will have crystallised. Secondly, I hope the teaching profession will be held in greater esteem by the populace, especially where payment for services is concerned ...'.

As they wrote, the eleven-plus was about to be abolished, comprehensive education was coming to nearby Caistor and schools were likely to be reorganised into age groups that would probably sound the death knell for many village schools. Primary schools were being asked to incorporate many new subjects and teaching techniques (there were mutterings about the Initial Teaching Alphabet and 'new' maths) but if they did so something else would have to go in order to make room for the additional subjects in the school day. The parents and the rest of the community, as they always do for village schools, were still busily raising money and supplying voluntary labour for the extras, but there were limits. Catchment areas were growing and there were justified fears that there would soon be no difference between rural schools and urban schools.

What, for example, about local dialects? Since 1870 children had been reprimanded for slipping into dialect at school, and in Wiltshire they were told to 'ta'ak oop and vurget their mother tongue' – except that the teacher would have pronounced this instruction in clipped tones. Who was to say what the 'right' language was? Many dialect words had been used for centuries before 'proper' words came into being – words like 'chimbley' instead of 'chimney', 'turmut'

rather than 'turnip', and so many more. A huge number of children's words for this and that started to be lost from the playground – phrases like 'I ballows that', 'Barley me that', 'Pike I'; words like coggy, shigs, laggy, croggies, screase, scribs, mardy and spahs. The language became greatly impoverished when there were no longer a thousand different ways to call someone a fool. Even Victorian strictness couldn't keep language wholly in its place; children and adults continued to create new words, and by 1890 schools were frowning on the use of local dialects. These were the beginnings of the loss of the rich vocabulary of old.

Flora Thompson, born in 1876 and writing her *Country Calendar* in the 1920s when she lived in Liphook, Hampshire, came up with the notion of appointing the school children of parishes to be local historians. 'What a multitude of little regarded facts, likely to be intensely interesting to future generations, those small, sharp eyes would note.' They would mark the passing of local landmarks – trees, cottages

and stories connected with them; they would report on village events and national celebrations; they would tell of weather, of wildlife, of work in the fields, of the planting of new woodland and the making of ponds; they would mention famous people who had passed through, or their own villagers who had become famous elsewhere. She ended her fantasy as follows: 'It would make interesting reading for the people of the year 2,000, this "New Domesday Book; or Every Parish its Own History".'

Fun and games

In 1908 Robert Baden-Powell published the first edition of *Scouting for Boys*. Scouting was born in the days of Empire, and 'Bee-Pea' wished to foster an interest in 'nature study and woodcraft'. 'We want to make the boy feel that he is a young backwoodsman and not an imitation soldier – still less a nonentity who does not count,' he said in 1918.

He had already created a junior branch of the movement – the Wolf Cubs (ages 8 to 12), about which he said: 'The prevalence

▲ PHYSICAL EDUCATION MAY HAVE BEEN PART OF THE CURRICULUM, *but in rural areas 'exercise' was often simply an extension of play, even if it was just going through hoops with your classmates and teacher. Most country children already had plenty of daily physical exercise in walking to school, playing in the fields and woods and helping with household and garden chores.*

of Juvenile Crime among boys between the ages of ten and twelve shows that propensities are then already forming, and points to the need of shaping their characters at an earlier age than that of Scouts'. He then instituted the Senior Scouts for the over-18s 'in sympathy with the changing psychology of the adolescent' and to retain the older boy 'under the good influences of the movement at the critical time of his life just when boyhood's pastimes cease to appeal and manhood's temptations are upon him'. He pointed out that scouting could be carried out in the towns just as well as in the country, and for many town boys scouting was their introduction to the countryside. The girls were not forgotten: the Girl Guide movement was only a little younger than the Scouting movement.

The range of self-made entertainments for country children seemed endless, as did their imaginations. There was an unbroken tradition of games, many of them seasonal, such as hopscotch and tag (in all its complex variations), and many games that children still play today, such as hide-and-seek and leapfrog – so many simple ways to use the playground! In the Lake District in the 1880s they were playing chivy, with 'dens' at opposite corners of the village crossroads; or cosolary, with someone standing in the middle of the square trying to catch people as they sprinted past; or 'ickly ackly aiko', which involved hurling a ball over a cowshed between teams; or the elaborate rituals of minny cuddy, which seemed to involve boys clambering up on top of each other in pyramids and chanting their gang chants. Knucklebones and spillikins, marbles and conkers, tiddlywinks and spinning tops, hoops for bowling and horseshoes for tossing, mock hockey played with hedgerow sticks and walking sticks, football and cricket – every evening, the village would be loud with the sound of happy children playing.

Then there were the sports days, at bank holidays or on other special occasions. School was school, but its rigours were

▼ SAMUEL WILDERSPIN (1791–1866), *pioneered the importance of playtime and playgrounds in schools, but his ideas were more suited to the greater restrictions of urban environments. In the villages, most school playgrounds continued to be rudimentary even after World War II, and the children devised their own games with simple equipment such as skipping ropes and balls, or marked out rough hopsctoch pitches. Many villages raised money during the 20th century to create separate children's play areas with swings and slides on the public recreation field.*

occasionally broken with high days and holidays – teas at the manor house with Punch and Judy shows and races (you could win a penny for coming in third), May Day parades, jubilee and coronation celebrations. These were always occasions for stuffing yourself with food but they were primarily for joining in various activities. There might be 'catch the train' races, in which there were piles of clothes and you had to run and put on first your socks, then run and put on your pants, then on to the next heap to find your shirt and put it on, finishing up with your shoes and racing for the finishing line to be not just first but also the best dressed. There was 'tilt the bucket', in which someone sat in a barrow with a long pole with a bucket full of water on the end of it, and they had to get the bucket through a hole without spilling the water. There were wheelbarrow races, egg-and-spoon races, sack races (easy to cheat if you knew how) and three-legged races (easy to fall if you didn't know how).

There was all this and playing pranks – simple things like tying a pin to one end of a reel of black cotton and a heavy button a little farther along, then secretly sticking the pin into a cottage window frame, reeling out the cotton while retreating across the field, and manipulating the button so that it kept going 'tink, tink, tink' against the window pane, irritating the occupants.

▲ A NATIONAL NATURE STUDY EXHIBITION *in 1902 encouraged village schools to teach science by having 'observation classes'. The children would bring their own exhibits of plants, feathers and the like to these lessons, or collect them on class nature walks.*

◀ HORSE CHESTNUTS *have played important roles in history, not least in school playground contests. Conkers were ground in World War I as feed for livestock, and in World War II boys were urgently encouraged by the Ministry of Supply to collect conkers for the war effort. School groups and Boy Scouts were paid 7s 6d a hundredweight for them.*

▲ HOOPS FIRST BECAME POPULAR
*in the 1800s. Made out of wood, with
metal strips or 'tyres' for weight, the hoops
would be pushed down the street either by
hand or with a stick.*

John Moore, writing evocatively about his
childhood in the late 19th century in a
village he chose to mask with the name of
Brensham, described how the only
commodities of interest to him and his
friends in the village shop were huge tiger-
striped bull's eyes, which could be used as
marbles, and thick square-sectioned elastic
for their catapults. For the latter, they first
had to persuade the shopkeeper that they
would only be shooting at empty tin cans
and bottles; she would always lecture them
on shooting at living things. 'If you hit a
poor little fluffy bird with a stone you might
hurt it very badly,' she would say, while the
boys tried to look solemn and at the same
time fingered the notches on the catapults in
their pockets. Her strong black 'cattie-lackey'
was just the job for what they really had in
mind. Then off they would scatter, out of the
village and up the hill past the last cottage,
inhabited by 'Goaty Pegleg', who had a
wooden leg and a long beard and kept a
long-bearded billy goat in his garden. The
old man always seemed to be leaning on the
gate at the end of the lane and usually was in
good enough humour to open it for the boys
so that they could explore the wilderness of

rough furze-bush fields leading to the old
limestone quarries and their magic jungle of
scrub woodland. Here they would hunt with
butterfly nets, catapults and rabbit snares,
though the creatures they caught were
usually imaginary ones. They saw merlins
and goldcrests that were real; they saw grass
snakes, slow worms, lizards and adders (even
a blue-bellied one); they saw the fallow deer
that belonged to the 'Mad Lord' – and once
they saw the Mad Lord himself, only he
looked neither mad nor a lord. He was
disappointingly dressed in 'an old jacket and
breeches, which would have been moderately
becoming upon a scarecrow' and he was
plodding along on a decrepitly ancient and
skinny grey mare. The boys opened the gate
into the larch plantation for him and he
searched his pocket for pennies but found
none, giving them instead a slow and gentle
smile. They raised their caps, as they thought
was fitting, and to their surprise he swept off
his own battered hat in return.

Moore highlighted another courtesy that
has long since disappeared. Along a lane in
the village were lots of very small cottages
that belonged to the Colonel, who owned a
farm at the top of the lane. Whenever the

Colonel passed by sedately on his motorbike, all the little girls from the cottages would curtsy to him, bobbing as they clutched their print frocks at the hem. The Colonel's blue eyes would twinkle and he would wave back, somewhat endangering his own stability on his chugging machine. Young Moore was just as respectful; he would tug hard at the peak of his school cap as the Colonel went by.

Children at work

Country children worked for the family as soon as they were strong enough to be of use. Each child helped with chores in the home, while girls were given household responsibilities from a very early age, caring for babies and toddlers. Children of all ages joined adults in the fields at harvest time, and some helped in their parents' trade or craft as well. Work was a vital part of family life and children were expected to contribute as soon as they could be trusted to do so.

Under the Poor Laws, small children from the workhouse were apprenticed to farmers. If the children were lucky, they were well looked after and received good training. Otherwise they were no more than slave labour. In the 18th and early 19th centuries children as young as six worked on the farms.

▶ CHILDREN'S GAMES AND RACES *would be organised at more traditional livestock markets and shows. The village fair would generally be held on the green at the heart of the village, and would include entertainment for all ages.*

◀ THE ORIGINAL GAME OF 'JACKS' *used anything that children could find near their home, such as sheep knucklebones and pebbles. Using only one hand, the aim was to throw one of the stones into the air and then scoop up another, catching the tossed stone before it landed. The metal, six-legged jacks with rounded feet and two balls that we are accustomed to today were introduced in the 1940s.*

▲ GLEANING USED TO MAKE AN IMPORTANT CONTRIBUTION *to the family income, and it was sometimes possible to gather enough ears of corn to keep the family in bread for the winter. The corn would be taken to the local miller who, in return for some of it for himself, would grind the corn to flour for home baking. The custom died out when harvesting machines became so efficient that there was little grain left in the fields for gleaners.*

'Many children
resented school as much
as their parents and
employers did, and
welcomed their 'duty'
to escape from it'

whose husband had deserted her, had a son of seven years old who went to work. When she applied for relief from Bicester's Board of Guardians, most of its members said it was good for children to begin work young and it would do them more good than going to school. In 1874, farmer Charles Brown on the same Board said he could not bear the thought of poor children having to go to school!

Many children resented school as much as their parents and employers did, and welcomed their 'duty' to escape from it to help with haymaking and harvest, when all the village turned out to work hard but also have fun in each other's company. There was a buzz, a great sense of the importance of getting in the crop, the culmination of the growing year. In Wiltshire some of the boys had the thrill of the annual all-day cattle drive, a 20-mile round trip through the villages to the market at Chippenham and back again, with all the excitement of rounding up animals along the way.

By the 1920s schoolboys were no longer automatically taking part in harvest and haymaking, though they were more than happy to earn pocket money after school within the restrictions of new laws about child work. They could deliver milk and groceries, for example. Children no longer went gleaning with their mothers, but they could still join their fathers under a hedge for tea during haymaking time, or help him on his allotment.

▶ THE ADVENT OF WORLD WAR II *meant that all the generations had to adapt to shortages and rationing, which encouraged much ingenuity in the kitchen. These two children have been making their own sweets, as it became increasingly difficult to buy them in the village sweetshop. Children became used to going without or finding alternatives.*

In 1875, a new Agricultural Children Act came into force, stating that no child under the age of eight could be employed in agriculture, except by its own parents, and that those between the ages of eight and 12 had to attend school for a certain number of days each year, though they could gain permanent exemption from attendance even below the age of 12 as long as they had reached the 'fourth standard' at school. The Elementary Education Act of the same year said that where 'out relief' was given to the parent of any child aged between five and 13 years, it was only on condition that the child received elementary instruction in the three Rs. The legislation was only going to become even more severe under the Education Act of 1876.

Many a farmer had young children working in the fields, and many (farmers, parents and all) deeply resented this new legislation and largely ignored it. Families continued to work together at peak seasons in the fields. In 1873 a woman named Savin,

▲ EVACUATION WAS NOT COMPULSORY,
but taking in evacuees was. Whole schools
would often be moved to the safety of the
countryside and billeted with local families.
Gosport – where these evacuees have come
from – was suffering heavily under German
bombardment as a result of its proximity to the
naval base at Portsmouth.

Pied Piper

In 1939, the government reckoned that more
than two million children would be killed if
they stayed at home in the cities. At 7.30pm
on Friday, September 1, 1939, Operation
Pied Piper was put into action – two days
before World War II was officially declared.
Parents took their children to the schools,
carrying only a toothbrush and comb, a
handkerchief, spare clothes (nightwear, pants,
socks and a mac), gas masks and enough
food for the day.

Over the first four days about one and a
half million evacuees were transported by rail
up to one hundred miles from home, the
government being certain that the enemy
would begin bombing immediately. Many
came back again by Christmas as the bombs
had not materialised, but were re-evacuated
when air raids began in May 1940. More
than three million children were evacuated in

the end, and some of them stayed away for
five years, becoming strangers to their own
families. It was not only children on their
own; there were also mothers with their
toddlers and babies, and the handicapped
with their helpers.

The local children couldn't help feeling
sorry for their visitors, who had been
separated from their families, taken away
from their homes and had arrived on the
railway station, clutching their gas masks and
with their names and numbers marked on
sacking satchels on their backs. A bus would
bring them to the village hall or school, and
there they were inspected like cattle, waiting
for strangers to take them to a new home.

Those strangers had little option: billeting
was compulsory, and this led to a fair amount
of resentment. But at least you could choose
which of the children you would take in,
which sometimes meant that a child would

be separated from its siblings. The government gave you 10s 6d for the first child, and 8s 6d for any others. The new country foster parents were often shocked at the state of the children, many of whom came from the city slums and knew not even the basics of hygiene, and were crawling with lice.

The children were equally shocked by rural life. Some were terrified of livestock and even of rabbits – they had never seen such things. Many were frightened of going down to the privy in the middle of the night, and by the sounds of owls and foxes, and were scared of all that open space during the day. Some would never be happy, missing their families and friends and the urban environment that was home, and sometimes being with foster parents who were severely strict, or treated them as skivvies, or even beat and abused them. Others settled in remarkably well and fell in love with the countryside, making the most of the fresh air and the fresh food; they would return in adult life to live there.

A clear future

The labourers' children described by Richard Jefferies in the 1870s had their future mapped out for them almost from birth. On leaving school, boys would immediately find work on the same farm as their fathers, or one close by, and their wages would augment the family's income. Times were good for agriculture (for a while) and farm labourers could find work and good wages easily.

The girls at this age went less and less into the fields, though they might help their parents at harvest (payment was by the acre, and extra hands speeded up the rate of production). Girls were generally destined for domestic service, and most of them by this period wanted to find jobs in the town, not in the farmhouse and particularly not in the dairy. Farmers' wives complained that they could only get young girls, mere children, whose mothers wanted them to have early experience of a servant's work; the farmer's wife would teach them the basics but they would leave as soon as she had done so, and she would begin all over again with another youngster, or perhaps a slow-witted girl who could find no other work, or a girl who also had to look after an invalid at home or her own illegitimate child.

Aiming for the towns, country girls of the 1870s had begun to dress 'as flashily as servants in cities, and stand upon their

▲ **MANY COUNTRY GIRLS** *went into domestic service in the towns and cities as soon as they left school, including this servant from Gartlogs House, Nether Wallop, in the early 1900s. Domestic servants, whether housemaids, footmen or butlers, would be required to wear a uniform that would vary from house to house.*

▲ THE LOCAL YOUNG FARMERS' CLUB
was an excellent place to meet potential marriage partners, though in theory the clubs were for learning about practical agriculture. A farming background was not an essential qualification for joining the YFC, and many members did not come from farming families. The 'young farmers' would take part in agricultural shows, exhibiting their skills at handling and caring for livestock.

dignity'. Jefferies was amused, and also thought that one effect was to reduce the rate of illegitimate births: the girls had more self-respect than of old and were perhaps wiser in the ways of the world. They began to marry out; the men they met when in service in the town were earning far better wages than the farm labourers at home and were more 'refined', whether working as footmen, grooms, artisans or general workmen.

When the girls first went into service, their cottage background was an obstacle that their employer had to overcome: they needed plenty of training if they had not already been through the hands of the farmer's wife. Mind you, should a girl choose to return to cottage life after marriage, she found her work a lot harder than it had been in service, because it was endless. Even Jefferies recognised that the lot of the agricultural labourer's wife was harder than that of her husband and that a woman's work was never finished. 'When the man reaches home he does not care, or will not turn his hand to anything, except, perhaps, to fetch a pail of water, and he is not well pleased if asked to do that.'

The young men began to travel in search of good wages, not just from village to village but farther afield, even to other countries. All over Britain they would turn their hand to other labouring jobs – find a spell of well-paid navvying on the railways, perhaps – and were not particularly interested in settling down with a wife and family yet awhile. When they did so, it might well be with a girl from a different parish, even a different county, not known in their own village. The tradition of marrying within a small circle of families that you had known all of your life was vanishing fast, and the allegiance to just your village was weakening.

So the problem of the young leaving the villages is far from being a new one. During the early years of the Industrial Revolution they left in their droves, seeking better opportunities in manufacturing than they could find in farming. The problem has persisted for generations.

In the 1930s, FG Thomas said it was important to discover what it was that attracted the young to the towns. 'Any youth will gladly accept an opportunity of escape. In this he is supported by practically the whole village of younger people, the "mobile generation".' He identified that the lure of the wider world began in the village school, with every head seeing the winning of scholarships as being the crowning achievement, putting a child on the first rung of the educational ladder to secondary school and the 'black-coated' professions. The brighter the rural child, the more likely it was that they would be pressed to aim for training colleges and university, preferably to become teachers themselves, ideally in a major urban area. That was where the bright lights went and were.

In the village schools only one or two would ever win a scholarship. The best of the rest might aspire to become office clerks or garage mechanics; the remainder would be encouraged to take a job working on the land. Everything between the wars was designed to encourage children to believe that towns were vastly superior to the country, and most teachers and parsons had urban backgrounds or tendencies anyway. Surely in town, where there were pavements and street lighting, indoor toilets and bathrooms, cinemas and shops, there must be

far greater opportunities for making a good living than in the materially poorer countryside, even if in the country you might pay little rent for your cottage and be able to offset costs by growing or catching your own food? Above all, there was a certain snobbery: townsfolk were deemed to be more sophisticated and worldly than clod-hopping farm boys. It was hardly surprising that the young villagers of the 1930s were on the move, by bike, by motorbike, by whatever means they could find. They would travel some miles to get to monthly meetings of the Young Farmers' Clubs, especially those of neighbouring villages, where they could meet new people of their own age.

Courtship and marriage

In most villages there were a lot of people who were related to each other, however distantly. The choice of marriage partners

▼ **DURING THE DEPRESSION** *of the 1930s Boy Scouts in Kent held a fundraising campaign for jobless youngsters whose fathers were unemployed. A fresh-air wash was all part of the fun at this campsite in Farnborough.*

was not very wide, but there were rules. For example, 'trade' was a superior stratum in village society, and it did not do for trade to marry beneath them.

Courtship was generally the talk of the village; it was hard to escape all those knowing eyes. Dances were the highlight of a young person's week – the village hop, or preferably a dance in another village or in town, where you had a chance to meet someone you hadn't known all your life.

Generally, weddings were quite simple affairs in the country until the end of the 19th century, when Jekyll remarked with horror on seeing a 'lamentable' photograph of a labourer's wedding in which the bride 'had a veil and orange blossoms, a shower bouquet, and pages!' She saw this as undignified burlesque. 'Such wedding parties do not walk to church; the bride's party, at least, hires the closed village fly, which for the occasion is called "the brougham". A wise old woman remarked, "When I was married we walked to church; and then walked home, and I cooked two chops. And then we changed our clothes and went to our work!"'

Sex education and birth control were non-existent – people simply did not talk about such matters. Even women born around the time of World War I might be quite shocked by their first period, having no

▼ **THE SEARCH FOR A SUITABLE GIRL**
would begin in the local parish, but if the men failed to find a match they would visit neighbouring parishes as well. Here, a tug of war was the challenge set by a group of bachelors from another village for the local stoolball team.

idea what it was all about, and if their mothers did think to explain sex to them they didn't believe a word of it. Yet if they fell pregnant before marriage the penalties could be severe: many girls were sent in disgrace to a boarding establishment for the duration, and after the birth would have the baby removed from them whether or not they wished to keep it. Nobody ever counselled or consoled them; they had done a dirty thing and their feelings were irrelevant. Nobody explained what they would go through during the birth, though many country girls had seen it in the cowshed and lambing pens or had seen their own mothers giving birth at home. The government's statistical review for 1939 showed that one bride in every six was pregnant on her wedding day and that nearly 30 per cent of all first-born children were conceived out of wedlock.

Babies were born at home; childbirth was not seen as an illness (although it often turned into one) and was such a regular event that it became a habit. Sarah Powell of Bucknell, Oxfordshire, produced five children in 11 months and her total tally was 23 (including six pairs of twins and one lot of triplets). By the time she was 51, only seven of her children were alive and her husband Samuel was 'ruptured amd quite unable to work'.

Friends and families would help at the birth and fathers were often on standby to summon the village nurse or midwife – they would probably set off on bikes at the first signs of labour, as of course there was no telephone to ring for help, and it was a matter of 'hunt the nurse' until they found her. Women paid pence a week to belong to their local nursing association, giving them the right to call out the district nurse when needed, and this was the situation until the National Health Service was created after World War II.

◀ THE WEDDING *of Christine and Angus McDonald – seen here being led to their reception by a piper – was the first time in the history of the Isle of Lewis that a traveller (or 'tinker') had married in white in a local church.*

9. Time Off

Getting the village together for a bit of fun had always been an antidote to the sheer drudgery of agricultural work, and the habit persisted long after the working lives of most villagers became less arduous and wearying. There were countryside entertainments of many kinds on village greens and organised recreation grounds and especially in village halls, with their range of clubs and societies. The village pub was another meeting place, where people sang and played games as well as quenching their thirst. Music and dancing took place out of doors as well as under cover, with village bands, village hops and folk dancing. Fairs, festivals, local customs, club processions, village fêtes and of course a wide range of sports were all part of the entertainment.

Country people knew how to enjoy themselves; in particular they knew how to make their own entertainment. One of the biggest changes in country fun is that, then, they created it; now, they probably watch other people doing it. The other big change is that the town now considers the countryside to be its playground. It was probably World War I that finally broke the chain of tradition in rural areas. After those four grim years, most of the old feasts and celebrations lapsed, despite attempted artificial revivals by individuals with more of a sense of nostalgia than of real life. Some customs did persist, like always planting your potatoes on Good Friday in Devon, though that was the most unlucky day of the year to plant anything if you lived in the north. But Plough Monday lost its meaning quite quickly after the war, especially when tractors took over from horses – somehow driving a decorated tractor through the village wasn't quite the same as taking a handsomely beribboned Shire horse with you to collect money.

Haysel, which used to be connected with St Barnabas Day, lost its meaning when girls no longer came into the meadow with wooden rakes to make 'sweet hay' with their lovers. Rush bearing at Ambleside, Shenington and Old Weston had no

'... every villager is usually within a couple of minutes' walk of open countryside and can find physical exercise and recreation there for free.'

▶ **WATER MILLS USUALLY HAD LARGE PONDS** *that were ideal for leisurely boating, swimming, fishing (if the miller allowed it, as fish and especially millpond eels were popular dishes at his own table) and for skating in winter. Punting (as seen here) is the art of standing upright in a boat and propelling and steering it by means of a long pole pushed into the bed of the pond (millponds tended to be shallow), rather than using oars to row it.*

◀ **SHOOTING-STICKS** *are portable seats in the form of a walking stick with a double leather-bound handle that folds out to form a small seat. The end of the stick has a sharp metal point, which is driven into the ground to support the sitter. Invented for 'guns' to perch on while waiting for the drive, they became popular also with racegoers and point-to-point spectators.*

meaning when churches were no longer regularly strewn with rushes; dressing the well, another ceremony with church connections, persisted at only a few places, such as Tissington, with any real vigour.

But there was still plenty of fun in the villages, albeit the nature of that enjoyment changed over the decades.

Meeting places

There are two aspects to be considered in catering for a village's leisure needs: the physical and the cultural wellbeing of the villagers. The needs of the former can be met easily, as usually every villager is within a couple of minutes' walk of open countryside and can find physical exercise and recreation there for free.

Village greens

The original communal meeting place was the village green, the place where entertainments were staged, sports matches were won, miscreants were mocked, children played, the village pump probably stood, people gathered to chat and argue and bargain and, naturally, there was an open-air market place where itinerants rang their bells to attract custom. Many a village would have an informal weekly market on the green, and many will no doubt do so in the future if they can negotiate the tangle of red tape that seeks to deter them.

Village greens can be the source of considerable conflict, especially when ancient laws governing commons and such are suddenly flourished by lawyers in the faces of

villages that have found better uses for their greens more in keeping with the times, for the good of the community in general, than leaving them empty. In most small villages there is so much 'open space' surrounding the built area that a patch of green in the middle of the village might seem superfluous. Also, the activities that traditionally took place on the green have either died out altogether or moved elsewhere. For example, people now prefer to be indoors for their communal meetings and they go to the village hall, the church hall or the school. It comes as a surprise to many that there are rules deterring a village from building even a cricket pavilion on its village green, let alone a village hall, though the green would seem the obvious place for either.

Recreation grounds

In the 19th century, many villages were granted recreation grounds for the exercise and wellbeing of their inhabitants. People also began to ask for facilities for more organised recreation, in the form of sport.

Football pitches, cricket pitches and general playing fields were often established on the edge of the village, on a piece of manorial waste or the parish's old allotments or in a field released by a generous landowner to the community, and the same landowner often built a small sports pavilion or club house of some kind. In other cases a squire or lord of the manor might have set up a village rifle range – this was particularly so during the second Boer War (1899–1902), when it was discovered that agricultural labourers were not necessarily the best of shots, and needed some practice. Sometimes these ranges go right back to the times when soldiers used longbows rather than rifles: they were archery ranges. Whatever their history, they very often became the village playing fields.

A more recent introduction is village tennis courts, built with the help of grants or donations or, more often, by the efforts of fundraisers within the village.

Halls, clubs and societies

Every village needs a communal centre where the inhabitants can meet and share less strenuous activities and interests. Initially this was the village green; next it was in the church vestry, which became the undercover equivalent of the village green. Finally it was the village halls.

As the 20th century rolled into the 21st, many villages marked the turn of the century by building new village halls, or at least renovating what they already had. Over the years the hall has become increasingly important in village life, the centre for so many community events on whatever scale, but to be so, halls had to move with the times and meet new needs. They also needed to be in the heart of the village, where available building land tends to be rare.

Fundraising is an important social feature of village life, for its own sake, and villagers are very good at it. Fundraising pulls the village together in a common cause, almost regardless of that cause, and it usually generates plenty of new social activities, which people enjoy so much that they hardly notice they are emptying their pockets at the

▲ INCREASING INDUSTRIALISATION IN THE 19TH CENTURY *resulted in growing numbers of people seeking rest and recreation in rural areas. As early as the 1820s, city groups were formed to protect old footpaths and, in the 1860s, to campaign for access to common land throughout the country. The National Council of Ramblers' Federations was established after a meeting in the Peak District in 1931. It officially changed its name to the Ramblers' Association in 1935.*

▲ BOXING WAS POPULAR AT THE FAIRS, *with professionals challenging all-comers to give the local lads a chance to show off their skills, and offering spectators plenty of opportunity for a spot of wagering. They were generally bloody bare-knuckle fights and at some of the huge sheep fairs the other gruesome attractions used to include kick-shins and cudgel fighting.*

▲ CHILDREN'S PLAYGROUNDS *were regarded as artificial and urban by many villagers, the general feeling being that in the countryside you used trees rather than frames for climbing. You also used trees for fixing up a swing made from a couple of lengths of old rope threaded through a board or wrapped round a stout stick. In recent years a huge increase in 'health and safety' regulations has forced villages to spend large sums on officially approved playground equipment and special matting and similar surfaces beneath the equipment to reduce the impact of a fall.*

same time. Looking back, fundraising has always been a part of village life: countless traditional celebrations, such as May Day, Plough Monday and Bonfire Night, included people collecting money from as many households as possible.

Raising money to build a village hall takes rather more. Many villages erected their first halls as memorials after World War I but they were often no more than wooden or corrugated-iron sheds, heated (if at all) by smoky stoves that cooked those close to them while the rest froze. These rough and ready buildings were greatly loved, and many a good dance and party would be held in them.

Between the wars the do-gooders haunted the villages and there were many worthy people organising 'amusements' in the form of music, drama, folk dancing (very false, that one), craftwork and all. The do-gooders meant well and tried to raise the standards to something approaching town levels. It was often a losing battle. For example, standards on village stages were usually so amateur that you could only put on a comedy: if you tried something dramatic or romantic, the audience would fall about laughing because they knew the actors far too well to believe the act. It could only be played 'for a laugh'.

' ... many villages were granted recreation grounds for the exercise and wellbeing of their inhabitants.' People also began to ask for facilities for more organised recreation, in the form of sport.'

'It is natural that people's opinions on what a village hall is for should vary, but the essence of halls is that they are places where villagers can come together for any purpose they choose.'

▼ THE BOY SCOUTS MOVEMENT *came up with the 'bob-a-job' concept as a way of raising funds and testing initiative in 1949. There would be a bob-a-job day or week once a year when local Scouts and Cubs offered to do jobs in the neighbourhood in return for a bob (one shilling) for each job. The jobs were usually polishing shoes, chopping firewood, cleaning windows, washing cars or, as here in that first year of the scheme, walking a neighbour's dog. With the introduction of decimal currency, the name was altered to the more cumbersome 'Scout Job Week'.*

Clubs, societies and other groups began to proliferate in the village, all seeking to build up their memberships. There were so many of them that the village hall, should there be one, was solidly booked, hardly leaving room for more spontaneous entertainment such as village hops, socials and Christmas fairs. Quite apart from the church and the chapel, there was the Women's Institute, the Men's Club, Boy Scouts and Girl Guides, Cubs and Brownies, the British Legion, Darby and Joan and the horticultural society, a variety of sports clubs and many more. The do-gooders were determined that villagers should enjoy themselves, whether they liked it or not. Then there was the more practical side: baby clinics, weekly surgeries and the like. In due course there were

monthly lunch clubs as well as Christmas dinners for the elderly; there were pop-ins and drop-ins, carpet-bowls clubs, drama clubs, choral societies – you would be amazed at the richness of village life once there was a hall in which it could be focused.

Halls could also be important centres for further education and for learning crafts and skills of all kinds. The Workers' Education Association (WEA) was financed by the Carnegie Trust to foster adult education, and though originally urban it became active in many villages between the wars. Its efforts, combined with those of the local authority and of individuals within the village itself, meant that villagers could walk to lessons on subjects as varied as history and maths, metalwork and soft furnishing. They weren't usually seen as 'lessons' – more a friendly get-together in which you happened to do something very interesting and came away knowing a lot more than you did before.

But the village was increasingly looking outwards as well, especially its younger generation. With glee, they discovered Young

Farmers' Clubs (first created in 1928), meeting people in different villages with broadly similar interests, though today most Young Farmers have no direct link with agriculture at all. Then they discovered the Young Conservatives – groups which, whatever your politics might be, became good hunting grounds for marriage partners outside the village and which often offered the only regular dance nights for miles around. The time had come when simply dressing up in your Sunday best for the evening promenade through the village had lost its sparkle; when courting monitored by the whole village had lost its appeal; and when even lovers' lanes had lost their magic. The village was looking for something more.

Gradually people's standards within the village also became higher and they raised money to improve the hall they had or to start again with a more solid edifice in brick and stone, sometimes (though too rarely) designed in the vernacular style that fitted in with the village-scape. Sometimes there was unexpected opposition to the idea of any village hall being built in the first place; sometimes there was opposition to improvement, as if it were an insult to a much loved old place that had seen better days. In recent years several villages have encountered quite bitter controversy when they have tried to extend the facilities of their halls. The opposition usually comes from people new to the village, who think that a bigger hall means more noise, more cars, more teenagers hanging around, and 'Why can't they all go to the towns anyway?'

It is natural that people's opinions on what a village hall is for should vary, but the essence of halls is that they are places where villagers can come together for any purpose they choose, even if it is nothing more than a cup of coffee. At Riding Mill, in Northumberland, they recognised this in the 1960s: 'Of all the activities at the Parish Hall none is more popular than the Saturday morning coffee, at which young and old gather to gossip,' they said, and the accompanying photographs showed more than 60 people enjoying themselves. That was more than 10 per cent of the village's entire population.

Halls are gradually expanding to become community centres. If they can work out what to do about their charitable status, some will include a small village shop to replace the one that has vanished, or an ever-

▲ THE VILLAGE WOMEN'S INSTITUTE *was one of the most regular users of the village hall and it was often the WI who had energised the community to get it built in the first place. The WI members shown here had formed their own 'canning club'.*

▲ BABY CLINICS IN THE VILLAGE HALL *encouraged mothers to bring in their babies for weighing and other basic health checks, and were usually run by health visitors and practice nurses with the help of local volunteers. There would also be a supply of health-enhancing goods such as orange juice and blackcurrant juice available at reduced prices, as they were bought in bulk for the clinic and even in some cases donated by local well-wishers.*

open informal coffee room with comfortable chairs and home-baked cakes, or will offer facilities such as photocopying, printing, computer lessons and access to the Internet. The possibilities are endless.

Public houses

Rural pubs, in contrast to many of those in towns, are important social centres for communal life. They give villagers somewhere to meet informally and mix freely with each other, catch up on the chat, exchange jokes and stories, shred a few local reputations and generally feel good about life, or not.

They are nearly all called pubs now, but in days gone by there would have been ale kitchens, alehouses and inns. And there were a lot of them in the early Victorian period.

Inns were places that offered food, lodging and stabling for a visitor's horses as well as drink; they tended to be sited on the road to somewhere, and often became the place where people did business, closed deals, paid their debts to each other, found jobs and put the world to rights.

Alehouses had been around forever, or at least since Anglo-Saxon times. They proliferated then, but in the 10th century a royal decree limited villages to only one alehouse each. They were really ale kitchens, set up in private homes ranging from farmhouses to cottages where the wife sold her home brew to the locals and let them sit around and chat. They often paid for their drinks in kind rather than in cash and it was all very amicable for the most part – just friends dropping in.

'Pubs provided other entertainments besides drinking, smoking, listening to old Joe on the fiddle and chatting.'

Gradually some of the ale kitchens grew to accommodate more 'friends', especially in homes that happened to be sited near places where villagers gathered anyway, such as the smithy or the village green. In Victorian times brewing had become an industry and the big brewers forced the homebrews off the market, either putting the kitchen brewers out of business altogether or taking over their premises. In 1850 the term 'public house' was first used, confirming that the premises were often used as a general local meeting place, in the days before there were such things as village halls. By the 1870s most villages had at least two or three licensed pubs and soon they were welcoming the tourists that began to pour into the countryside by train, by bicycle, by motorbike and finally by car. By 1914 nearly all the pubs were tied to large breweries.

Pubs provided other entertainments besides drinking, smoking, listening to old Joe on the fiddle and chatting. For many a country man, the alehouse was, as Richard Jefferies put it,

… at once his stock exchange, his reading room, his club, and his assembly rooms. It is here that his benefit society holds its annual dinner. The club meetings take place weekly or monthly in the great room upstairs. Here he learns the news of the day; the local papers are always to be found at the public house, and if he cannot read himself he hears the news from those who can. In the winter he finds heat and light, too often lacking at home; at all times he finds amusement; and who can blame him for seizing what little pleasure lies in his way. As a rule the beerhouse is the only place of amusement to which he can resort: it is his theatre, his music hall, picture gallery, and Crystal Palace.

▶ **MANY VILLAGE PUBS** *invented their own traditions. In this case the 'Bone Trophy' was the prize in a village football competition, and its winning required due celebration in the pub. In the Sussex village of Ebernoe a centuries-old Horn Fair on the village common centred around a cricket match against another village, and the highest-scoring batsman was presented with a set of horns removed from a sheep roasted on a spit for the postmatch celebrations.*

▲ **FOLK SONGS OFTEN FOUND A VOICE IN THE PUB,** *where many of the old songs were kept alive. The locals here are Devonians having a sing-song at the Fox & Goose in the small Exmoor village of Parracombe in 1954. The village has an interesting old church, largely reconstructed in the early 16th century but with an early 13th century chancel: its Georgian interior is unspoilt, with musicians' gallery, box pews, screen and tympanum, period hat pegs, whitewashed ceilings and walls. This old church, up on the moors above the village, is rarely used, as a new one was built in 1878 but locals, supported by John Ruskin, saved the older building from demolition.*

There was a wide range of traditional pub games, such as dominoes, draughts, cribbage, bagatelle, skittles, darts and shove ha'penny, but pubs changed. Even in the 1870s new laws had practically forbidden pub-goers to play ninepins and dominoes, in an attempt to stamp on gambling. The reign of 'skittle sharpers' was more or less over. Yet skittles was usually played only for a quart of ale (to be drunk by the loser as well as the winner), which was hardly heavy betting.

In more recent years some villagers have felt pushed out by the innovations – changes that seem to be designed to pull in outsiders rather than give the locals what they want. Outsiders bring their vehicles, and villagers start complaining about cars parking outside their homes. But the pubs are fighting to survive and will do what it takes.

Village music

Music was very much a part of country life. People sang local folk songs and understood them; many an old boy had just the one song, which he could be 'reluctantly' persuaded to sing at the drop of a hat as his party piece, usually in exchange for a pint of ale. Children were always singing, especially girls in their games; women sang at their housework or in the field; everybody sang in church (with fewer people going to church these days, the joy of singing together is being lost); men whistled as they worked long before that became a catch-phrase. Singing and playing music were an integral part of any march or procession.

In recent years all that singing has disappeared, except in a more formal context such as the church choir or a local choral society or at school. Nobody bursts into song at the pub any more (unless they play rugger or support a town football team) or pulls out a fiddle or pipe and gives the locals a tune. They don't even tickle the ivories now.

There was a time when many villages had their own band – not just a couple of men with penny whistles and a shaky tambourine but the full works: brass instruments,

▶ **VILLAGE BANDS** *helped to celebrate big village events and often evolved from the local musicians who used to play for services in the days before village churches had harmoniums or organs. Much pride was taken in the band's uniforms and much care was lavished on the brass instruments – cornets, trombones, euphoniums, clarionets and all, and usually a big bass drum.*

big drums and all. Many a country church had a band of fiddlers and pipe players in the days before they all had church organs. In 1878 George Dew noted in his diary that a new organ had been installed in Lower Heyford church in Oxfordshire, replacing the old harmonium which had in turn replaced the 'fiddle, bass-viol, bassoon, clarionet, & such instruments' that had played in Rector Faithfull's time. When the harmonium first arrived, the Lower Heyford choir refused to sing, but then, that choir had always been a law unto themselves. Dew could remember their behaviour in the gallery during services 'and all sorts of strange memoranda were written on the seats there; for instances such as when "Polly Hore", the landlady of the "Bell" Inn was last at church. But after the harmonium was placed in the gallery matters in this respect were much improved.'

Travelling bands visited Victorian villages too, including the old one-man band with cymbals on his knees, a drum at his back and a pipe to his lips. Another musical itinerant was the ballad seller, singing from the sheet music that he offered for sale. There were also visits by itinerant acrobats (there are several hamlets where the crossroads is still known as Tumblers Corner).

Dances

Oh, those village dances and hops! Can you imagine it when the lads (who by day worked in the fields) dressed themselves up in breeches and gaiters for the dance, but kept on their hobnailed boots? Can you imagine the sheer noise, the boots thumping on the floor and more often than not on other people's toes as well?

In Victorian villages you would often see a dancing booth set up in the square or on the green near the pub on one of the various feast days. It was popular with all age groups,

▲ THE GREAT WESTERN RAILWAY INSTITUTE, *formed in 1855 at the company's Stafford Road works in Wolverhampton for men attached to the works, organised an annual three-day excursion (by train, of course) for members and their families from 1858. In that year a brass band was formed and a few years later an Institute Choral Society. Soon there were fortnightly entertainments, in which music naturally played a major part.*

▶ MORRIS DANCING, *with its colourful costumes, clacking sticks and flourished handkerchiefs, has a recorded history of some four centuries but, like many traditions, it began to lose its meaning during the Industrial Revolution, and very few local teams or 'sides' remained by the mid 19th century. The tradition was artificially revived by English folklorists from the early 20th century. In 1911 the vicar of Thaxted, in Essex, encouraged the formation of a 'revival' morris side and its members are photographed here in April 1938.*

married and single, male and female, sons and daughters and parents, of the labouring classes, all of whom had a merry old time. It was also another good excuse to get drunk.

And then there was morris dancing, a custom that is supposed to be pagan and Moorish in origin and was introduced into England from Spain by John of Gaunt.

Fairs and festivals

Sometimes the green was the site of a fair – a time of great local excitement which attracted the crowds from miles around. Fair days were almost the only weekday holidays into Victorian times; fairs slotted into the calendar as regular as clockwork and punctuated the mundanity of everyday rural life. For a day, or two, or three, the site of the fair was buzzing with life and excitement and crowds, and the next day it was all over until the next time, gone, quiet again and back to the old routine.

Some fairs had a specific purpose: say, a sheep fair, a horse fair, a toy fair, a simple pedlary fair, a hiring fair where people looked for new jobs, a cheese fair. Some fairs combined many purposes, and threw in a wide range of entertainment for good measure. But above all a fair was a market of some kind, and you went to the fair prepared to spend your money or to make it. You also went to have fun and to meet lots of people.

The animal fairs would mean herds and flocks filling the lanes and spilling over the hills for days beforehand, all heading for the fair, and all splitting off in different directions afterwards in the hands of new masters. Lewes Sheep Fair would attract up to 30,000 sheep in the 19th century, and not far away the ancient Findon Fair on the South Downs filled its pens with more than 10,000 sheep (nearly all of the Southdown breed) in the 1920s, with the added attractions of roundabouts, coconut shies and refreshment tents. In 1925, for the first time, sheep due to travel a long distance after Findon Fair were sent by rail, drifting over the Downs to the station at Steyning: Southern Railway laid on a special shunting engine with 56 trucks to transport them all over the country. In 1928 the first lorries were seen at Findon, loading sheep to and from the fair; until then the animals had used their own legs to get there. At its peak in 1950 some 18,000 sheep were sold at Findon Fair, most of them travelling in

▲ THE POLE FAIR *at Corby, Northamptonshire, probably dates back to the 13th century but it is only held every 20 years. Historically, petty criminals would be carried into the village astride an ash pole, for people to throw objects and insults at them as they were paraded through the streets.*

▲ TRAVELLING FAIRGROUNDS *were essentially transient, paying regular visits to selected villages and towns usually to coincide with a market of some kind, setting up stalls and sideshows, bringing plenty of colour, noise, light, music, entertainment and excitement, and then moving on to the next venue leaving no traces except in memory.*

> *'Today the big agricultural shows and county shows attract huge numbers from towns and cities as well as from the rural areas they originally served.'*

▼ **VILLAGE FÊTES** *featured simple games such as the greasy pole: contestants sat astride a greased pole and did their best to knock each other off with pillows. Sadly this, like many other fête games, has lost favour in recent years because some village voluntary groups have found themselves being sued for damages when someone falls off the greasy pole (as intended) and breaks a wrist or twists an ankle.*

lorries (rail transport would cease entirely when the Steyning line was closed in the 1960s), but today only a fraction of that number of sheep, of various breeds, comes to the fair, though buyers still come from all over the country.

Any fair would mean the convergence of a wide range of itinerants, eager to set up their pitches and bringing the lanes alive, mingling with the crowds who tramped fairwards with cheerful anticipation of selling a wife, buying a bonnet, seeing a bearded lady, chancing their arm against a wrestler, hearing their fortunes, shying coconuts, bowling for pigs, taking a turn in the dancing booth, watching a dancing bear or an organ grinder with his monkey, drinking themselves silly, finding a new lover, making faces at caged wild animals, and from the middle of the 19th century also enjoying the thrills of steam-driven fairground rides. Oh, those were the days!

Local fairs were rapidly declining in Victorian times, though the bigger town ones and the county shows were still exciting and opened village eyes to the rest of the world and its goods and inventions. Today the big agricultural shows and county shows

attract huge numbers from towns and cities as well as from the rural areas they originally served. That must surely indicate that the country exerts a strong pull on urban man even now, though they cannot really compete with the events that villagers would have attended in the 12th century. Where Salisbury now stands, there used to be a large open space between the lofty palace of Clarendon, the fortress of Old Sarum and Wilton Abbey, and here they had a tournament ground. Villagers would set off from home a day or two before the great day dawned, to be there in time to see the host of armed men riding out from the castle in the early morning, banners fluttering and arms gleaming, while from the direction of the Abbey came the royal princesses (they were being schooled there) and the soldier priests from the crusading knights of Jerusalem's establishment at St John's Priory at Ditchampton; and from Clarendon would come a horseback procession of gaily dressed courtiers. Villagers would be overawed by the richness of the clothes and the presence of queens, lords and ladies. The tournaments themselves would be full of excitement, colour and courage, with the knights and

their horses gorgeously arrayed as they took part in these martial sports, and their retinue of pages and esquires and minstrels and heralds all dressed up to the nines as well.

There were tournaments here for four centuries, and, four centuries after they had finished, the military theme took centre stage again in the form of searchlight tattoos in the grounds of Tidworth House from 1923. By 1938 the tattoos were attracting 150,000 people and excursion trains were coming from as far away as Wales, Cornwall and Wolverhampton. There were massed bands, pageants, physical training exercises, sham tank fights and gunfire, circus episodes and a grand multicoloured torchlight procession. (Why 'tattoo'? Apparently it is from the Dutch *taptoe*, with *tap* meaning alehouse

▼ SOMERSET BOASTED SEVERAL *female friendly societies to provide insurance against sickness, unemployment and old age. Hannah More established a women's friendly society in Wrington, Cheddar and Shipham in 1797 and it continued until 1948, when it distributed its balance of more than £900 to its 45 remaining members.*

▲ MERRY-GO-ROUNDS *were the essence of the fairground and were originally turned manually or were horse-driven. An early developer of the steam-powered merry-go-round was the 19th century agricultural engineer Frederick Savage, mayor of Kings Lynn, who had been a carpenter and smith repairing fairground machinery. Other thrills included helter-skelters, chair-o-planes, switchbacks, swingboats, ferris wheels and the 'wall of death', where centripetal force pinned your body to the rotating circular wall as the floor dropped away.*

▲ THE BRITISH LEGION *launched the first 'Poppy Day' on 11 November 1921, a date chosen to commemorate the formal ending of World War I on 11 November 1918. The poppy tradition began when Moina Michael, an American War Secretary, inspired by John McCrae's 1915 poem 'In Flanders Fields', started selling poppies to friends to raise money for ex-servicemen. The idea caught on, however, and the Poppy Appeal now raises money for those at war, as well as ex-servicemen and dependants.*

and *toe* meaning to close. When William of Orange reorganised the British Army in the late 17th century, the signal for troops to return to barracks was the sounding of 'Taptoe', at which the alehouses closed and the men had nothing better to do than come back for the nightly muster.)

Fêtes, feasts and fiestas

The village fête – what visions that phrase conjures up! They don't do them like they used to, you know. There was a fête at Blenheim Park in the 1870s in aid of the Great Western Railway Widow and Orphan Fund, with excursion trains laid on from all parts of the country, and people came in their many thousands. Early shades of Woodstock, without the mud. It must have been rather more than the typical village smattering of stalls with bash the rat, homemade cakes and second-hand books. An August fête a few days later in Middleton Stoney Park was typical: it rained.

Some villages had fiestas and carnivals, complete with people in fancy dress on floats mounted initially on horse-drawn wagons

but later on tractor-drawn trailers (which also carried carol singers around the villages and farms). Other had elaborate pageants, perhaps telling the history of the village; these essentially outdoor plays involved as many of the village as possible, including the animals, and sometimes included a tableau. Some villages had their annual Revels, usually connected with May Day; others have invented new traditions such as rural fairs, raft races, duck races (with plastic ducks down the river), rare breed shows and revived goose fairs.

Feasts and festivals used to punctuate the village calendar and had an important social role at both the community and the personal level that perhaps has not been widely acknowledged. They were a dramatic change from the daily routine that on the one hand confirmed community bonds, as they were essentially social occasions, and on the other gave individuals a moment to pause and lift their eyes from the everydayness of life, to reflect that there could be more to it, and perhaps even to meditate on the meaning of it all.

The biggest bash in the rural calendar had always been the harvest feast. It meant food and it meant drinking, both to extremes; it meant dancing to the pipe and fiddle, and it meant fully grown men bedecking their hats with flowers. But Richard Jefferies was bemoaning the demise of such village feasts even in the early 1870s:

> *Here and there the clergyman of the parish has succeeded in turning what was a rude saturnalia into a decorous 'fête', with tea in a tent ... A village feast consists of two or three gipsies located on the greensward by the side of the road, and displaying ginger beer, nuts, and toys for sale; an Aunt Sally; and, if the village is a large one, the day may be honoured by the presence of what is called a rifle gallery; the 'feast' really and truly does not exist. Some two or three of the old-fashioned farmers have the traditional roast beef and plum pudding on the day, and invite a few friends; but this custom is passing away. In what the agricultural labourers' feast nowadays consists no one can tell. It is an excuse for an extra quart or two of beer, that is all.*

Villages tended to celebrate various royal occasions, such as jubilees and coronations, with great vigour (any excuse for a party). Food was important for such events; many a parish celebrated a coronation with a 'Tea' (children's tea, knife and fork tea, a 'good meat tea'), combined with sports and games and usually a bonfire with a few fireworks. Others were more practical; Victoria's jubilees prompted many of them to open a parish reading room, dedicate a stained-glass window in the church or plant a tree.

Club days

A Victorian innovation was the festivities held annually by local Benefit Clubs ('sickness societies' to which you subscribed your pence as a form of early health

'Villages tended to celebrate various royal occasions with great vigour'

▼ THE VILLAGE'S CLUB WALK *was led by men with flags and the village band as members marched to church traditionally bearing 'wands' or poles (the club's officers had emblems at the top of theirs). Afterwards they would have a meal at the local inn and probably an afternoon of sports to round off the day. These were the 'benefit clubs', forerunners of the 'friendly societies', and many had strict rules about how their members should at all times live 'religiously, honestly and soberly'; they were expected to attend church every Sunday, and it is possible that the Church was instrumental in the formation of such groups originally.*

YATELEY CLUBS ANNUAL FEAST. CHURCH PROCESSION.

'Men lie on their backs
and never take the
wooden harvest bottle
from their lips'

insurance), usually on the old village feast
days. Jefferies described the annual village
club dinners in Wiltshire at which farm
labourers 'gormandised to repletion'. One
man ate, in quick succession, a plate of roast
beef, a plate of boiled beef, a plate of boiled
mutton, a plate of roast mutton and a plate
of ham and said he could not do much to the
bread and cheese but devoured the pudding.
Jefferies had heard of men who stuffed
themselves silly and then retired from the
table to take a mustard emetic so that they
could come back for more gorging. As for
beer, he had seen men lie on their backs and
never take the wooden harvest bottle from
their lips until they had drunk a full gallon.

The Benefit Club at Kirtlington held its
annual gathering, with much feasting,
drinking and general debauchery, and music
from two bands for the procession, on the

day of what had formerly been celebrated as
Lamb Ale. At the Lamb Ale they would
have had a Lord and a Lady (the
community's most respectable inhabitants),
with 12 attendants, processing with a lamb
with a blue ribbon around its neck. This
occasion of much merrymaking had died out
by the 1860s, but the Benefit Club annual
days continued. The clubs soon added stalls
and amusements to their annual holiday, but
the main activity seemed to be drinking. One
Charles Hickman extended the idea of
Lamb Ale by drinking himself to death on a
non-stop week-long binge. On the day he
died the local policeman said that he would
have had difficulty in finding 12 sober
jurymen in the whole of the village.

At nearby Chesterton they had an old
feast known as the Chesterton Barrel on the
same day as Kirtlington's Lamb Ale: they

played all kinds of games with barrels of beer under a large tree along the old Roman road of Akeman Street. Everybody was given a day's holiday and would meet with friends and relatives from miles around, but in the 1860s the local parson decided the whole matter was a disgrace and he discontinued it.

Customs and traditions

There was a time when a wily traveller could find a free meal every day of the year if he was in the right place at the right time. But the doling out of flour and bread – the Tichborne Dole, the Biddenden Cakes, the Lenten Doles of bread and herrings at Dronfield – seemed spurious as poverty became less abject. What happened to Paignton's amazing puddings (seven years to make, seven to bake and seven to eat) or the mammoth Denby Dale pies, and Colchester's oyster feasts and the great Buckinghamshire cherry pie feasts? Who still gives their landlord a goose at Michaelmas?

What happened to the candle auctions at Tatsworth, Chard and Upwey, or the drawing of balls at Yarnton? Do they still 'bump the mayor', or do they still bump new freeholders on the dunting stone on the Northumberland moors at Newbiggin? Do the boys of Helston still beat the bounds and place a clod of earth and a sprig of hawthorn on the boundary stones? Do they still ring the church bells of Kirton-in-Lindsey to guide people home from market? Do they still ring the pancake bell, and do Midland cottagers still throw the first pancake to their chickens to make sure of good luck and plenty of eggs?

What about Mothering Sunday: do they still eat frumenty and simnel cakes; do they still make special wafers in Chilbolton? On Palm Sunday do they still eat figs in Northamptonshire or fig cakes on Silbury Hill? Do young men still race up Dunkery Beacon at Easter for luck in love and work? Do they still go Peace Eggin' at Easter in West Yorkshire, and do they still scramble for hare pies and penny loaves at Hallaton on Easter Monday before playing football with a small beer barrel?

Do the hobbyhorses still prance at Padstow on May Day, and does the Minehead horse still have a long tail of knotted rope to chastise those who don't put coins in the collection box? Do they still understand the Horn Dance at Abbots Bromley, or the Furry Dance at Helston?

Does Abbotsbury still take flowers out to sea on Garland Day as an offering to Neptune, and do they bury cakes and ale as luck for the fishermen? Do they roast lamb on the bed of a dammed stream at Kingsteignton on Whit Tuesday? Do children go souling in November in Shropshire? Do they still observe Salmon Sunday at Paythorne Bridge? And if they still do these things, do they know why?

In the 19th century, there was a traditional Whit Monday fight between the 'Kaffirs' (originally Cavaliers) of Coneyhurst Hill, in the Surrey parish of Ewhurst, and the Diamond-Topped Roundheads of Rudgwick, a Sussex village just over the border. It always took place on neutral ground, at the Donkey Inn at Cranleigh. Countless villages had regular rivalry with

▼ THERE WERE MANY 'DOLE' TRADITIONS *in which food – usually bread or flour – was handed out to the deserving poor once a year. One of the best known is the Tichborne Dole, dating back to the tragic story of Lady Mabella, wife of Sir Roger de Tichborne of Hampshire in the time of Henry II. On her deathbed, she implored her frequently cruel husband to donate the grain from a small part of his estate as flour for the poor each year. He agreed to do so only for as much land as she could walk around. The dying woman crawled around an area of 23 acres and today some 2 tons of flour represent-ing the yield of that area are distributed each year to the villagers. (The dole photographed here is at Biddenden in Kent.)*

▲ THE WELSH NATIONAL EISTEDDFOD *is held at different venues each year, alternating between North and South Wales and celebrating the arts, especially poetry. In 1937 it was the turn of Machynlleth, a market town in old Montgomeryshire (now Powys), and the photograph shows Anna Davis representing 'Fruits of the Earth' as she and her attendants, including Druids, process through the town. The celebrations are on a large scale, requiring plenty of open space for all the pavilions and stands and for the many people who camp in the fields for the festival.*

▲ MAY DAY IS AN ANCIENT FESTIVAL *dating back to pre-Christian Europe. It celebrates the birth of summer, and used to be an occasion relating to fertility and a good excuse for couples to head for the woods for a playful spot of 'romance'. The Victorians quashed such vulgar behaviour and by the 1870s May Day had become a children's day, when they would be dressed in white decorated with brightly coloured adornments, and march around the village with May garlands and flags to collect money for a good 'tea' in the afternoon, after dancing round the maypole to weave it with ribbons.*

neighbouring ones, though usually on the more informal basis of a gang from one village taking it into their heads of an evening, probably after a drink or two, to go and sort out the other.

In Cumberland, many old customs persisted into the mid 20th century, though only just. For example, if a farmer was selling off his stock and implements, he provided a meal for everybody who attended the farm sale and he supplied stronger liquid refreshment for those who spent a good deal of money there or were his neighbours; each neighbour, by tradition, would buy something at the sale (often the piece of equipment they had most often borrowed) and would pay more than it was worth.

Neighbours were also important at burials, for it was they, never members of the family, who bore the coffin, and must make sure that the deceased left his home by the front door, feet first. At weddings, the bride and groom would find the church gate firmly tied when they came out of the church, or a flower-decked rope stretched across their way; the custom was for the groom to throw copper coins to the village young before they were allowed to pass.

May Day

The beginning of summer – marked by May Day – was celebrated throughout most of the 19th century with all the paraphernalia of maypole dancing by the children (and quite tricky it can be, too), crowning the May Queen, going a-maying to fetch hawthorn blossom (terribly unlucky if brought indoors), dancing and feasting. The 'tradition' was deliberately revived after World War I, but by then it meant nothing. Gertrude Jekyll, who could remember the chimney sweeps' Jack-in-the-Green in the streets of London in the 1840s, when she watched an 8ft-tall tower of greenery dancing and revolving along the street, said of the 20th-century May Day: 'The continuous chain of ancient tradition has been snapped and nothing can restore it.' That is why modern attempts to perpetuate morris dancing and other 'traditions' always seem so uncomfortable, so unnatural. So many of these traditions were country ones, based on agricultural realities that people no longer experience or understand.

In the real old May Day celebrations, children would carry bunches of flowers on top of peeled willow sticks, chanting, 'The first of May is Garland Day, so please to remember the white wand; we don't come here but once a year, so please to remember the Garland.' Some would have a more elaborate arrangement of an intersecting double ring of hoops of flowers and foliage, carried on a horizontal stick by two children.

Bonfire night

Bonfire Night was sometimes not quite the occasion it is now in many villages: it might be no more than a peal of bells, not even a bonfire, though some individuals would fire off several rounds of cartridges from their pocket revolvers in private remembrance of the Gunpowder Plot. In other villages they gave it the works, the village boys having been collecting money for the bonfire for some time before the day itself, and all around the countryside you could hear the explosion of fireworks and see the flare of the fires. In some places the blacksmith's anvil would be charged and fired.

Villages often had a bonfire club, which did very little for the first nine months of the year but then would wake up and start its complicated preparations for the Fifth of November. There would be flaming torches to be prepared, hundreds of fireworks to be bought (and in the old days home-made, very dangerously), the display to be planned meticulously, and materials to be found for a carefully constructed bonfire, not to mention the guys to be burnt on it.

Christmas

Isn't everyone's image of the traditional Christmas set in a village? The village church, the carol singers, the handbell ringers whose brass tunes echo gently across the meadows, snowy landscapes with misty-breathed cattle and sunset-lit sheep, robins on the twig, skaters on the pond, frosted trees.

In the village, you knew all the carol-singing children and they took their rounds seriously. They would have been trained by the schoolmaster or the parson for weeks in advance but only give the village the benefit of their carols on Christmas Eve, visiting every dwelling (but especially the bigger houses) where they would be given goodies

▼ GUY FAWKES *failed to blow up the Houses of Parliament on 5 November 1605. In his boyhood home village of Scotton, near Harrogate, they do not burn an effigy of Guy Fawkes on their annual bonfire but they do have fireworks. In the Somerset village of Enmore, the 1795 will of a disinherited man decreed that effigies of his own father and sister should be paraded around the village and then thrown on the Bonfire Night pyre.*

▲ ARTHUR GIBBS, *who died in 1899 at the age of 31, recalled Yuletide revels when 'the whole hamlet (for farmers as well as labourers honoured us)' came to 'a big feed' at his family's manor house in the Cotswolds, including every man, woman and child of the hamlet plus visiting carol singers and musicians: there were 72 revellers in all, the brass band played, people danced and four or five 18-gallon casks of ale were consumed. Gibbs remarked that the Yuletide festivities sealed the bond of fellowship and goodwill between the classes.*

to eat and ginger beer to drink. Individual carols were often peculiar to a local area, unknown beyond it, but they've all been forgotten now.

Do any West Country farmers still wassail their apple trees? Does anybody remember the rhyming play of the Mummers and recognise the paper-clad St George, the Turkey-land Knight, Father Christmas, the Doctor and the Old Woman, Betsy Bub? Read Arthur Gibbs if you want all the details about a Mummer's cure that involved eating a bucket of hot dry ashes, being groomed with a besom and drinking a yard and a half of pump water, recommended by the Doctor, who could 'cure the itchy pitch' and much else besides.

Christmas in the village was a real excitement, followed by the Boxing Day meet of the hounds somewhere not too far away. Then at midnight on New Year's Eve the church bells rang out the old year and rang in the new; they had also pealed to mark the shortest day on 21 December, at six in the morning.

Sports and games

In the early years of the 20th century, some sports and pastimes could still be closely identified with particular regions. For example, hawking was popular on Salisbury Plain and its first day always coincided with the week in which the wild violets suddenly scented the Wiltshire valleys; the old hawking club's members always wore green velveteen coats. Wrestling was enjoyed in the dales of the north west as well as in Devon and Cornwall; in Somerset they went eel hunting with dogs; in Cumberland they had hound trailing and fell running; in Yorkshire it was arrow throwing and billets; in Cornwall they hunted seals for sport.

Quoits, also known as horse shoes, involved iron quoits, made by the blacksmith, and a 3in-high peg known as the hob, set in a square yard of moistened clay surrounded by a wooden platform. With a flick of the wrist, a player would send his quoit (which weighed more than 5lb) from the wooden platform to another hob 11 yards away; at the same time another player would probably be throwing his quoit in the opposite direction. Two points for a quoit over the peg, and one if your best shot was nearer to the hob than your opponent's, though in fact the scoring was much more subtle than that.

Singlesticks was a rural game that harked back to the days of swordsmanship. You cut a slender stick of ash or hazel from the hedge, about a yard long and thicker at one end. The thick end was thrust through a basketwork hilt to protect the hand and, basically, you sparred with it. In the time of the first and second Georges, the stick was rather stouter and the 'game' was called cudgel play.

At Tinsley Green they have been holding marbles championships for more than 300 years. At the model village of Ashton in Northamptonshire, built by Lord Rothschild in 1900, they have conkers championships. And can anyone remember the village that hosts the international tiddlywinks championships? In some villages they still have cheese rolling.

Cottage-dwelling metalworkers and Black Country miners were passionate about pigeon racing, and at one time also enjoyed cock and dog fighting, until their bosses dissuaded them and swung them around to playing in brass bands instead.

'With the flick of the wrist, a player would send his quoit from the wooden platform to another hob 11 yards away'

▼ THE SPORT OF HOUND TRAILING *originated in Cumbria in the 18th century, when two packs of fell foxhounds competed to prove which was the fastest. Trail hounds have since been bred selectively to improve their speed, and a Hound Trailing Association was set up in 1906. The races are a form of drag hunting: rags soaked in aniseed, paraffin and oil are dragged over the course to leave a scent trail.*

Much more to most people's taste was horse racing. Mary Russell Mitford wrote in the 1820s that all people loved Ascot Races 'but our country lasses love them above all. It is their favourite wedding jaunt, for half our young couples are married in the race week, and one or two matches have seemed to me got up purposely for the occasion.'

Cricket

Cricket. The very word suggests village, and the game was born in the village. Every village had its cricket club and every boy in the village aspired to share in its glory. Most of the village would turn up to watch the Saturday inter-village matches and pass judgment on the players and of course on the umpires. Literature is full of wonderful rural cricket matches, described with passion and wit – the perverse pitch, the cowpats, the subtle needling between the classes, the way in which the crowd could so easily sway the umpire's decision, the wifely bickering over the teas.

The young Arthur Gibbs, in his book, *A Cotswold Village*, thought that cricket was too energetic for hardworking farm labourers. But he remembered Peregrine, an 80-year-old yeoman farmer of the old type, who took cricket very seriously if his own sons were playing. He wouldn't speak to you for the rest of the day if you took one of them off the bowling. The rest of the team included a couple of farmers, the miller, two carpenter's sons, a footman, a 'somewhat fat and apoplectic butler' and the tall village curate as captain. Another of Peregrine's sons, the local gamekeeper, was the umpire, always with a cigar clamped between his teeth.

Cricket had been much more fun in the earlier years of its four centuries (at least) of history, but then in Victorian times the killjoys came along, as in so many other old village games, and produced official rules. These tablets of stone were spread about the country by a rail-travelling MCC All-England XI. Marylebone? Isn't that

◀ **CHILDREN WERE PLAYING CRICKET,** *or something like cricket, a thousand years ago, batting at lumps of wood or claggy sheep's wool with a stick and defending a tree stump. Adults apparently only took up the game in the late 16th or early 17th century. In 1611 two Sussex men were prosecuted for playing cricket on a Sunday and a dictionary of the same date defined cricket as merely a boys' game.*

somewhere near London? How dare they tell the villages how to play cricket (even if their club was established in 1787)! William Beldham of Hambledon would have turned in his grave, carefully minding his top hat or velvet cap as he did so. Incidentally, did you know that Julius Caesar played for England in 1861 against Australia?

In Nottinghamshire in the 1870s they claimed that the excellence of their village cricket was due to the local cottage industry of hand-frame knitting. It is difficult to see the connection, but it is a fact that the prevalence of this village industry in Nottinghamshire and Leicestershire could be judged by the endless long, low frame-shop windows that fronted row upon row of old cottages in the two counties.

Cricket clubs were often run by the parish institute, a committee of villagers of all classes and a wide range of occupations, from field labourers to schoolmasters, which evolved of its own accord in the days before lots of well-meaning sets of initials started coming into villages between the wars to improve rural lives.

Quite often a local lord would build a cricket pavilion for the village and then join in the match himself, as Lord Jersey liked to do in the 1870s – preferably with a band playing at the same time. Shortly after World War I, cricket played in the grounds of the big house was quietly being eased out as squires turned their attention to golf or polo – hardly village games.

In Chobham, Surrey, they started a ladies' cricket team after World War I. They played in long white dresses, which made bowling interesting. Each woman paid an annual subscription of half a crown, and once a year they played against the men, with tea provided by the ladies. A more typical team game for women was stoolball, said to have evolved from milkmaids using a leg from their three-legged milking stools, or simply their hand, as a bat and the stool itself as something for the bowler to aim at. The game has affinities with cricket, softball and rounders and may even be the forerunner of cricket, but is a much quicker game. Stoolball has a long history in rural areas and is still played today, especially in Sussex.

▼ VILLAGE CRICKET *was traditionally played on the village green, but as standards grew higher the condition of the pitch became a greater matter of pride and villagers often sought a field that could be devoted to the game. Sometimes a local landowner would allow the use of one of his fields in return for a peppercorn rent (literally a donation of one peppercorn a year, or perhaps one red rose). This sometimes caused problems for later generations when the field changed hands and the new landowner refused to honour what had in effect been a gentlemen's agreement.*

▲ STOOLBALL TEAMS HAVE ELEVEN PLAYERS *and the batting team defends a wicket. The differences between stoolball and cricket are that the willow stoolball bat is like a long-handled table-tennis bat; the wicket is a small square board set up on a stake; the ball is bowled underarm at full toss (so the pitch does not have to be pampered); and there are eight balls in an over. After being played for more than 500 years, this game that predates cricket and baseball was finally recognised as a sport by the Sports Council in 2008.*

Football

It probably all began with an inflated pig's bladder being kicked about by the lads on the village green. Or did it?

Several centuries ago, when Shrove Tuesday was the nation's favourite day for sports, a company of saddlers in Chester started presenting the drapers with a wooden ball decked with flowers, held on the point of a lance. In about 1540 the wooden ball was changed into a silver bell, to be awarded to the man who could run 'the best and farthest on horseback' on Shrove Tuesday. Later, the shoemakers of Chester started presenting the drapers with a leather ball, called a 'foote-ball', and naturally they started kicking it around. But the leather balls had a tendency to break windows and so the ball was changed for a silver trophy and was given for foot races instead of kick-abouts.

A more complicated version of football was played in the streets of the Derbyshire village of Ashbourne: they called it Uppards and Downards and it lasted for several hours. The Uppards team comprised native villagers born above the river; the Downards had been born down of the river. Others could join in as well but their goals wouldn't count.

Shrove Tuesday games

Shrove Tuesday games also included tug-of-war and cock-throwing. The latter bestial sport involved tying live birds to a stake and throwing things at them until they were dead. In the Scilly Isles, having enjoyed a spot of cock-throwing, the local boys would then chuck stones at people's doors. In Dorset, on Shrove Tuesday, they went in for the similar pastime of 'Lent crocking'.

As for tug-of-war, that very villagy event is said to have sprung from an argument at Henry VI's siege of Ludlow. One group in the town supported the Duke of York, another group wanted to give in to the

◀ ASHBOURNE, IN DERBYSHIRE, *is the home of the ancient Shrovetide Football match, in which the Uppards play the Downards. The goals are three miles apart and each period (one on Shrove Tuesday and the second on Ash Wednesday) lasts for eight hours. It has been played at Ashbourne for hundreds of years. In 1943 the ball was 'goaled' by women for the first time – both of them called Doris and both on Ash Wednesday, for opposing sides.*

King, and this, it seems, led to an annual controversy which they would settle every Shrove Tuesday with a tug-of-war.

Wrestling and boxing

Charles Vancouver, in his Devon survey published in 1808, said that the local 'young farmers and peasantry' were addicted to wrestling. Purses of up to ten guineas (a year's wages) would be put up by the promoters. A ring some 15–20 yards across would be made in a field near a large village, marked out with stakes and a single rope, within which the winner had to throw down five of his adversaries before he could claim his purse. The rules seemed to be almost non-existent: it was a case of no holds barred, or almost so: 'the collar, arm, or any part above the waistband, that most conveniently presents to the combatants during the contest'. The fun usually started at between two and three o'clock in the afternoon and often continued until midnight (by lamplight). Each bout lasted from ten to 15 minutes, 'in which is displayed much activity, strength, and adroitness, whilst the shins of the party are often found streaming with blood from the sharp and violent blows they

▼ GEORGE STEADMAN *was a famous wrestler, the star of Grasmere Sports along with fellow wrestler Hexham Clark, who eventually took over from him at the end of a long career. Steadman was still wrestling just a couple of years before he died in the early 1900s. The two men, locked in a wrestling hold at Grasmere, featured on a sign at the Cumberland Wrestlers pub in Carlisle until recently.*

◀ SUMMER CAMPS *were an excellent outlet for boyish energy in the 1930s. These two lads from Woking in Surrey are locked in battle at Ingham summer camp, Norwich, in 1934. The popular 'snake belts' are much in evidence in the onlookers as well as the wrestlers: these adjustable woven striped belts had a metal snake-shaped clasp, complete with scales and head, and had many uses other than as a belt.*

receive from each other, but which on no account are ever permitted to be given above the knee'.

The first rule was to shake hands before and after the contest 'and it rarely happens that the play is followed with boxing, or that any grudge or ill will is continued from the conquered to those that may have thrown them'. The men of the Devon moors were celebrated for their hardiness 'in bearing excessive kicking upon their shins'. It would have hurt – the Devon style allowed opponents to wear heavy shoes.

Arthur Beckett described a boxing match at a village fair before World War I. A large crowd of men and boys stood before a booth with a poster proclaiming 'Professor Gillam's Troupe of Athletes, Boxing and Wrestling'. Beckett found himself a place near the roped-off circle to witness a match between the 'ex-champion lightweight corporal boxer of the army' and a local lad who had volunteered to put on the gloves for the honour of the village. The local lad was the favourite, stripped to the waist, clean-limbed and fresh-faced in contrast with the 'low-browed, bullet-headed' ex-champion. Beckett described the fight through the rounds until the local lad landed a punch that made the champion stagger, lose his balance and fall over the rope among the crowd of rustics.

▶ AT THE SUMMER CAMP IN PENDINE EDGE, *South Wales in 1936, boxing was the sport of the day. Pendine also offered the boys a seven-mile stretch of beach.*

Skating and sledging

As soon as the winter had set the ponds to ice, the whole village would take to sliding, with or without skates. In January 1879 the flooded valley at Somerton in Oxfordshire froze over and a large number of skaters arrived by rail to skate on it. Some brought small sleighs in which ladies sat while a couple of skating men propelled them over the ice. At Christmas the boys had been happily sliding about on the River Cherwell at Islip, and on Christmas Day the ice was 'as busy with sliders and skaters as a fair day'. Mary Russell Mitford described a winter

scene: the road was gay with 'carts and post-chaises, and girls in red cloaks, and, afar off, looking almost like a toy, the coach'. The walkers seemed much happier than the riders in the coach as they were all off to the glassy ponds for a bit of sliding and skating. The children on one pond had made 'two long, smooth, liny slides', skimming down the bumpy, snowy bank to land on the rough ice, falling over backwards and toppling the whole line, collapsing in a heap of sprawling laughter. At another pond it was all much more sedate: the lieutenant was skating elegantly with his little sons, on blades rather than boots.

Field sports

Hunting and shooting were for the most part the sports of the upper classes. In some regions farmers and tradesmen often rode to hounds as well, and most of the rest of the village followed on foot. Many locals found employment in both sports – as huntsmen and gamekeepers, as kennel workers and

stable workers, as beaters, as lads earning a few pence for holding a horse or fetching buckets of water, or indirectly as farm labourers helping to maintain the landscape that suited the sports and had often been created to some extent directly for their purposes. There would be fewer spinneys, copses and hedgerows in the countryside if the hunt had not needed cover for foxes and the shoot had not needed cover for the birds; there would be much more barbed wire in hunting country if it were better jumping material than hedges and gates.

The quarry hunted was not confined to foxes. As well as foxhounds, there were staghounds, beagles and harriers, bloodhounds and basset hounds; while coursing hounds (lurchers and the like) pursued hares (a species that has vanished from many of its old haunts), legally or otherwise. Deerhounds and wolfhounds used to be worked against larger prey; dachshunds used to be badger dogs.

There were working otter hounds until otters became virtually extinct, within living memory; otters are now very gradually re-establishing in areas where they have not been seen for many a year. At Rousham there is a marble tablet inscribed to the memory of a favourite otter hound. Otter hunters on the Cherwell wore a uniform of blue serge jackets and knickerbockers with red stockings, caps and waistcoats; on the front of each cap was an otter's paw. Their followers would be on foot but were not averse to hopping on a train to go home again at the end of the day; the hounds did the same.

Sir Archie James, a man who so loved hunting of all kinds, in England and in Africa and India, that he entitled his memoirs *Nimrod*, wrote a rousing piece in the late 1970s about how there would be no foxes in Britain without the hunts to preserve them, and how the very fact of hunting kept the species more healthy;

▲ ICE SKATING *was accessible to many in rural areas, if the winter was hard enough to freeze the ponds and fens, and sledging had always been every child's delight at the first hint of a snowy slope. But skiing was limited to the upper classes, who could afford to travel, and to the military. It was not until the 1950s that the middle classes, now with money to spare, began to take skiing holidays in the Alps.*

▲ **THE HISTORY OF BRITISH FOX-HUNTING** *with horse and hound is not as long as some might think. It can be dated back to the late 17th century but it was not until the 18th that hounds and horses began to be bred specifically for the sport. Most sporting horses had been bred for racing on the flat and a very different mount was needed to tackle the cross-country jumping (carrying a possibly portly rider) that was involved in hunting.*

▶ **THE YELLOW LABRADOR CLUB** *held its first field trial meeting in 1925, at Wootton, near Bedford. Black labradors are more common than yellow in modern shoots, and some guns prefer chocolate labradors. The essence of the labrador is its eagerness to please, its joy in retrieving shot game and its 'soft mouth' for bringing back that game undamaged.*

then he spoiled it all by saying that it meant nothing to him at all – he hunted purely because he enjoyed the sport, the thrill of the chase, the glory of the ride, and the good company of his friends.

Hunting animals with hounds has recently been banned. Some thoroughly unpleasant 'sports' have been banned by law in the past – horrors such as badger baiting, dog fighting and cock fighting – but are still carried out by people in search of an illegal and violent thrill.

Shooting

Shooting is now very big business indeed. John Moore, in his tales of the fictional Midlands village of Brensham in the 1930s, described the dreaded Syndicate that gradually took over much of the land for shooting. The Lord of the Manor was always close to bankruptcy and kept selling bits of land to the Syndicate to stave off his creditors, until finally he was isolated on his own island of the rabbity Park (home to gypsy caravans for years), the crumbling Manor with its ruined chapel and muddy moat, the Home Orchard and a handful of cottages and smallholdings. Even the

lord's Folly fell to the Syndicate, who promptly evicted the harmless old hermit who lived there.

Then the Syndicate took over the river as well, sticking up 'Private Angling' notices where villagers had always been able to fish for roach and chub with homemade bamboo rods and bent pins. Those who ferreted for rabbits along the railway embankment, seeing it as their moral duty to keep down the plague-like numbers of the little beasts that were undermining the tracks, found themselves turned off so that keepers could snare and trap rabbits and sell them for ninepence a brace in Birmingham. Boys who had always collected rotting colic-inducing green windfall apples found themselves being prosecuted for theft; footpaths that the villagers had used for generations were suddenly closed. When the Stock Market plummeted in 1938, the Syndicate managed to grab the rest of the lord's land but allowed the lord to live in his own lodge along with the cowman's family. The trouble with syndicates was their shadowiness; they were not an identifiable individual you could punch on the nose.

Many modern gamekeepers know a great deal about the countryside in which they roam – they probably study wildlife more closely than most and many are excellent conservationists, but their job is to rear birds for the guns. The 'conservation' stance has been adopted in recent years by those who enjoy hunting and shooting but feel they

▲ THE TRADITIONAL BOXING DAY MEET *is at the heart of many an English village. The Cattistock Hunt, in the heart of Dorset's Thomas Hardy country, would meet outside the village pub for a stirrup cup before setting off across the fields. In 1806 JJ Farquharson established the first pack of hounds in Dorset in Cattistock 'country'. Cattistock formed its own separate hunt in 1869, 11 years after Farquharson retired.*

must justify their sport. This has created a whole new area of antagonism, with the arguments being shouted loudly by both sides, in a strange mixture of emotion and 'science'. Looked at more dispassionately, both sports unsettle the balance of nature and that is always a dangerous game to play. In the case of shooting, dispassionate conservationists and those who study nature point out the dangers of creating a monoculture in which one species – pheasants, for example – is reared in huge numbers in a limited area in which many other species are deliberately eliminated as vermin that threaten the monoculture species, thus creating a gross local imbalance with consequences that do not seem to have been studied seriously and without prejudice. And then those monoculture species are shot. It's a funny old world.

It is perhaps something of a leftover from the dominance of the squire that both shooting and hunting are seen as sports in which the 'countryman' has a right to participate, regardless of what others may think about it. The sports are divisive in that they tend to perpetuate the age-old anger

of the peasant, feeling helpless against the power of the king and his 'barons' – it harks back to the days of the royal forests when the abundant game was preserved as the sport of kings while the ever-hungry everyman was denied food for the pot and was punished with disproportionate severity when hunger led to poaching. The anger was refuelled by the equally harsh laws against trespass and against the traditional taking of game during the widespread enclosures by major landowners in the 18th century.

More recently it has been fanned again by the sometimes arrogant behaviour of some shooting landowners whose sport impinges on the lives of those who happen to live locally. Thus the perception of this social divide lingers today, even though in many country areas people at all levels of society might be involved in the sports directly or interested in maintaining the traditions of them. There

seems to be a gut reaction among those who live in urban areas against these major rural sports and it is unfortunate that such a strong urban/rural divide is seeking to dominate the debate about the countryside. There are far more important rural matters to be discussed.

'There would be fewer spinneys, copses and hedgerows in the countryside if the hunt had not needed cover for foxes and the shoot for the birds'

10. Changes in the Countryside

The Victorian farmer would be amazed at the changes in the countryside, should he be able to return to his home today. The first of the major social factors that have altered farming and village life was emigration to distant parts of the world, starting in the 18th and 19th centuries and, with different aims, continuing into the 20th. But the biggest factor of all was two world wars, which changed the entire class structure in the British countryside and radically altered people's attitudes, aspirations and way of life. The wars also had a huge effect on agriculture: food supplies imported to these islands were blockaded by the enemy and so production at home had to be massively intensified, changing farming ways forever. The wars also brought many more city people into the countryside, as evacuees and then as settlers, opening the eyes of villagers to a new way of life. The Cold War had its effects, too, and by its end the village was not same one that was known by our ancestors.

The great countryside drift to the towns has already been described, and the later drift in the other direction by town and city dwellers trailing their urban habits behind them in their baggage like security blankets, as if they were settlers heading for the outback or the Wild West. Here be bears; here be dragons.

In the 18th and 19th centuries, many a rural family or farmworker made the journey into the unknown, emigrating to North America or to Australia and New Zealand in search of a better life, and hastening the depopulation of the countryside. They continued to do so in the 20th century, but by then they were seeking employment and good weather rather than wanting to settle on a piece of virgin land and farm it.

In the 1830s much of that emigration was enforced. After the rural Captain Swing riots of 1830, nearly 500 men (and two women) were found guilty of crimes such as breaking a threshing machine or setting fire to a rick and were transported to Van Diemen's Land (Tasmania) and New South Wales, Australia. They were not criminals by nature and the Superintendent of Convicts at London Docks said that he 'never saw a finer set of men'. Of those sent to Tasmania, only one in three had ever been in prison, usually for things like trespass, poaching, fathering a bastard, petty larceny, leaving their master's service or cutting a fence. Of those who were sent to New South Wales only one in 12 had any sort of a record.

George Dew, whose work brought him in close contact with the poorest in the local villages, frequently mentioned emigration in his diaries in the 1870s and the scale was surprising. Nearly all of his cousins living around Banbury had emigrated to America by 1871, and in that year he recorded in July alone that seven people from the small village of Lower Heyford had emigrated to Canada. Three months later 20-year-old James Dunn left the same village and sailed for the United States. In the following year Dew noted that there were more empty cottages in the village than ever before, all due to 'emigration to the north of England and America'. In 1874 he reported two shiploads of emigrants setting off for New Zealand in January, including two local families. Within three months two more local families had left for New Zealand 'and nearly all over the Bletchington District the Agricultural Labourers are on the move,

emigrating to New Zealand or else migrating into the northern counties'. These emigrations had been arranged through the National Agricultural Labourers' Union, whose local officials were recruited as agents by the New Zealand government.

A few years before World War I, a special training farm was established at Woking Park in Surrey for those who wished to emigrate. At the time many people were emigrating to Canada with high hopes of wealth and adventure in the wide open spaces, but the 'farms' they leased there were often just a square mile of virgin prairie, perhaps with a basic log cabin if you were lucky (if not, you built your own immediately) and your nearest neighbour 20 miles away and the closest store a day's journey. Ah well, at least the Canadian government provided you with a telephone, even if it had not built a road yet.

Many of these hopeful emigrants to Canada knew very little about farming; many came from the towns and had done hardly any physical labour in their lives. The creation of the training farm at Woking Park was timely, and soon there was a similar

▶ FAIRBRIDGE FARM SCHOOL *near Pinjarra, Western Australia, was the brainchild of Kingsley Fairbridge (1885–1924), a South African who came to Australia in 1912. His dream was of 'migrants who would one day fill the empty dominions' and when he saw the overcrowded cities of England he realised that the most successful migrants would be the children. So he created his Farm School, in which the children lived in small groups under the care of 'Cottage Mothers' and were trained to be farmers. Between 1920 and 1950 some 1,200 children passed through the school – including this group from an English farm school setting sail for Australia in 1948.*

▲ THE 'BRING OUT A BRITON' CAMPAIGN *in 1957 by the Australian government was intended to lure a larger proportion of British migrants into the country. Australians were encouraged to sponsor a British family and help them to settle.*

'Wars radically change people's lives, even those not involved in the fighting, even those who did not lose loved ones'

scheme for young women – most of them town-bred and middle-class, often used to having a servant at home and certainly not ready to be a farmer's wife on the Canadian prairies. But World War I brought an end to emigration and the training farms.

War punctuates lifetimes. People talk about 'before the war', 'after the war' and 'during the war', as signposts in their lives and in the history of their communities. Wars radically change people's lives, even those not directly involved in the fighting, even those who did not lose loved ones. Wars leave too many holes in the fabric of the community.

The countryside was changed more suddenly and more thoroughly than the urban areas by the two world wars of the 20th century. It may not have suffered the terrible bombings that gutted cities and city

lives (though it was by no means safe from the bombs), but the entire rural way of life was changed by those wars, probably more so than during any war since Harold fought at Hastings.

World War I

World War I was very different to any that had preceded it. The Crimean War, the Boer War and the fighting in India had been distant affairs carried out by professional soldiers and not directly impinging on life at home, except for the excitement of reading about the battles in the papers and occasionally celebrating a victory. The new war was far more serious.

Very soon, there were recruitment drives in village halls and village schools all over the country. Many of those who joined up so eagerly would never come home from the trenches or, if they did, would be physically or mentally maimed. As the war took hold, there was a constant flow of farmworkers, estate workers and servants in the big house, along with the sons of the gentry, out of the villages and across the Channel, younger men enlisting as soon as they were old enough to replace the huge numbers being killed. Every village family had at least one member or a close relation out in the trenches or at sea, and many never returned.

When German submarines began to interrupt the imported food supplies on which Britain had come to depend, it was all systems go in the fields: grass was ploughed, the downlands were ploughed, committees were set up to tell people what to do, labour and machinery pools were created. Between 1916 and 1918 some two million acres of

grassland were ploughed up (it was still horses), the production of wheat rocketed and the British farmers beat the blockade.

The children did their bit as well, picking rosehips, crab apples and blackberries at the government's behest; they gathered conkers for grinding into an alternative livestock feed so that there would be more grain for the people. Families knitted socks for sailors and collected eggs for soldiers; they raised money to buy tents for the troops and money to help wounded warhorses in France. Everybody was much more involved in this war than in previous ones.

In some parts of the country, enormous army camps were set up on commons and farmland and the nearby villages suddenly found large numbers of strangers in their midst. For some, this was exciting; for many, it was an invasion that disrupted their lives.

Then there were the women – the land-girl volunteers of the Women's Land Army that was formed in 1917 to put women in the fields to replace the men who had enlisted. They were joined on the land by urban women and public schoolboys, taking working holidays on the farms. In the massive drive to feed the nation, everybody in the village from the squire to the poorest would be working out in the fields too. But the scale of 'invasion' of the countryside was

▼ MANY WOMEN HELPED ON THE FARMS *during World War I out of a sense of patriotism, and had no previous knowledge of land work and often came from comfortable homes, utterly unaccustomed to physical labour. They learnt to milk cows, manage working horses and hoe the fields and after the war they continued to work, in order to make a living in hard times.*

> *'It was said, during World War I, that pheasants in southern England could hear the sound of the heavy artillery across the Channel'*

as nothing compared with World War II, and in many villages there was little disruption to everyday life.

The aftermath

After the American Civil War, the phrase they used to express how life had changed was, 'Gone with the wind'. It was also an appropriate phrase for the British way of life that vanished with World War I, and perhaps even more so with World War II.

In 1916 a concerned reader wrote to *The Field* for advice. The editor's response (the reader's question was not published) was:

> *Men are now acting as their own chauffeurs, who before the war thought they were too old to learn to drive a car. Others who had hardly handled a spade in their lives are now manfully digging over their kitchen gardens, and finding it not unexciting though laborious work. There is a piquancy about coming across stray potatoes in patches which purport to have been thoroughly explored long ago. When a man by force of circumstances becomes his own gardener, he realises a good many essential truths, one of which is that the proverbial slowness of the professional is due quite as much to the stubborn character of Mother Earth as to the restful proclivities of the sons of Adam. Orderly rows of vegetables represent a great deal of solid and patient labour, and some of us are learning this lesson for the first time now that we realise that the rows of vegetables are part of the country's economic strength.*

No doubt the reader who had sought advice was hoping that, after the war was over, life would return to normal and he would have servants again to do these things for him.

▼ **THE HUGE MOVEMENT OF TROOPS** *through the countryside in the build-up to D-Day in 1944 filled the lanes with camouflaged tanks and jeeps, all heading for the south coast. In southern England, many roads became dedicated convoy routes, and on D-Day itself the skies were almost black with swarms of gliders and Dakotas heading for France.*

World War II

It was said, during World War I, that pheasants in southern England could hear the sound of the heavy artillery across the Channel: they reacted by shouting their heads off in the middle of the night. And, yes, some people living near the coast could hear those terrible shellings too, though not the screams of the wounded. But the war did not come to Britain on a large scale then.

It did in World War II. The enemy crossed the Channel and invaded the air above Britain, so that very few areas escaped from the noise of the aircraft and the sound of bombs dropping on cities and docks. Almost every village experienced the influx of evacuees (mostly children and women, and in some cases whole city schools), billeted soldiers taking over the squire's house, perhaps new airfields in the meadows, air-raid shelters in the garden, blackouts and of course rationing.

Many people can remember watching the dogfights between aircraft in the skies over southern England. Many can remember

▲ MOST OF THE D-DAY TROOPS TRAVELLED UNDER COVER OF DARKNESS *and sometimes villagers were quite unaware that the local woods were giving them shelter. Children who came across Canadian or American soldiers catching a nap under a hedge soon discovered that a chat with them on the way home from school was often rewarded with a big handful of sweets.*

▲ TEMPORARY TROOP CAMPS *sprang up in many areas on the edges of villages and towns. In rural areas they could put a considerable strain on local resources.*

▼ THERE WERE ABOUT 145,000 MARRIAGES *between American or Canadian soldiers and British women, many of them taking place during the D-Day build-up. Women whose villages were near American and Canadian bases had had their social lives greatly enlivened by dances and other get-togethers with the visitors but marriage was another matter: GIs needed to gain written permission from their commanding officer two months ahead of any wedding, after he had personally interviewed the prospective bride. But more than 70,000 British women sailed across the Atlantic after the war to rejoin their husbands and start a new life.*

the drone of German bombers heading for the cities and ports and airfields, the distant explosions and ack-ack responses, and the frightening sound of the bombers releasing their 'spare' ammunition at random in the countryside on the way home. Many have stories of planes crashing in the fields and woods, streaking like comets across the sky with their tails on fire before exploding as they hit the ground, and tales of parachutists tumbling among the mangolds. Many remember the terrible fear that one day their village would be bombed, and then how the thatch would burn! And sometimes it did.

Those who could not join the forces served with the Local Defence Volunteers (later renamed as the Home Guard), prowling the countryside at night armed with shotguns and knives that they were expected to use against invading Germans.

After World War II those heroes and heroines in the services who could come home did, and the village welcomed them warmly but went on talking about crops and

weather and rationing and horses and dogs and rabbits and cricket and fetes, as if the war had never been. But the lives of all of them had been changed, even those who had not seen active service. For a start, the women who stayed behind had discovered that they could cope on their own, they could handle the fieldwork, they could pay the bills, they could keep a trade going all on their own and still manage the household, they could earn their own living and they could wear the trousers, both literally and metaphorically.

The Cold War

The next war was the Cold War, with its unthinkable threat of the atomic or nuclear bomb. Despite the enormity of the mushroom cloud that we lived under for so many years, the villagers were ready for it. Parishes were encouraged to set up emergency planning committees, which they did with all the enthusiasm of boy scouts building campfires, relying on local

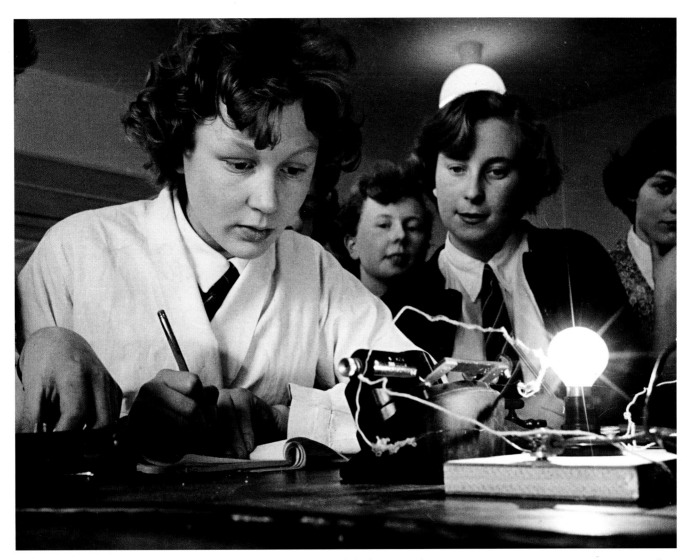

knowledge of essentials such as water supplies, fuel supplies, which houses had cookers that did not rely on mains power, what useful equipment was held by farmers and householders such as generators, boats, thick ropes, cutting equipment and horses, and all the other minutiae that would mean survival in the aftermath of disaster. If a threat is so huge and so unimaginably awful, you tame it by ignoring its scale and concentrating on the little things that you can control. Villagers found themselves learning about digging latrines, making field ovens, building nuclear shelters, setting up radio communications and using geiger counters to monitor local levels of radioactivity, just in case. They drew up plans to feed the village on stored provisions and to accommodate refugees from the cities in the village hall and the school and the pub. The pub dug out the old air-raid warning siren, blew the dust off it and prepared to let the village know when a nuclear attack was imminent – though

just what people could do about it in the allotted four-minute warning was difficult to say, except that the committee would have trained them to dive under the stairs and stay there, with a goat for fresh milk and a tin opener and Calor gas stove and bottled water, and instructions not to eat the vegetables growing in their own gardens in case they were contaminated by fallout.

When the nuclear threat was lifted, most villages retained their basic emergency plans in case of a different threat, and many have since put those plans into action – for example, after the major storm of October 1987 that cut off countless villages from the rest of the world for a fortnight when trees blocked roads and brought down telephone and power lines, or when coastal villages became swamped by exceptionally high tides in stormy weather, or when others suffered severe inland flooding after torrential rain. Villagers always were self-sufficient, and sometimes they still can be even now.

▲ THE COLD WAR EFFECTIVELY LASTED *from the end of World War II until US President Ronald Reagan and Societ leader Mikhail Gorbachev finally broke the ice in the late 1980s. In 1956 it was suggested that the Cold War could be won in the classroom – especially in the training of young scientists.*

The future of the village

Yes, the village has changed, much of it for the better, some of it apparently for the worse (until you remove those rose-tinted glasses when you look at the village of old) and some of it with genuine regret. The kinship has gone but so has the claustrophobic atmosphere it could create. The village bobby hardly exists, his place taken by the occasional passing patrol car whose occupants know none of the names or even faces of the villagers and certainly don't have the time or inclination to take a young lad to one side and point out the error of his ways before his petty mischief turns into something more serious. It is no longer possible to put a culprit in the stocks on the village green, to be ridiculed by those who have known him since he was born; instead he now goes to a town prison and disappears into a safe anonymity where nobody inside knows his mother.

The squire has gone, his place usurped by the state. The parson no longer dominates the village; again his role has been partly usurped by the state but partly lost through the reduction in his flock and the lessening of unquestioning respect from villagers who now are often as well educated as he is. But the village still cares for and respects its older folk, boasting with as much pride as they do themselves about their age, and listening to their memories. The village still cares for its children and raises money to ensure that they have a school and playing fields and playgrounds. The village still cares.

There may seem to be more unhappiness, more abuse, more depression, more suicides in rural areas, especially at times of trouble for farmers, but in reality it is probably less than of old – it's just that the news of it is more widely broadcast. In the old village you might have known of such problems within the village (and possibly put it all down to a combination of witches and bad luck) but not elsewhere, so you would not have had the impression that the problems were on a large scale. Some say there is hidden rural poverty, but it is again a matter of scale: a 19th-century villager would not recognise it as poverty in comparison.

People say that the spirit of village life is dying but in reality it is only changing. There is still in many villages a strong desire to be involved for the general good of the community, albeit there are conflicts about what that 'general good' might be. The children in today's village will look back at their childhood in years to come and shake their heads, telling their grandchildren that life was wonderful in those days, those good old days, when there were still fields and woods and streams, before the village was engulfed by the tidy concrete suburbs of the town. Oh yes, believe me!

▶ **MANY OF THE CHILDREN** *who were evacuated from the cities retained good memories of their enforced stay in the countryside. Their stories are gradually emerging in memories books published by villages all over the country, often as Millennium projects, and more recently on village websites.*

▼ **WORLD WAR II** *marked several turning-points in rural life. Children during that war were among the last to see working horses playing a serious role in agriculture. This 1941 photograph has an added poignancy: the child was not a country boy but an evacuee from Croydon who found himself living on a farm in Buckinghamshire.*

Index

ACKNOWLEDGEMENTS

The author would like to thank the villagers of Chobham, Lyndon, Grittleton and Milland for sharing their personal memories of the past.

PICTURE CREDITS

Andover History & Archaeology Society 39, 116 / BT Sanitation 47 / Buckinghamshire County Museum 161 / Friends of the Lake District 59, 64/5, 73, 90.119, 133t, 140, 141, 226 / Getty Images 10, 11, 12, 13t, 13b, 18b, 21t, 21b, 22, 24, 25, 26t, 26b, 28/9, 30, 31t, 32, 34, 35, 36, 37, 38, 40, 46, 48, 49, 54, 57, 58, 60t, 62, 63t, 63b, 72/3, 78, 79, 81, 82t, 93b, 97, 100, 101b, 102, 102/3, 104, 105t, 105b. 107, 110, 111b, 112, 113, 117, 118, 123t, 124t, 124b, 125, 126, 127t, 128/9, 139t, 143, 144, 146, 151, 154, 155, 157, 162t, 163, 165t, 165b, 166, 167, 168, 170, 177t, 172/3b, 174/5, 177t, 177b, 179, 180, 181, 182/3, 188, 189, 190/1, 192, 193, 194, 195, 196, 197b, 199t, 201, 205, 206/7t, 210, 212t, 214, 215t, 215b, 216, 217t, 220t, 220b, 221t, 228t, 229, 230, 231, 234b, 235, 236t, 236b, 237, 238t, 238b, 239, 240/1, 242, 243, 244,245, 247t, 248, 249, 250, 251 / Gosport Society 202 / Courtesy of L Brownlow and www.picturethepast.org. uk 148/9 / Courtesy of Burton Joyce and Bulcote Local History Society and www.picturethepast.org.uk 135 / Courtesy of Derby Museums and Art Gallery and www.picturethepast.org.uk 55 / Courtesy of Nottingham Evening Post and www.picturethepast.org.uk 171 / Courtesy of Nottinghamshire County Council and www.picturethepast.org.uk 44, 75, 93t, 99t, 108 / www.picturethepast.org.uk 130 / Hampshire Record Office 16, 20, 53t, 69b, 77t, 101t, 164, 198, 203, 225, 246, 247b / Doug Bone Collection 19 / James H Smith Photographic Collection 71t / Kilford of Botley Collection 212b, 222 / Mary Evans Picture Library 74 / Milland Memories Group 14, 14/15. 17t, 17b, 18t, 23, 27, 52, 53b, 71b, 76, 77b, 86/7, 91b, 98, 162b, 184, 185, 187, 204, 206b, 210/11, 217b, 218/9, 232 / Museum of English Rural Life 2, 4/5, 33, 41t, 45b, 50/51, 60b, 66, 67, 69t, 70t, 70b, 80, 88. 89, 92, 96, 99b, 106, 109, 111t, 114/5, 120, 121, 122, 123b, 127t, 127b, 131, 132, 133b, 134t, 134b, 136, 136/7, 138, 139b, 142, 145, 147, 159, 169, 200, 221b, 223t, 223b, 227, 233 / Tom Quinn 144/5, 153 / Sutcliffe Gallery 31b, 68, 95, 156, 186, 197t, 199b / The Odiham Society 45t, 228b / West Sussex Record Office 94b, 160, 175, 176, 178/9, 213, 224, 234t / West Sussex Past Pictures for Amberley Working Museum 158 / Marlipins Museum Shoreham 61, 152 / Steynings Museum 83 / West Sussex County Council Library Service 8/9, 41b, 56t, 56b, 82b, 84/5, 150 / Weald & Downland Open Air Museum 42 / Wyn Voysey 43. Front Cover by Eric Guy Collection / Museum of English Rural Life / University Of Reading. Back Cover by Reg Spiller / Fox Photos / Getty Images. Back Cover Inset by Topical Press Agency / Getty Images.